About

Ian Plenderleith is a Frankfurt-based football writer and journalist. He is the author of the football short-story collection *For Whom the Ball Rolls* and the non-fiction *Rock 'n' Roll Soccer: The Short Life and Fast Times of the North American Soccer League*. He has been writing about football in the UK, Switzerland, Germany and the US for the past 25 years, for *When Saturday Comes*, the *Guardian*, the *Wall Street Journal*, *Soccer America* and numerous other newspapers, magazines and websites. A lifelong fan, player and coach, he also writes a weekly blog, Referee Tales, about how much he enjoys receiving non-stop abuse for his unconscionable attempts at refereeing in the German amateur leagues.

Ian tweets at @PlenderleithIan and @refereetales.

THE QUIET FAN

THE QUIET FAN

IAN PLENDERLEITH

This edition first published in 2018

Unbound

6th Floor Mutual House, 70 Conduit Street, London W1S 2GF

www.unbound.com

ISBN (eBook): 978-1-912618-43-9
ISBN (Paperback): 978-1-912618-42-2

Design by Mecob

Printed and bound in Great Britain by Clays Ltd, Elcograf S.p.A.

With love, for Mum, Dad and Carol. Thank you for coming with me to Boston on a Monday night. And thank you for everything else besides.

Dear Reader,

The book you are holding came about in a rather different way to most others. It was funded directly by readers through a new website: Unbound.

Unbound is the creation of three writers. We started the company because we believed there had to be a better deal for both writers and readers. On the Unbound website, authors share the ideas for the books they want to write directly with readers. If enough of you support the book by pledging for it in advance, we produce a beautifully bound special subscribers' edition and distribute a regular edition and e-book wherever books are sold, in shops and online.

This new way of publishing is actually a very old idea (Samuel Johnson funded his dictionary this way). We're just using the internet to build each writer a network of patrons. Here, at the back of this book, you'll find the names of all the people who made it happen.

Publishing in this way means readers are no longer just passive consumers of the books they buy, and authors are free to write the books they really want. They get a much fairer return too – half the profits their books generate, rather than a tiny percentage of the cover price.

If you're not yet a subscriber, we hope that you'll want to join our publishing revolution and have your name listed in one of our books in the future. To get you started, here is a £5 discount on your first pledge. Just visit unbound.com, make your pledge and type LINCOLN18 in the promo code box when you check out.

Thank you for your support,

Dan, Justin and John
Founders, Unbound

Super Patrons

Colin Anderton
Ursus Arctos
Konstantin Atanesyan
Wadiah Atiyah
David Baillie
Duncan Batchelor
Roger Bates
Richard Bates
Phillip Bennett-Richards
David Bentley
James Bentley
Dominic Blore
Matthew Bowers
Rhona Bradford
Tim Bradford
Marian Brent
Andy Bulley
Scott Cahoon
Annie Canby
Jonathan Carr
Martin Cawsey
Karla Chaman
Doug Cheeseman
Lincoln City FC
Andrew Coburn
Lane Cooper
Susan Curran
James Curtis
David Danielson
Trevor Denton
Ann Dickson
Marion Dickson

Mark Dickson
Stephen K. Doyle
Suzanne Fitzpatrick
Michael Gantenberg
Andre Gazdag
John Gilardi
Jason Goldman
Colin Green
Michael Greenhill
Helmut Guesten
Sean Hallam
Paul Hamnett
Adrian Harte
David Hawley
Andy Hayes
Edward Heppenstall
Charles E Herbert
Andy Hockley
Mike Hoyer
RAY HUDSON
Gary Hutchinson
Andrew Isbester
Peter Johansson
Alison Johnson
Malcolm Johnson
Tim Jones
Ben Jones
Alex Jones
Fiona Kelly
Steve Kester
Dan Kieran
Kate Langdon
Jimmy Leach
Dave Lifton
Mark Longden
Gerd Lotze

Conny Lotze
Caterina Lotze-Kaufhold
Joseph Mapother
David Matkins
Neal McCleave
Kevin McGill
David Miles
Reed Miller
Steve Mills
John Mitchinson
Jens Mueller
Martin Mühleisen
Simonetta Nardin
Clive Nates
Thomas O'Brien
Mark O'Neill
David Pankopf
Dorian Patchin
Kenny Pieper
Carol Plenderleith
Roz Plenderleith
Robert Plenderleith
Ann Plenderleith Ferguson
Justin Pollard
Cathy Poole
Moni Port
Ian Preece
Susan Pukall
Brent Quigley
Dan Roberts
Neil Ruane
Marc Silverstein
Amanda Slater
MTA Smith
Ally Spicer
David Squires

Thomas Stavrou
Elmar Sulk
Scott Thomas
Simon Thompson
Ruth Thomson
Roy Thomson
Laurens van der Tak
John Van Laer
Connell Vaughan
Kenneth Vaughan
Paul Vincent
David Wallis
Ruth Walters
Drew Whitelegg
Gerrit Wiesmann
Sonja Wild
Ernest Wohnig
Julius Wohnig
Kelly Young

With grateful thanks to Lincoln City FC for helping to make this book happen.

'If I fall down dead tomorrow then there will be a funeral, and then on Friday there will still be eleven players on the field.'

Thomas Müller, Bayern Munich and Germany.

Contents

1

Introduction

Football, like life, is generally a disappointment, but there are ways of getting by. Due to the limited number of trophies, fans of most teams will learn to dampen expectations, develop a self-protective layer of stoicism, and prepare themselves to experience only the rarest moments of triumph. Some goals may be attained, but most of them won't.

Following a football team merely reflects the way that most of us quietly lead our lives. Perhaps too quietly most of the time, but that's the way we deal with adversity and the likelihood of defeat. We are neither violent nor fanatical, but mainly loyal, stable and steady. We persevere and make do with what we've got, despite our doubts, our complaints and our threats to leave or give up completely.

A friend of mine, Fiona, once told me that she found it hard to go out with men who didn't like football. When she was growing up, her dad and two brothers watched the game a lot. Maybe she was biased, but she thought her dad and brothers were all grounded, reliable blokes. Therefore, any man she went out with who watched football could well turn out to be a grounded, reliable bloke too.

With Fiona's approval, you could misquote Humphrey Bogart here and say, 'Never trust any bastard who doesn't watch football', but that's not really true either. I have a number of quite sane friends and relatives with little or no interest in sport, and sometimes I envy them. They make me wonder what more worthwhile pursuits I could be involved in if I wasn't on the train to Woking, say, to spend a Saturday afternoon watching Lincoln City lose 3–1 (in fucking *Woking*, of all places). Then the longer I think about it, the fewer worthwhile pursuits come to mind. I could read more books, watch more films, walk more hills, but I'm fine with the amount of book-reading, film-watching and hill-walking that I already do. Some days, I'd simply rather be watching Lincoln lose at Woking.

Now most of the people I know who watch football would not make the effort to go to Woking to watch Lincoln City, or whoever it is they support. In truth, it's something I only do on rare occasions, when the opportunity arises. I no longer even live in the same country as Lincoln City (my team, in case you hadn't worked that out), let alone the same county. And that's just the point. It's quite normal not to be incessantly possessed with a football team, because the vast majority of football fans are completely normal. For the most part we are not, as commonly portrayed, obsessives. The completist programme collectors, the serial ground-hoppers or the fan who hasn't missed an away game for 36 years – honestly, although you might want to have a conversation with these characters, you wouldn't want it to last for longer than a few minutes. And for the most part we are not, as previously portrayed, hooligans – see select front pages of every pre-1990 British tabloid. Like the hooligans, the obsessives are the minority who gave (or, occasionally, continue to give) the rest of us a bad name.

Since the dawn of the Premier League, the idea of the obsessive fan has been played up, mocked, exploited, patronised and flogged by the media. Once the hooligan ran away, was locked away or was finally told to grow up by his wife, it was necessary to conjure up a new stereotype after a lachrymose Paul Gascoigne Changed Football Forever at Italia '90. Our mundane hobby was no longer a platform for anti-social miscreants who were threatening to bring down the state by taking the away end at Gresty Road. It could now be packaged as something harmless, ludicrous and laughable, backed by a banner with the word 'PASSION!' boldly painted in 6-feet-high letters. Have you got 'I Love Chelsea' tattooed across your arse? The journalist from the *Sun* would love to meet you and harness your flabby but impeccably etched rear cheeks to write a story that will help to sell a few thousand more Sky receivers.

Yet, as Fiona knows, watching football is the most normal activity you could want your man or woman to do. Millions of us have done it for decades, without hitting anyone or feeling the need to name our children after Northampton Town's 1987 Division Four championship-winning team. Some of the things you have read about fans in memoirs and colour supplements may have been exaggerated to suit the needs of the marketing department. Football fans may be more interested in the fate of their teams than is perhaps healthy, and they may spend too much time and money on their interest (but then what's a hobby for?). Some of them may, for a short while, take defeat far more seriously than is rational. These are all parts of being a normal football fan.

Do we show up for every game, home and away, no matter where or when, no matter where we are in the table? Do we suffer genuine long-term clinical depression purely because our team has failed to win a trophy? Do we stand outside the chairman's house at midnight and scream abuse at the upstairs windows? Do we collect every replica home, away and third kit, every season? Such fans do exist, but there aren't that many. And although the excessive cases attract the most attention, the same patronising portrayal of the supposedly eccentric football fan who eschews all other considerations in life in order to follow his or her team is a leaden, preconceived fallacy. It's possible that if you look an obsessive in the eye, you may find yourself being subjected to a four-hour appraisal of why a bad refereeing decision away at Gillingham in 1978 permanently changed the course of your club's history for the worse and the referee *will never be forgiven* (even though he died twenty years ago), but most of us generally avoid these borderline headcases. Just as, back in the days of the hard men, we'd steer clear for fear of getting punched, and keep our eyes down lest we be accused of looking at something we shouldn't have been looking at.

Football Fans Do Other Stuff

My belief, nonetheless, is that sport is, on some level, important. Once, when I was visiting the house of family friends who weren't into football, I tentatively asked if I could watch a game that was about to start on television. 'Is it an important game?' asked the head of the house. I looked him in the eye and replied, 'All games are important.' He laughed heartily and seemed to understand. I gratefully abandoned the dinner table and was allowed to settle in front of the TV.

For all that, though, football is not as important as some people would like to think. It's not important *in itself*, meaning that if people stopped playing football tomorrow, the world would continue to turn and few would die as a direct consequence. And it's not important enough to make you punch someone, or neglect your family and your hill-walking, say.

It's important because it's a fixture of so many people's lives. For between 10 and 12 months of the year, it's there, mainly in the background but sometimes at the forefront of our daily existence. Football's a barometer of stability. And the fact that I can trace and memorise so many events in what has so far been an averagely dysfunctional life to football matches that happened to take place at the same time – to me, that's normal.

Put simply, most football fans do other stuff too. The lives of those employed full-time in the game are consumed by football – like the manager who spends 14 hours at the stadium and then returns home and sits up half the night studying videos of his team's next opponents. But we fans, the majority, play a minority role. Of course, the cliché is true that without us there would be no game, and in recent years fans have played significant and creditable roles in rescuing a number of smaller clubs, or setting up new ones. But most of us are on the periphery of the game, literally. We stand, and now mostly sit, as a mass, reacting to events on the field that are beyond our control. We come, watch, emote, and then we leave and return to jobs, families, friends and food.

At the same time, there are lots of terribly dull games where nothing ever happens. During these matches the mind can start to wander or wonder, thinking about a problem at work, about a boy or girl and how you'd rather be with them now than standing here, or about how much longer you'll be freezing your rear off in front of 22 Division Four hack-and-run journeymen before you can hotfoot it to the nearest warm pub for a pint. You might think about how you could be at home finishing off that Murakami novel. Or wonder whether Mercury Rev will ever make a decent album again. Is that a chaffinch on the roof of the main stand? Shit, I wish I'd brought along my binoculars and my *Mitchell Beazley Birdwatcher's Pocket Guide.*

The fans who are relieved when the season ends, or when their team is playing away so that their Saturday is free, or when they simply decide on a Tuesday night (that would typically be a very wet and windy one in Rochdale, in January) that they can't be arsed – these fans really do exist. This is perfectly normal behaviour. We don't believe it's the end of the world if we miss a game, or even several. We go happily to our brother's wedding instead, or take the dog for a long walk. Of course fans are deeply attached to football and largely profess to love their team. And most of us love our mothers too, but we wouldn't want to spend every day of our lives with them.

Why Football Has Little to Do with Philosophy

A few years back I was working with a literary agent who said she'd heard that a certain publisher was keen to solicit proposals for a football book based on the well-worn Albert Camus line about how everything he'd learned about 'morality and the obligations of men' he owed to football. Although I thought the quote was dubious, I cobbled together an outline. If anyone was going to write such a book, then it might as well be me. Reading that book proposal now, I'm glad that the commissioning editor in question never even deigned to reply.

In a second-hand shop in Lincolnshire a few months later, I found a superb book published in 1962 called *The Footballer's Companion*, a collection of football essays, match reports, poems and short stories edited by Brian Glanville. The book contains the original essay by Camus, published by *France Football* in 1957, that included the famous quote. It's called 'What I Owe to Football'. *At last,* I thought, *I'm going to find out what Camus actually meant. In what way, exactly, did he learn all about morality and the obligations of men through our favourite game? And how can I follow his philosophical path and become a better person?*

Unsatisfyingly, the closest the essay comes to philosophy is when he writes about playing football on a bumpy pitch in Algiers. Here, the writer learned that the ball never comes to you where you're expecting it (a wordier paraphrase of the German coach Sepp Herberger's famously pithy statement that 'the ball is round'). The unexpected bounce of the football, Camus goes on, helped him cope with life in the big city, where people are 'not always wholly straightforward'.

Well, that's lightly amusing, as is the rest of the essay as he nostalgically recounts his playing days. Finally, he comes to the great quote, which is translated as learning all he knows about morality and obligations from *sport*, rather than football, and that's it. The rest you have to guess – namely, that when he wrote *The Rebel* and *The Myth of Sisyphus* he was perhaps sitting in the stands of his favourite team, Racing Club de Paris, siphoning all that he saw on the field through his head and on to the page. Perhaps Racing Club went one up after 10 minutes and Albert immediately wrote: 'It is futile to be amazed by the apparent paradox that leads thought to its own negation by the opposite paths of humiliated reason and triumphal reason. 1–0 to Racing Club. Get in!'

Why am I going on about this? Because it's not just football's commercialism and endless frothing hyperbole that have become rampant and bloated; it's the significance that the game has now been burdened with. It's not just football, it's deep! Camus said so, and he knew bloody everything. Er, no, I've never read anything by him, but he used to play in goal for Algeria. And Shankly too, he said that thing about life and death. Football, philosophy, death – it's not just about kicking a ball into a goal, is it?

Except that, basically, it is. For kids down at the park with all the requisite dreams and fantasies, football is fine the way it is – just a game where you kick a ball between two posts. There is no purer form of football. But once their parents and the media and older fans have polluted their innocence or shattered their dreams, they may fall prey to football's ludicrous, latter-day loss of perspective, reflected in the widespread use of that Camus quote, which they might have seen on a T-shirt or quoted by an unimaginative hack, usually along the lines of: 'As Albert Camus once said…' Yet when you look into what he *actually* said, it was just a throwaway line in an article for a French football magazine. The next day it was the wrapping for some Parisian's pommes frites. No one took it seriously enough to say, 'Oh yeah? You're one of France's foremost thinkers and you learned it all from football? What the fuck are you on about? How about one or two examples, at the very least?'

So I certainly haven't learned much about morality and my obligations to man through football, although I've learned a ton of completely useless statistics and player names, mainly without even trying, but none of which is useful except at a pub quiz, or when someone asks, 'Hey, Ian, what year was it that Lincoln reverted from an Arsenal-style shirt back into their red-and-white stripes?'[1]

I've learned a lot more from one Siegfried Lenz radio play I studied for my German A level than I have from a lifetime of watching and playing football. All I have learned from football is that it's a game that too many people take too seriously for their own health. Me included. When I started playing for a men's over-35 team in the US, I also started shouting at referees. For years I had been a calm, model player who never got booked. I received my first yellow card for dissent at the age of 36, and my first red card at the age of 45, also for dissent, followed by swearing at the referee for booking me for dissent (he deserved it). It's as if the older I become, the *less* football teaches me about morality and my obligations to man.

The Quiet Fan – What This Book Is About

I would like to reclaim at least some of the game for the quiet majority of fans. Neither the self-styled vandals and their banal tales of mindless violence nor the manic collectors and itinerants with their meticulous lists and spooky rituals say anything to me about my own experience of watching football. And although I've been verbally violent towards referees and players from the safety of the mass, and although I go on about football too much at times and watch too many games, I know approximately where the boundary lies, and so, I believe, do nearly all my fellow supporters. Otherwise they would all be in jail on assault charges or locked up in institutions for the statistically insane.

Football hasn't formed my personality, or unduly influenced my life, or made me think anew about myself and life in general in a profoundly radical manner. However, imagine that if I die tomorrow and a complete stranger is commissioned with sorting out my possessions and writing my life story. My sporadic and mainly navel-gazing

1. 1973–4.

diaries aside, they wouldn't have a lot to go on. But if they looked through a pile of my football programmes, they'd have a good idea of where I've lived and the places I've visited. I grew up in Lincolnshire, and when I was a teenager I used to go to Scotland a lot during school holidays. I lived in Birmingham, and later London, and then Germany and Switzerland and the US, and in between I watched games in different parts of Europe.

These programmes serve as the material markers to games that have been mostly forgotten, but which occasionally stood out either for an event that was connected to the time and place of the match, or an incident that happened at the game itself that reflects the way I developed. Football is a part of the foundation of my life. If I'd grown up in America, it might have been another sport or another pastime altogether. I haven't lived my life through football, but football's been living through me ever since I could read a league table and understand the concept of results and victory.

A handful of games, then, conveniently map out and reflect the course of my life's narrative. They are a random selection, at times concentrated in certain locations, but always there as an accompaniment, like a loyal dog. If the dog died, you'd be in shock because for years it had always been around; it didn't do much but wag its tail and bark and divert your attention from time to time, but you loved it nonetheless and you associate it with a fixed period of your life. Football's even more of a constant than that because it's far less likely to die. It's always been there, and so it's more convenient to use the game as a milestone.

The matches we've been to mark our time for us – our growth and decline. Football's like the grandfather clock in the corner of the room that never stops, the cyclical seasons ticking relentlessly on, and since World War II there's always been a new one to follow the last, no matter what else is going on in the world. This book is an anti-memoir for the majority of us who watch football from the edges, mainly following crap teams and a crap country (Scotland), to help us muddle through life in a similar fashion. We will never be part of the big time – in either football or history – but always part of the crowd at the side looking in on the glamorous world, struggling on, but essentially laughing at both what's going on in the middle and in the crowd around us. Occasional moments of joy and glory punctuate years of blackly cheerful stoicism, which is the way it should be.[2]

Fiona and I, incidentally, went on a date shortly after we first met, to watch a match between Ireland and England in a Notting Hill pub, but halfway through the game she went to phone her not-quite-ex-boyfriend (a neurotic, not a football fan), then made her excuses and left. Clearly, I wasn't doing it for her. Probably, I was paying too much attention to the game – I was just a bit *too* normal for her tastes. Still, I obviously wasn't that upset as I stayed in the pub on my own until the final whistle (it ended 1–1). She ended up having two boys with another bloke altogether, a Spurs fan who's about as normal as they come. Which was just what she needed.

2. Fans of self-appointed Big Teams who think that one trophy a season constitutes failure are warned that reading on will take them into a world where the point is not really to win, it is just to be.

2

Cursing

Lincoln City v. Exeter City, Football League Division Four, 3pm, Saturday, 13 January 1973

Telling It Like It Is

'Come on, Lincoln, you useless twats!' These words caused a shocked quiet to spread across the main St Andrews Stand at Sincil Bank in January 1973 for the home tie with Exeter. Not because Lincoln fans were prudish about bad language back then, but because the words came from a mouthy seven-year-old boy. I had not yet become the quiet fan.

At that time, when we bumped into my mum's friends out shopping, they would ask me questions, and I'd hide behind her, refusing to answer. They called me 'taciturn', which was a word I didn't understand. At the football ground, by contrast, I had a voice with more power than the collective speakers of the tannoy system that blared out a scratchy and hardly encouraging version of 'The Lincolnshire Poacher' prior to every home game.

One of those friends we often met shopping was the wife of the town butcher, Bill Lancaster, and she arranged for me to go with Bill and their son Richard to another Lincoln game around that time, on a day when my dad was on call and couldn't make it. It was a 1–1 draw, and I can't remember anything about it except that it was during that strange time in the early '70s when they played a lot of games on a Sunday, and the reason was nothing to do with television scheduling. Maybe it was to stop thugs getting drunk, or to discourage them from travelling. All I remember is that we drove the 15 miles back to our home town of Market Rasen, and when we came in Bill's wife asked me the score. When I told her, she said, 'You didn't shout loud enough, Ian.' To which Bill almost exploded in a combination of repressed anger, bemusement and lingering incredulity, 'Loud enough? I'm surprised you couldn't hear him in Market Rasen.'

My mum, who was there to pick me up, and Bill's wife both laughed, but Bill never offered to take me to a match again. I was clearly a loose cannon, and if I sat there yelling obscenities at the players, he didn't feel he had the remit to clout me round the ear and tell me to shut up. Still, he was always friendly enough when I went into his shop over the following years to pick up some of his excellent Lincolnshire sausages, and he never mentioned his afternoon of hell with the fledgling foghorn of the east.

I've no idea what I was yelling that Sunday afternoon with Bill the Butcher. The day of the 'useless twats' against Exeter, though, is still very clear in my head. I stood up to shout. I can also recall that as the words came out of my tender, unsoaped gob, my dad sort of jerked, which made me sit back down and think that something wasn't quite right.

Years later, he told me that he was trying to stop himself from laughing.

I can also recall that an uncanny silence settled upon the fans around us. Either they were disgusted at my dad's moral laxity and were perhaps waiting for him to wallop me one, or they were laughing up their sleeves as well. At the time, though, I was genuinely disgusted at Lincoln's inability to beat their counterparts from Exeter. I'm not exactly sure why, because I'd been coming to games for over a year by that point, and they must have played like useless twats before. But something about their ineptitude really struck me that afternoon, and it was enough for me to want to offer my own high-pitched brand of motivational loud-speaking.

Shortly after I moved from Zürich to Washington DC in 1999, I discovered what my dad had lived through at Sincil Bank that day. I was sitting in a crowded underground train carriage with my two daughters, then aged one and three. The train emerged from the noisy underground tunnel and out into quieter open space, somewhere near the Pentagon. The carriage was conspicuously silent when Nina, my three-year-old, chose to break it with the single, clearly enunciated word 'Fucking'.

At that moment I bit my lips and sucked in my cheeks. If anyone else in the carriage had laughed, it would certainly have set me off. On the other hand, I didn't really want Nina to see that I thought what she had said was funny. At that age kids don't need much encouragement to repeat the same joke 18,000 times in quick succession. So I sat rigid, wondering if I should turn around and explain to those nearest me, in a thick German accent, that Fucking was in fact the name of the Austrian village[1] we had just moved from and that my daughter was feeling homesick. Like my dad, however, I opted to pretend that nothing had been said, all the while knowing that everyone in that train carriage was thinking the same thing. 'Fucking fucking fucking fucking fucking.'

Where did I learn a word like 'twat', without knowing what it meant? And where did my three-year-old daughter learn the word 'fucking'? I could hardly blame the Swiss kindergarten we'd taken her out of only a few weeks earlier, any more than my dad could have placed the blame on the small but strict private school I was attending at the time in Market Rasen, which was run by a Victorian-style headmistress who seemed around 95 years old.

So I hold my hands up and, if anyone from that Washington DC underground train carriage is reading this today, admit that my daughter learned the word from her foul-mouthed dad, probably through listening from the back seat while I was driving. But please, ma'am, don't be too hard on me. I'd have known better if *my* dad had whacked me round the head at Sincil Bank that time. But he couldn't, because he must have known I'd picked the word up from him. God knows where he got it from, because he came from a family of stringent Scottish Presbyterians. It must have been all those slanderous professors he encountered during his five years at veterinary college in Glasgow.

1. It really does exist, and I hope they have a football team and that they're called Fucking FC. Though the village only boasts a population of 93, so it's doubtful.

None of this detracts from the truth of what I was shouting. Lincoln were a bunch of useless twats. Newly appointed manager Graham Taylor, a fresh-faced 28-year-old, who had started the season at full-back but ended up as manager the month before – after impressing the board with an analytical dossier of how he would turn the club around – had said as much in his programme notes, although he was a little more circumspect.

'Every team would like to dominate the whole 90 minutes play,' he mused, 'but it is common sense that as there are two sides playing, one team at certain times during the game is going to hold the upper hand.' I can imagine the fans before the game assenting to this penetrative wisdom, and the board of directors nodding at each other knowingly, as if to say, *Yes, this is what we bought into. This is dossier-speak.*

'I feel that it is during the times that opponents dominate that we become aware things are perhaps not going as we would like,' the future England manager continued, 'and we tend to become slightly frustrated in our efforts to correct matters.' Oh yes, Professor Doctor Taylor. Absolutely. Hang on a minute, what are you trying to say?

That we're a bunch of useless twats.

Taylor even anticipated my anger. 'The crowd also sense this feeling and things go from bad to worse, even though a tremendous amount of effort is being put into our play.' (Hey, not from where I was sitting.)

The young boss was effectively telling the spectators that they weren't helping matters much by getting on the players' backs. The game against Exeter proved to be the 13th consecutive match where City had failed to win, and a promising early season top-four promotion placing had now become something slightly worse than mediocrity. Looking back on it now, I can't believe that men didn't stand up beside me and yell, 'The squeaky little lad's right, you're a bunch of useless twats!', causing more and more of the 3,729 voices present that day to chime in in agreement and profanely chant, 'Useless twats! Useless twats!' until the players hung their heads in shame.

Being Irish in 1970s Lincolnshire

Lincolnshire football crowds have never had a whole lot to cheer about, and my memory of watching football in the 1970s across the so-called Scunny Triangle – a trilateral linking of the footballing flatlands of Grimsby, Scunthorpe and Lincoln – is of being in the company of men who gave off an air of sullen resignation, and who rarely allowed themselves the indignity of being overwhelmed by emotion. However, there were certain things that seemed to get Lincoln fans worked up, and it wasn't their team playing like a bunch of useless twats. Blacks and Irish, for example.

When I was six, I consciously saw a black man for the first time. He was playing for Aldershot against Lincoln, and it was only my second-ever game. Aldershot were 2–0 up at half-time, and I remember feeling embarrassed when I said to my dad, 'Huh, 0–0,' and he corrected me. Because no one had cheered when Aldershot scored, I assumed that the goals hadn't counted.

The other thing was that Aldershot had this black player called 'Sambo', at least according to the men around me. They seemed to be genuinely angry at Sambo, and kept telling him to get off the pitch every time he got the ball. I looked in my match programme for the line-ups, but was confused that Aldershot had no player called Sambo listed on their team sheet. No one explained to me what was going on, and I didn't ask because at that age you tend to presume it's all something logical that's beyond your ken. I've lost the match programme for that game, so I've no idea who he was, but I sure as hell hope he scored.

On the day of the Exeter game in 1973, Lincoln fielded an Irish striker called Brendan Bradley. He'd come from Finn Harps in the close season and had started brilliantly, and in Lincoln's early-season run had scored several goals with his attacking partners Dixie McNeil and Percy Freeman. At one point he netted seven times in five games, and overall he'd scored 12 times in 24 appearances, which is pretty good considering that McNeil and Freeman would have been the main target men. I liked him because of his alliterative name, and because I'd seen him scoring goals for Lincoln. I'd no idea, of course, that he was Irish or what 'Irish' even was.

Before the Exeter game I was astonished to hear Bradley, one of my favourite players, being booed by the crowd when they read out the line-ups. Then, during the game, he was booed as well. True, his scoring rate had dropped at the same time as the team's, but he could hardly be single-handedly called to account for a 12-match winless run. There was nothing overtly anti-Irish in the catcalls (though would I have known?), and I'm not trying to retrospectively single out people – who could now be dead – with harbouring prejudices that were sadly par for the course at that time. It just makes me sad when I look at Bradley's playing career as a whole.

A few games after the Exeter debacle, he was dropped for good and returned to Finn Harps. Apart from his sortie to Lincolnshire, he spent his whole career, from 1969–86, at the Irish club, scoring 181 goals, an overall record for his team. He was obviously a natural goalscorer, as he proved during that early flash in the 1972–3 season. But when things turned a little rougher, the crowd singled him out. You could see Graham Taylor's dictum about crowd abuse just making things worse in Bradley's performance. He'd lost all confidence and was playing terribly – even a seven-year-old could see that. And at the time I probably thought, *They're right, he is rubbish after all.*

Now I think of a homesick Irishman in 1970s Lincoln. For a while he's scoring goals and things are okay, but then all of a sudden, when the goals stop going in, being called 'Paddy' by the other lads isn't quite as good-natured as it was before. He's recognised in the main street, maybe in the pub, and people take the piss. Now he just doesn't feel like playing at all, and after he's dropped everyone agrees it'd be best if he just packed up and went home to Donegal and the Irish League. People at Lincoln say he doesn't have the mental strength. Brendan tells his family and mates back in Ireland that as far as England goes, and Lincoln in particular, you can stick it; the people are a bunch of ignorant gobshites. It's not like Division Four was a footballing nirvana where soaking up the hassle was worthwhile.

Forty-two years after watching Bradley play for Lincoln against Exeter, I got talking to Johnny Lyons, a Dublin FM radio host, after

I'd appeared on his Sunday-morning show to promote my latest book. I mentioned Bradley and his time at Lincoln, and Johnny promised to get me his number. And so I finally got to speak to my former hero, now 65, about what had driven him away from Lincoln. I braced myself for harsh tales of dressing-room mockery and caustic comments from the locals.

'Lincoln was a nice wee city,' Bradley told me in his gentle, genial manner. 'In the end, I was just a home bird, that's the truth of the matter. I couldn't settle really. It was nothing to do with Graham [Taylor], or the players, or the city itself. I felt happier back home.' Oh. Alright then, but how did the other players treat you? 'Oh, they were a great bunch of fellows.'

My finely honed skills as a muckraking journalist had taken a rapid battering, but I had one more ace in the hand. What about the booing? Wasn't that upsetting to a young player in a strange land?

'No,' he said. 'I didn't actually hear anything. There's always someone in the crowd doesn't fancy you. When you're not playing well, and when supporters have paid to get in, they're entitled to do that – I've done it myself.'

I told him that I was relieved, that I'd been very upset as a seven-year-old to hear him booed, and that for over four decades I'd harboured a quite different idea in my head about his fate as a player in my home city.

Bradley thought about this for a second and then said, 'That must have been quite traumatic for you. But I suppose you've got over it by now.' We both laughed. For him, it was just part of his career that he looked back on fondly, although he did say that he regretted not having tried to stay longer in the English game. For me, though, it was pure closure. Lincolnshire in the early 1970s was shit, but not *quite* as shit as I'd always thought.

'Affectionate' Monkey Chants

In the mid-1970s Lincoln signed two black strikers on loan: the Nigerian Ade Coker from West Ham and the West Indian Bert Bowery from Nottingham Forest. They didn't hang around for more than a handful of games. In 1979 Tony Cunningham became the first black player to thrive at Lincoln, and even he was greeted with monkey chants every time he got the ball.

It's hard to believe, but those monkey chants were meant to be good-natured, and the lanky, powerful Cunningham was genuinely loved by Lincoln fans at a time when attitudes were, in any case, slowly beginning to see some light. The chants, which came mostly from the Railway End terrace, made me feel uncomfortable and I didn't participate, but you could argue at a stretch they were reclaiming the idea of the monkey chant and rendering it inoffensive – it would be heard when Cunningham scored or came close to scoring, an ironic mimicking of racist taunts (I think, I hope). By this time, opposition black players were not chanted *at*, and although Sincil Bank in 1980 was hardly an Islington Council-sponsored multi-ethnic love-in, it was definitely a more tolerant place to watch football than it had been seven years earlier.

By 1980 I was no longer mouthy, and was an almost silent teenage observer, sitting with my mum behind the goal and joining in with the occasional 'City! City!' chant initiated by a weird bloke in the front row called John, who would stand, emotively raise his fist to get the chant going, and then promptly sit down again, mute. Or I was standing on my own on the Railway End terrace, too shy to call out individual abuse, but taking part in the general singing from around five seconds in, when my croaky adolescent voice could be safely lost in the choir.

At seven, though, I had no such self-consciousness. I called it like it was – we were a bunch of useless twats. It wasn't just Brendan Bradley, it was the whole damned team: that victory-shy crowd of nobodies who went another six games without winning after the 2–2 draw with Exeter, before finally scraping a 1–0 home win at the 20th attempt, against Darlington, with a goal in the 90th minute. That I received no backing from those around me shows that my impromptu analysis was just too close to the bone. Especially issued from the tender gob of such a screeching skinny little oik.

Cursing through the Ages

When you are aged seven you swear because you're trying out new words and you have no idea that they depict subjects that make your parents, for some reason, uncomfortable, such as genitals, acts of copulation and masturbation, Jesus Christ our Lord and Saviour, and children born to unwedded parents. I can still remember the scandal caused by Mark Hawley, the producer who later married Tori Amos (that's not relevant here, except as a piece of unashamed name-dropping to show that pre-celebrities used to come to my house), when he called out to someone 'Open the bloody gate' at my sixth birthday party (tsk, rock and roll). The mothers talked about it in hushed voices for weeks after, although they never actually came out and explicitly said, 'His parents should be flogged and stoned.'

Up until around the age of 10 you are serving your apprenticeship. It seems that no matter where you are, you are allowed to hear adults and older kids say all these words, but God forbid if you make the mistake, knowing no better, of saying them yourself. My dad's policy of not reacting probably worked the best. If he'd beaten me savagely and dragged me from the ground to gain the approval of those seated close by, it might have not only put me off Lincoln City and football for life (yes, I know, that might not have been a bad thing…), but it would have made me think, *Wow, swearing is a big deal. Twats! Twats! Twats! Twats! Twats!*

So, from age zero to 10 you start by unknowingly parroting bad words, then once you've realised their shock value, and that the same parents who say these words go ballistic if they hear their kids saying them, you recite them secretively in quiet corners. At the football stadium you listen and absorb, getting ready for the next stage.

From around the age of 10 through your teenage years comes that glorious epoch of released, but limited, profanity. You spend less time with parents and guardians, and much more time with your mates, making up for lost time. Fuck this, fuck that, fuck everything. True swearing outlives all slang – these are wonderful words you'll keep for life.

You still can't really get away with it while your mum's around, however, even if you have one of those fantastic feral mums who make a fishwife look like the Virgin Mary (my mate Chris's mum, two doors up, was like that – I was terrified of her, though also her most attentive listener). There's always that inexplicable double standard, with its savagely unjust, unwritten rule: 'I can swear all I fucking want in my house, but you can't – at all.'

Meanwhile, that teenage awkwardness and reserve is reflected at the football match, where there are crowds of unknown people, many of them older and harder than you. You would never dream of trying to initiate your own chant at this age because your voice might still be too high-pitched and wayward for a heart-wrenching cry of 'Come on, Lincoln, you useless fucking twats.' Heads would turn, and then they'd look at each other and laugh and say, 'You what?' Your football-swearing at this time comes mixed in with the rest, when it's noisy and there's general dismay and condemnation of whatever outrage is happening on the field. You just want to be one of the crowd, tagging along and desperate not to be left out.

Between 20 and 30 you've become an adult, at least physically, so you can swear all you want. And you do. There will be the odd ageing secretary at work who might be shocked, but you know what? Fuck her. And if you're good enough at your job and you choose the right moments to drop the appropriate curse of frustration at some incompetent colleague or the sly tactics of a hated competitor, then so much the better. Swearing can help you on your way up.

Going back home to visit, your mum can't say a lot either. What's she going to do? Throw you out? Stop your pocket money? You go to the game and you let it all out there too. 'Fucking ref, fucking cheating bastard opposition striker.' No one cares. No one looks at you. You might make new mates down the pub before the game, effing away, all unattached young blokes getting it off their chests. It's as natural as the very act of fucking itself (which, it's no coincidence, you're also now obsessed with).

Beyond the age of 30, though, you might be taking your kids to the game. You try to be on your best behaviour, though you'll refuse to buy seats in the Family Stand. The bloke next to you swears at the ref, and your daughter looks up at you and says, 'Daddy, that man just said a bad word.' You ignore her and she insists, as if she wants you to do something about it, like tell the man off. Maybe you could turn the tables and say, 'How do *you* know it's a bad word?' – even though that would be extremely unfair. Remember, though, that's the natural order you had to put up with 30 years ago. Parents are unfair. But next time you buy tickets for the Family Stand.

There are other times when you go to the game on your own or with your ageing mates. And this is when you really let go. At work you're now in a position of responsibility and can no longer throw the curse words around like you've just swaggered into the saloon. You're not the cocky young Turk, you're the middle-aged fart in middle management. You have to hold on to your job so you can pay the mortgage and feed the kids.

And at home you're treading carefully since your daughter's teacher sent a note home complaining about her foul language in the classroom, where she said the same word you used last Sunday afternoon while you were watching the game on television. All bottled up, now is the time for release. It's neither the self-conscious muttering of Stage Two, nor the posturing yells of Stage Three. It's closer to the honest and sincere cry of despair and fury that the seven-year-old Lincoln City fan let loose. You're over 40 years old and you *really* mean it again. 'Pass the fucking ball in a straight line, you useless twats!'

Lincoln v. Exeter and the Cyclical Futility of Life

All these years later and I haven't learned a thing. You'd think that I would be using my vast experience to sit back in my seat exuding an air of Zen serenity, explaining to my kids that football is a game where players have always made mistakes and frustrated the fans, and they always will. It's a game played with a perfectly round, rolling ball, using nothing but the feet, so it's inevitable that passes and shots will not arrive at their intended destinations for much, if not all, of the time. So let's just chill out and enjoy the fresh air and the sporting spectacle.

Yet there I am, on my feet, worse than ever. At a Major League Soccer game between D.C. United and the New England Revolution in the summer of 2004 I stood up and yelled at one of the D.C. players, and saw Nina, now a sensible eight years old, looking at me with an expression of surprise, bewilderment and embarrassment. I quickly smiled at her, reassuringly, although I didn't tell her that I'm quite often like this when she doesn't come along. And that, in fact, this is the very reason I prefer to leave her, her mum and her sister back at the house.

It's fitting to the cyclical nature of life and football that this all started at Lincoln City v. Exeter City. If ever there was a fixture I feel has typified my life as a fan, it would be this one. I feel like I've seen it dozens of times, even though the five programmes in my collection suggest otherwise. Mind you, I've lost some programmes down the years, and on other match days – especially when I was on my own and had to pay for it myself – I didn't bother buying one. And this doesn't detract from my point, which is that I *feel* as though I've been watching this fixture all my life, and even when I go back to Lincoln, it seems they're always playing Exeter, even when they're playing Mansfield or Barnet.

Out of all those Exeter games, the only things I can remember are calling Lincoln a bunch of useless twats and standing outside the ground at the start of the 4–1 victory during the 1975–6 season and missing the first goal – the only time this has ever happened to me, and the only time I can ever remember us being late for kick-off. (And do you think that I and my fellow Lincoln fans who were also still outside the ground cheered when we realised that our team had gone 1–0 up? Did we hell. We all looked embarrassed that we were stupid enough to have arrived late and had already missed some of the action. Ever since, I've annoyed dozens of companions by insisting that we leave the house or the pub way too early, and so we end up arriving way too early. Then they say, 'Nice seats. Now we have 75 minutes until kick-off. Any suggestions for Things to Do?')

Even when Lincoln City were stuck in the National League for six years and there was no chance of the two teams meeting, I knew we'd go back up some day and that Exeter City would return to Sincil Bank – as they did (twice) during the 2017–18 season. Those won't be the last times we meet. Even though both teams have been threatened with bankruptcy and dissolution a number of times over the years, Lincoln v. Exeter is like the houses I lived in and the schools I went to as a kid – they'll always be there to go back to. The teachers' names will have changed, and the houses will have new bathrooms and kitchens, but fundamentally everything will be just as it was before. The school's there to educate, and the houses are being lived in. And although all four sides of Sincil Bank have been completely replaced since 1973, there's every chance that the players, as Graham Taylor would say, are still 'putting a tremendous amount of effort' into their performances. And that they're still playing like a bunch of useless...[2]

2. Although at the time of editing this book, Lincoln had – thanks to managers Danny and Nicky Cowley – mysteriously stopped playing like twats and started playing like a very decent football team. It's been hard to get my head around.

3

Tears

Lincoln City v. Plymouth Argyle, Football League Division Three, Saturday, 18 November 1978

Death on the Glorious 12th

The 1978–9 season began on the 'glorious' 12 August, Lincoln going 2–0 down at Bradford City in the first round, first leg of the League Cup, and my uncle John falling to his death at the age of 40 from the roof of his house in nearby Leeds. During the following winter, strikes and heavy snow brought the country repeatedly to a halt, and the media-deemed Winter of Discontent signalled the end of the Labour government and the imminent rise to power of Margaret Thatcher. My grandfather set his flat on fire while drunk and died from smoke inhalation, my dad left my mum for a younger woman, and Lincoln finished at the bottom of Division Three after a miserable season. If only I'd been able to sing and play guitar, I could have written a country, western and blues album and made a fortune.

My uncle and I understood each other perfectly because he was a football fan. My dad is a fan too, but not in quite the same way. My dad is a cynical, pessimistic fan who always expects the worst, and who also manages to affect an air of detachment if his side is losing. He'll generously acknowledge talent on the opposition team and accept defeat if it was fairly handed out (except when Scotland lose, which is always somehow unfair and always will be). But my uncle was a fan who saw each fresh game as an empty palette of sporting possibilities. Whereas my dad would set out for Lincoln City with a stoical sigh, as if about to embark upon the 100th battle of a grim and futile war, my uncle went to Leeds United and came back full of it – Eddie Gray's dribbling, Peter Lorimer's shooting, Billy Bremner's fighting or Norman Hunter's fouling. He loved every moment, good or bad, because it was all part of the spectacle, and once he got going on the subjects of Leeds and Scotland he would talk twice as quickly and twice as fervently as at any other time.

'When Leeds are away from home,' he once told me, 'there's no greater pleasure in life than running a hot bath on a Saturday afternoon and listening to the second-half radio commentary and the final results.' This is possibly the wisest thing that anyone in our family has ever said, although once my cousins were born I doubt that he ever managed this on more than one or two occasions. I can still remember the way he said it, though, in a tone which implied that although he didn't regret for a second getting married and having three kids, he would be willing to pay several hundred pounds for the chance to sit in the tub on a Saturday afternoon, undisturbed but for the bubble bath and the bubbling voices of Peter Jones and Alan Parry, and 40-odd thousand screaming people in the background.

My uncle gave me all his Leeds programmes, including the ones from Jack Charlton's and Billy Bremner's respective testimonial games, which are probably worth a bit of cash now. I recently gave them to my oldest cousin Mark, who was delighted to see that one of the programmes, Leeds v. Burnley in 1975, was the first game he'd ever been to. His dad would take a milk crate along so that he could stand on it and see. The best thing my uncle ever gave me, though, was a pair of Leeds number 12 tags, the kind players used to wear tied around the tops of their socks. He'd got these one day when he went to watch Leeds Reserves and the players had thrown their tags into the crowd at the end of the game, presumably as some sort of compensation to the fans for their troubles. He couldn't remember if it had been Joe Jordan or Trevor Cherry who'd been sub that day, but it didn't matter to me. I told everyone at school they'd been worn by Joe Jordan. When I played on my own in the thistle-pocked turd-covered cow field next to our house, I'd be the hard-bitten gap-toothed Scottish striker, coming off the bench to save the game. I'd tie the tags round the tops of my socks, even though they came halfway down my calf and felt a little awkward. It didn't matter. These were authentic football wear. They had been worn by a genuine professional, a Scottish international to boot (or perhaps an English one, if it was Trevor Cherry). My leg was feeling, through a sock, what a professional footballer's leg had once felt, through a sock, while playing in an actual game. I still have them today, although I can't see them fetching much on eBay with the following claim of authenticity: 'My uncle, who died 40 years ago, once said they might have been worn by Joe Jordan or Trevor Cherry, although he was a bit vague about it.'

I have many fond memories of my uncle John, but the one image that moves me more than any other is one that I never actually saw. It's just in my imagination, where I see him and a few dozen other devotees on a weekday afternoon in an almost deserted Elland Road watching Leeds United Reserves. Maybe it's half-term or the Easter holidays – he was a biology teacher, and it's just the sort of thing I can see him doing on a free afternoon. It's mainly old blokes smoking pipes and moaning about how crap the players are (why else would you go to watch the Stiffs?). There's no question of him leaving early. He's got out of the house and he's staying out of the house – he's probably the only one happy to be there, toking on a crafty ciggie. At the final whistle, he's already jostling his way to the front of the terrace, thinking about a present for his nephew in Lincolnshire as the players hand out material rewards to those fans who've lost an afternoon of their lives to 90 minutes of already forgotten football. Then he heads for home with a spring in his step because he has Joe Jordan's number 12 tags in his coat pocket. Isn't that the sort of thing that would warm the blood of any normal fan?

The Spectator's (Keith) Fear of the Penalty

A season that started with defeat and tragedy hadn't much improved by the time Lincoln played Plymouth at home on 18 November. 'From past events it does not seem that as supporters you have much to cheer about,' understated new manager Colin Murphy prior to his first home game. 'This I can understand is difficult, for you the one thing that is important is to see your team win and score goals.'

No kiddin', Colin. They had won only once, and were six points adrift at the bottom of Division Three with six points from 17 games, having hit the net only nine times. Former Leeds and Scotland player Willie Bell, who'd semi-successfully taken over during a relegation struggle the previous year, had been sacked a few weeks earlier, and Murphy – previously manager at Southern League Hastings United and then for two brief months at Derby County – was brought in to take on the thankless task of finding the way out of a darkened sewage labyrinth with neither a boat, a paddle, a torch nor a visible outlet in sight.

Reading between the lines, the programme basically acknowledges that Lincoln's season is already over. 'I hope… at the very least, you will see a hearty, spirited, hardworking performance from which we can see light at the end of the tunnel,' said Murphy in a typically tortuous conclusion to his column. Put another way, 'We're up shit creek, there's no way back down shit creek, and shit creek has uncountable bends ahead. It's going to be a long time before the smell of shit subsides. And no, we don't know how long it will be before the water and the air clears – next summer, at the earliest.'

'After a very good result at Hillsborough last week [0–0], let's hope we can continue picking up those precious points to get us away from the foot of the table,' said the Supporters Club section, with a gritted smile. The Red Imps Association was no more bullish: 'Let us hope that things will start to go our way a bit more,' it offered lamely, 'and we can get back to our winning ways.'

Meanwhile, *Lincolnshire Echo* writer Maurice Burton carefully posited that 'the task of scoring 34 points, which should be enough, from 29 matches, is not beyond the capabilities of a Lincoln side playing to form'.

Those final three qualifying words are important. Lincoln were nowhere close to playing to form. Burton stated that now would be a good time for Lincoln's strikers 'to start putting the ball into the net'. Because if they don't, you know, they 'are going to be wide open to defeat every time the opposition manages to slip one in'.

(When it comes down to it, all the football experts, pundits, analysts, fans and journalists that ever expressed an opinion about the game have been saying exactly the same thing: 'The team that scores the most goals will win.' If only I knew how to get one of those jobs where you're paid £100+ grand a year for repeating this week after week, using a different combination of words every time.)

As a 13-year-old fan who was not used to seeing Lincoln at the foot of the table, I was certainly reading these lines from an optimist's point of view. Mathematically, we could still do it. Lincoln could still manage 34 points from 29 games, and so until they had failed, what was the point of saying they couldn't?

I was a bad loser. I hated losing. I hadn't yet understood the one defining characteristic of defeat – its inevitability. During the previous seven years as a Lincoln fan, they had rarely lost at home when I had been there, even when mired in the lower reaches of Division Four. From 1974 through to 1977, under Graham Taylor, they had finished fifth, then first (in the Fourth) and then ninth in the Third. In those three seasons they'd only been defeated at home on three occasions, and I hadn't seen any of them.

So far that season they had already lost at home four times, including a 0–5 humiliation to newly promoted Watford, now managed by Graham Taylor. I missed that one, thankfully, though according to Ian and Donald Nannestad's official club history, the home fans were cheering the away team by the game's end. I don't recall if I was at the other games or not. I can only remember Plymouth and my naïve greenhorn hopes that Lincoln could still turn its season around, while wilfully ignoring Maurice Burton as he approached the conclusion to his column: 'I wish him [Murphy] well in his task. Any man who is prepared to take on such an ominous job, with the inevitable consequences of bitter failure known to him beforehand, deserves to succeed.'

I can only remember one incident from the game. Lincoln were winning 3–2 and it was the last minute. I think Plymouth had pulled one back from being 3–1 down, but I couldn't swear to it. I do know that I had already mentally added the two points to the six we already had. We had increased our points rate and our strike rate by 33 per cent, all in one satisfactory afternoon. We had a new manager. We would keep on winning and everything was going to be alright.

Plymouth had a few 'name' players because their extravagant manager, Malcolm Allison, didn't know a whole lot about managing a football team, but he was good at covering up the fact by being constantly active in the transfer market. He'd just bought Barry Silkman from one of his numerous previous clubs, Crystal Palace, and that summer had also taken Keith Fear from Bristol City. I knew Keith Fear because he was in my Football '78 Panini sticker album. 'A tricky ball player', it says in his Panini profile. *Complete and utter bastard*, I thought for several years afterwards. On his sticker he looks like a hirsute and slightly melancholic gnome.

Fear struck the Plymouth equaliser from outside the area, a left-foot volley that crept into the bottom-left corner past on-loan keeper Ian Turner. Turner did that thing of looking around from his prostrate position, asking with his eyes, 'Why did you let him shoot?' He was blameless, of course. The players' heads hung like this was the sort of thing they'd come to expect. Worst of all, the Plymouth players were jumping all over each other like they really had more than a sole point to celebrate. I thought it was outrageous that Fear, who'd come from First Division football, could get so excited about scoring against Lincoln, of all teams.

When the final whistle went shortly afterwards, I started to cry.

Tears on Tap

Not just a sore loser, I was a cry-baby too. There was no other word for it. As a boy, I had a huge problem holding back the tears. I had no major physical affliction that other kids could have picked on other than a pair of bandy legs which had not yet evolved their full cowboy-like curves. But there were times when I'd have traded my inability to stay cool and dry at the eyes for a huge schnozzer, Dumbo ears, buck teeth or a chronic limp. There was no one like me for letting it all out. Looking at my pale wiry body in the mirror made me think that I should have been born a girl. They got to cry all the time and no one seemed to bother. On the contrary, girls were expected to cry. It's what they did. Shakespeare's embittered King Lear called tears 'women's weapons'. For boys, they were more like inviting, open wounds.

Here's how long my crying problem lasted. I was in a German class, and the teacher picked me up on a basic pronunciation point. Then he said that my pronunciation was typical of the whole class, the whole year, even. We weren't good enough. We were pathetic. I felt tears flush into my eyes. My classmates all stared at me in horror. *Is he going to beal*[1]*?* I was 21 years old at the time, in the final year of my German degree at Birmingham University, just a few months from graduating. I was supposed to be fluent in the language. Professor van der Will was right, I was the manifestation of a collective miserable failure. It was enough to make you cry.[2]

That day, I just managed to hold back, even if the evidence of my idiocy had been welling up. When younger, I'd had no such luck. Even my best friends delighted in my tearful ways, and I can't say I blame them. I was no better when it came to other people's physical and mental weaknesses, and everyone knows the school playground is just a learning field for the general shittiness of the working world beyond. You feel better when someone else fails. It's a natural reaction. Just like crying.

There were plenty of occasions when I roared, but here are my three favourites:

At nine years old I played in only my second-ever football match for Market Rasen Methodist Church Sunday School. I was in defence and doing okay. We were 3–2 ahead, then in the final minute I did the opposite of Keith Fear, sticking my leg out to block a shot and sending our keeper the wrong way. I can still see his incredulous face – just like Ian Turner's. Being Christians, they were all very good about it. I walked to my dad's veterinary surgery to get a lift home. He took

1. 'To beal' in northern Lincolnshire means 'to cry'. In practice, its implied meaning is 'to cry like a snivelling, pathetic little baby who wants his mammy'.

2. Professor van der Will was notorious for speaking his mind. At the start of our first year he asked a group of students in his seminar what A-level grades they had achieved in German. When one told him that he'd got a C, the Prof exploded, 'Well then, you're fucking lucky to be here!'

a look at my face and said, 'What's the matter with you?' I began to wail. Only now does it occur to me that around this time I became an atheist.

At eleven years old my best friend, Tim Bradford, ganged up with an older lad to steal my fruity men. These were plastic fruit-shaped figurines that you put on the end of your pencil. I was very attached to them. Tim and the older boy threw them to each other as I whined, 'Give us 'em back.' They laughed, and in the end I broke down and cried. They gave me back my fruity men, and the older boy, with whom I later played football and cricket on the same team for several years, enjoyed spreading the story about how 'Plenderleith bealed when we nicked his fruity men'. Around this time I stopped believing in the secret mystical powers of the fruity men, although Tim Bradford is somehow still my closest friend. The bastard.

At twelve years old, on the day we received our second-year physics exam back, I scored 46 per cent, a result I knew would get me a severe bollocking from my dad. As we went through the paper, question by question, I realised that I'd got one of the questions right, but that it had been marked as wrong, and this would give me an extra 2 per cent. I brought the attention of our teacher to his mistake. True, 48 per cent isn't a whole lot better than 46 per cent, and wouldn't save me a bollocking, but I was clutching for any lifeline. The bearded git didn't want to admit it, and claimed he hadn't been able to read my handwriting. He wouldn't give me back my lousy 2 fucking per cent. Like it would have killed him. Quietly, I began to weep, and to hide this I pretended to be looking for something in my bag under my desk. Tim Bastard (as he shall be known from now on), sitting next to me, noticed, and began to gesture to the class by pointing at me and then rubbing his eyes gleefully. There was a low buzz of appreciation across the class, and around this time I lost all desire to be a physicist, or ever to grow a beard. (Three years later, the same teacher punished me with an essay for talking in class. I hadn't forgotten the lost 2 per cent. I can't remember exactly what essay title he gave me, but I distorted its premise into a long and thinly veiled acerbic attack on his personality that so infuriated him that he marched off, red-faced and speechless, to show it to our admirably bemused headmaster. Despite the subsequent trouble – I had to write him a letter of apology – I felt that I was suitably avenged. A malevolent part of me even likes to imagine that he went to the bog after reading it and broke down in tears.)

So it wasn't exactly the school of hard knocks, not even a concerted bullying campaign, a bare-knuckle fistfight (curiously, I had a few of those and *didn't* cry) or 18 strokes of the headmaster's quivering cane. Just an own goal, some fruity men and a lost 2 per cent on a physics exam. When Lincoln conceded a last-minute goal against Plymouth Argyle, my tears were not caused by pent-up grief at the death of my uncle, or even by the fact that my mum and dad had, over the previous few weeks, suddenly started fighting like feral wildcats. It was just the goal. It was Keith fucking Fear. It was too late for us to get another one. It was the squandered point and the floating, lost sensation of hopelessness that comes with being anchored to the foot of Division Three.

'Crying Is for Jessies'

My mum was probably too soft on me for crying (cuddles, sympathy, etc.), while my dad, a traditional male in every respect, veered towards the other extreme. 'Don't be such a big Jessie,' was his customary response when drops began to cascade down my cheeks because he'd yelled at me for failing to complete some extraordinarily basic practical task (another speciality of mine).[3] Given the things that upset me (see above), he was probably right. I was a bit of a big Jessie. But that day at Sincil Bank, in the very same stand where six years earlier he'd hidden his laughter at me yelling 'Come on, Lincoln, you useless twats,' he just looked at me, slightly surprised. He didn't say anything, though. He looked like it was the first time he'd seen me crying for a worthwhile cause. I wasn't howling, I was just letting the tears out,

3. My family nickname was Useless Eustace, which in retrospect I love. At the time, I was probably not so chipper about it. Both Mum and Dad claim they have no recollection of calling me this and that I must have made it up in order to garner retroactive sympathy and to make them feel bad. 'I suppose you'll want counselling now,' was my dad's response.

soundlessly, so I wasn't creating a scene or anything like that. In fact, just as I had done when I'd cried at the physics paper, I tried to hide it, and I wasn't even sure that he'd seen me.

When I was sitting at tea that night, though, I knew he must have noticed. Without any explanation, my mum came up to me, hugged me from behind and gave me 10p. If I'd had any hint of manhood in me, I'd have stood up, outraged, and thrown her money back at her while shouting, 'I don't get paid for crying, woman!' But although even in 1979 10p was hardly a fortune, it was still 10p, and it would stretch quite far at Garnett's Sweet Shop. I would have preferred the extra point, but as consolations go it was better than nothing.

Of course, I was almost 12 years ahead of my time. When Paul Gascoigne burst into tears during the 1990 World Cup semi-final upon receiving the yellow card that would prevent him playing in the final, crying was suddenly okay. If a hard-drinking working-class Geordie could cry in front of millions of people, then anyone could. Gary Lineker was making the same gestures to the England bench that Tim had made to my classmates in second-year physics. But this wasn't in order to get Bobby Robson and the whole squad to jump up and down, point at Gazza and shout, 'Ha ha, look, he's *roaring*!' Lineker's gesture was one of concern and compassion. Everyone just loved Gazza for bealing. He cared, and we all cared back. This was the day that football, for the first time, was something you could cry about. Nowadays, if you believe the cameras that pan the stadium for sorrow at the end of 90 minutes, it's almost obligatory.

Crying through the Ages

Up until about the age of nine, you can let it all out. You lose, you cry. Other kids don't get too worked up at you crying right now, because they know they'd do the same. Parents may lightly chastise you for being a bad loser, but mostly they understand. Kids have to get used to losing, like they have to get used to all the other sordid disappointments of life. When I was coaching my daughter's class at school, an eight-year-old boy threw himself to the ground at the end of the game because the other side had scored the winning goal. He was especially upset that the winning goal had been scored by my daughter, and that when I'd kicked the ball back into play it had gone straight to her, standing in front of an empty net (it was almost time to pack up). He screamed, wailed and beat the ground with his fists so hard that at first I thought he was having some kind of fit. I ran over, ready to call the emergency services, until I realised he was shouting 'That's not fair!' over and over.

'No, son, it's not,' I said. 'It's football.'

Then, overnight, it seems, boys learn to stop crying. There are certainly a handful, like myself, who don't get the memo and slip through the net. We stragglers are imbued with a special sensitivity that sets us aside from the mob. Or, interpreted another way, we're spoilt little cry-babies (or big Jessies). While others are moving on and growing up, we still care so much about losing a stupid game that we get upset about it. Although, in my defence, as a rule I didn't cry about losing; it was just the odd exception, like the own goal and the fruity men, and the physics exam, and Man United losing to Southampton in the 1976 FA Cup Final, and Scotland losing to England at Hampden in 1978. And Lincoln conceding Keith Fear's last-minute equaliser later that same year. But, mostly, I could take it. If my school team lost, I'd be depressed for the day, but it wasn't worth *roaring* about. And if we'd lost and I'd scored a goal, I almost didn't give a toss at all.

The changing of perspectives and the dominance of oscillating hormones means that from around the age of 14 until the age of 30, tears dry up for good, unless you really, really give a shit. Former German international Andy Möller weathered the nickname 'Heulsuse' (translated literally as 'crying Susan', more loosely as 'cry-baby') throughout his career, because whenever he disputed a referee's decision he looked as if he was about to burst into tears. There is a famous picture of the less than charming Lothar Matthäus, during a Bayern Munich v. Borussia Dortmund game, standing in front of Möller with his balled-up fists up to his eyes doing the Tim Bastard imitation of a small child crying – 'Look at Möller! He's roaring!' Thomas Müller did a similar imitation of Giorgio Chiellini to his face during the Euro 2016 quarter-final between Germany and Italy.

After Gazza, though, crying players became a tediously common sight. Now, all of a sudden, you were allowed to be sensitive – as long as you were crying at the end of lost but crucial encounters – because the media had decreed that it made for great visual and written copy. At the end of the game, the cameras no longer focus solely on the victors. There are enough cameramen at the ground, covering every breath of every game – both important and less important – that we can see the expression on every player's face as they sit down on the turf and start the process of coping with defeat. When this trend started, the talk would be about the one big Jessie on the team who'd let it all out, and who was then ensured cult status among fans for years to come because he was the one who really showed that he cared. He'd mop his eyes with the club badge, then kiss it, tear it off the shirt using his teeth, then have the club physio stitch it on to his raw left nipple with a red-hot needle.[4] Now, any player who doesn't cry comes in for criticism because he or she wasn't seen to emote enough for club or country.

Among fans in the 14–30 age bracket, though, this is a time to swear at defeat and spit on the floor rather than wet your sleeve. You're old enough to control the emotions and channel them towards vengeance. You could live to see another 40 or 50 seasons, maybe more, so this is not the final word, this bitter Cup Final defeat at the hands of local rivals, or this relegation on goal difference on the last weekend of the season. You'll get over it. So will the players. In fact, it will only be a few more weeks until pre-season training begins. As the manager of the Market Rasen Wanderers Under-15 team said week after week during our disastrous 1979–80 season, 'It'll be different next year' (see 'Hope' chapter).

Then, at the first signs of middle age, your eyes start once more to become a source of salty water. In the spring of 1995, just a few weeks shy of my 30th birthday, I went to see the semi-final of the German women's FA Cup, between FSV Frankfurt and Grün-Weiß Brauweiler, which took place within walking distance of my flat.

4. Not really, but you get the point.

There were around a hundred people in the Bornheimer Hang stadium, and the final score was 1–1. After extra-time, it went to penalty kicks, and Frankfurt won. The women celebrated with such unadulterated joy that all of a sudden I was overwhelmed by an old sensation that hadn't plagued me for years: the waterworks were creaking back into life. Fortunately, there were so few people in the ground that no one else spotted me, although somehow I felt that at any moment a gang of German teenagers were going to appear from nowhere, and one of them would point at me and yell to his mates, 'Ha ha ha, *guckt euch die große Schwuchtel an, der heult wie ein Mädchen!*' ('Look over here, lads, this big poof's crying like a girl!')

I was surprised to have developed such an affinity with this team over the course of a single afternoon that their victory had led me to tears of happiness – the only time I'd cried in a stadium besides the Plymouth game. But it was just my body preparing me for parenthood. Around one year later I became a father, and from then on my body let its defences down again. Not at football grounds; just at really soft stuff, like sentimental kids' films and my daughters saying something cute. The sort of stuff that you don't tell other people about, so I'll stop right here.

Programme Highlights

Profile on Tommy Tynan

The month before the Plymouth game, Lincoln had signed Tynan from Sheffield Wednesday as a solution to their striking ills. Two years earlier, he had played against Pelé for the Dallas Tornado in the North American Soccer League. At £33,000 he was a record buy, and like many record buys before and since, he was a flop (although he didn't get much of a chance), scoring one goal in nine games, before Colin Murphy sold him on in February to Newport County at a loss.

'He says he is happy at Lincoln,' the programme reports doubtfully, 'and his ambition is to be successful and he looks forward to many goals, and a revival in the club's fortunes.'

His hopes and expectations were thwarted on all fronts. Neither was he 'successful', at least not at Lincoln, nor did the club revive, finishing the season at the foot of the table and going down to Division Four while most of us were shaking the remnants of tinsel off our hands.

Just as record signings inevitably fail, so Tynan fulfilled the other rule of spurned front men, returning to Sincil Bank on numerous occasions and scoring for whichever club he was playing. Wherever he went, he scored goals, including 66 for Newport County and 126 in three different spells for… Plymouth Argyle. But nothing seemed to be going well in Lincolnshire that season, not even for a born goalscorer like Tynan. What started with death and defeat ended with relegation and my parents divorcing (but don't switch off, this is a football book, so I'm only going to mention it in passing).

Lincoln City FC Social Club

A list of forthcoming attractions in the programme on that tearful day included George Perry, 'a vocal entertainer who hails from Doncaster', who would be appearing that night. If that wasn't enough, the following night the club welcomed Gail Sinclair, who 'has the unusual distinction of being a female guitar/vocalist'. You can just see the social club's secretary during the sound check asking, 'Are you sure you know how to tune that thing, luv?'

The following week, we were asked to make space in our diaries for Sandra Dean, 'a personality who has appeared on TV many times. Sandra comes from Durham.' Exactly how she was set to entertain us was not revealed.

Match-Day Entertainment: New Ollerton Blue Jays Children's Jazz Band

I can't recall this pre-match jamboree, which consisted of 'about seventy children of ages varying between six and fifteen… in three sections consisting of Mace girls, Banner section, Drum and Cymbal Section'. Quite how they performed jazz with maces, banners, drums and cymbals is, therefore, just a guess. Perhaps this was part of a youth-inspired avant-garde improvisational music scene in the county that passed me by at the time.

There's a picture of them gathered in a cow field, all wearing tall white fur hats. They look cheerful. I hope Keith Fear is happy that he spoilt their day as well.

4

Kissing

Lincoln City v. Scunthorpe United, Football League Division Four, 3pm, Saturday, 27 September 1980

Breaking the 'Code'

This date marks the first time I officially copped off with a girl. It was official because it was seen and talked about by lots of people. It was in the full public glare of the disco lights at Tealby Village Hall, and so was recorded in the verbal annals of Lincolnshire snogging incidents, dated autumn 1980. I can't remember much because I was drunk, but I know that it didn't feel right because the girl I was copping off with had dumped one of my best mates, Neil, the day before. And he was staying at my house that weekend. Only hours earlier we had been watching Lincoln v. Scunthorpe together.

Among American women, I recently discovered (and, alarmingly, I've been told by non-American women that this applies elsewhere), there's some sort of rule about not dating your friends' exes, otherwise you can consider the friendship automatically destroyed because you broke the 'Code'. It doesn't matter if the friend only went out with the guy in question for a month, 12 years ago, and she broke up with him and doesn't care about him any more and has since married and had children. You just don't do it because it will piss her off that you broke the 'Code'.

I think it was around the same time that I received a similar piece of advice from my German teacher. One night at Market Rasen Rugby Club, being underage and having no money, I drank some of his pint when he went to the loo. 'A bit of advice for you, Plenderleith,' he intoned wisely the following week in front of the whole class. 'There are two things you should never steal off a man: his woman and his pint.' I wasn't quite cocky enough to tell him that although I had enjoyed his beer, he didn't need to have any worries on the other account.

Neil, though, was quite chipper about me having snogged his ex. Almost congratulatory. He'd been putting in serious snogging time for a couple of years by then at least, and was obviously feeling sorry for me. Also, he'd only actually been going out with this girl for three days when she gave him the axe, so it wasn't like he was suffering too profoundly. And as there was a limited number of vaguely attractive females in Lincolnshire, a certain amount of sharing was inevitable. This was the countryside, after all, where sometimes generations of an entire family could live undiscovered for decades on a small farm hidden up a bumpy track where no one had bothered to look.

Still, while I was relieved enough at finally notching my first goal in adolescence's seemingly interminable season, it didn't feel quite right. It was like wanting to make your mark with a screaming 30-yard thunderbolt in front of 40,000 fervid home fans, only to be presented with an open goal from three yards out in a pre-season friendly at Hendon Town. True, the stats showed I was listed that night as a scorer, and of course they all count, but they didn't show the true story. Which was that I had almost pushed a better placed teammate out of the way in order to get on the score sheet, wheeling away with my arm in the air while everyone else stood around with their hands on their hips staring at me like I was a bit of a wanker. But then who would expect moral fibre from a 15-year-old?

Moral Fibre, Part One

Scunthorpe are one of Lincoln's local rivals. Despite our friendship, Neil was perceived as my rival at school in most sports. Snogging his just-ex was the first time I'd 'beaten' him at anything. Lincoln had often beaten Scunthorpe, but that day they could only draw 2–2.

Neil was a promising young footballer who trained with the England set-up at some age level or other, and went on to play for the Grimsby Town youth team. He was also the best rugby player in our year and the fastest cross-country runner, and the fastest at middle-distance athletics and probably at sprinting too. I was the second best at cross-country and 1,500m, every time, and way back in the field in the other sports. In races against him, I couldn't figure out if it was a psychological block, whereby he simply possessed the greater will to win, or if he was just faster and nothing I could ever do besides putting him in a wheelchair would change that.

When we'd first come across each other at De Aston Comprehensive School at the age of 11, he'd been a right little shit: utterly full of himself and all the stories of his goals and first-place finishes. With some ruthless long-term ego-bashing, we'd managed to turn him into quite a bearable kid, and it helped that he was a very good footballer who made our school team look much better than it probably was. We became friends, even if there was always this running undercurrent of competitiveness. It was something we could laugh about, but we also took it dead seriously. I wanted to beat him, so badly, but I never expected to. By the time we were 15, I was so used to coming second, or worse, in all sporting endeavours that I had long since learned to cope with the disappointment of not being number one. ('Why can ye no beat him?' my dad would ask. Er, because I can't.)

His parents were in the RAF, and they had moved away from Lincolnshire to Scotland the previous year, leaving him in the school's cliquey, 70-strong boarding house. Boarders 'got' girls as boarders were imbued with a sexual mystique, either because they played rugby or because girls preferred not having to meet their boyfriends' parents. Perhaps boarders were – as with Neil's football, rugby and athletics skills – simply *better* at getting off with girls than day-schoolers. They could talk in the dark dorm at night, exchanging tips on chat-up techniques, whereas we day-schoolers were too timid to even admit to our best mates that we fancied someone in case they started snickering and told the rest of the school. We were sexually backwards, and boarders were cool and mature. And they put in the extra effort to avoid the label of being gay (because they all slept together), while saps like me just sat around with crushes, waiting for the girls of our dreams to come up and snog us. Which happened as often as me beating Neil at cross-country and 1,500m.

So Neil, once he became a boarder, started copping off with girls, while the rest of his old day-school mates could only stand and admire his prolific tongue movements. Yet despite his superior rugby skills, he was never entirely accepted by his new cohorts in the boarding house, even though they took rugby almost as seriously as they took masturbation (the boarding-house porn stash allegedly took up more space than the British Library). 'You'll always be a scabby day-schooler at heart,' a particularly odious cretin sneered one night when the pack closed in on Neil for the (absolutely not homoerotically charged) humiliating rite of shaving off one of his eyebrows. It was strange that in the middle of a bog-standard modern comprehensive school there existed this anachronistic vacuum of ritualistically inclined, academically dull *snoggers* who seemed to believe they were attending Eton in the 1850s.

Seeing as he was the best athlete in the school and could barely move for queues of doe-eyed admirers, and as he was still a bit of a cocky little bighead at heart, it didn't seem to bother Neil much that he deftly kept a foot in both camps. So every now and again he would be 'released' to come and stay at my house for the weekend, especially if there was a party on, and Tim Bastard and I would sit around and laugh at his tales of sadistic boarding-house punishments and obligatory nightly doses of Judas Priest.

Moral Fibre, Part Two

Since the Plymouth game almost two years earlier there had been a few changes. My parents had divorced and my dad had moved to Scotland with my future stepmother. I was living with my mum and sister on a bland middle-class housing estate (think Privet Drive in the *Harry Potter* books) in the village of Middle Rasen, just about joined to the town of Market Rasen. But Colin Murphy was still the manager at Lincoln. Relegation had been followed by a year of consolidation in Division Four, and now we were sitting in second place after eight games. 'I am so pleased that at long last it would appear that we can see the light at the end of the tunnel,' said Murphy in his by now notoriously rambling programme notes. Remember that light in the Plymouth programme? Well, if you don't sack your manager after six games and give him a chance, sometimes that metaphorically hackneyed luminescence will appear. Eventually.

My dad's move to Scotland meant that for the next few years I lived a life largely free of direct parental control. My mum showed a commendably libertarian attitude towards me going out, with no curfews and a few unspoken boundaries that I was careful not to overstep. It wasn't that she didn't care, it was just that she was quite self-absorbed around this time and, like the attacking midfielder I was, I happily made runs down the left wing to exploit the spaces she left free. We certainly had our share of run-ins, but it was over stuff like me leaving skid-marks on the toilet bowl. Left unsupervised to do my school work, I actually did it, whereas I know that under pressure I tended to rebel. (During my annual exams, when I was 12, my dad had gone to watch Lincoln one night on his own because he said I had to revise. I was so peeved that he'd gone to a football match without me that I sat in my bedroom reading comics all evening, deliberately avoiding my school books. Yep, I really knew how to stick it to The Man.)

That Saturday, instead of looking ahead to how we would buy a bottle of Martini from the off-licence, despite clearly being underage, and then secretly chug it down before the party, Neil and I should have been paying closer attention to Colin Murphy's column. The last home game, against Aldershot, had seen Lincoln's first defeat at Sincil Bank for a year, but they had bounced back the following weekend with a 0–1 win at Wimbledon. Murphy accredited this to a 'clear-the-air' chat following the Aldershot defeat.

'At times there is nothing like a bombshell and a serious discussion between players and management to effect confidence, attitude, determination, concentration and general application,' he wrote, beginning to sound like an ad for household paints. 'The moral fibre shown by the side ensured that these particular qualities were not missing… From a managerial point of view, it just shows what a fine bunch of determined men, irrespective of footballing skills, we have on our staff.'

So it wasn't necessarily skill but moral fibre that you needed to be a footballer. My PE teacher, Mr Brewis, had been telling me that if I wanted to make the grade as a player I needed to lift weights, because I was too light in the tackle. But what Neil and I should have done was go home, watch *Match of the Day* for tactical tips, have an early night and then be bright and fresh for our 10am kick-off with Market Rasen Wanderers the following morning.

Years later, I met Mr Brewis again at Tim Bastard's wedding. 'Neil was a good player,' he said, 'and he was good enough to be a professional. The problem was that he didn't *want* it enough.' As Colin Murphy might have said, he didn't have the attitude, determination, concentration and application, although the confidence was definitely the one thing he did have (the ball-hogging bastard). He just didn't have the moral fibre – unlike, say, Craig Bellamy, Lee Bowyer and Joey Barton – to make it to the top. Okay, bad examples. I suppose sometimes you can be good enough to not have to work that hard to reach the point where you earn several grand a week, moral fibre or not.

Mr Brewis politely didn't mention why I hadn't become a professional footballer. And I didn't bring it up either, although it may be emblematic that while we were having the conversation I was knocking back several pints of Guinness (plenty of fibre, just not the moral stuff) and toking on a cigarette.

Match Report!

Relations between my mum and dad had deteriorated to the point where it was not possible for him to phone me at home, so we began writing letters to each other. In early 2005 he told me that he was clearing out his things and had found all the letters I'd ever sent him. Did I want to see them? Otherwise he'd probably throw them out. What was in them? I asked. Well, mostly stuff about Lincoln City, he replied. That was hardly a strong justification for literary curators to rush and throw themselves in front of the incinerator, but I asked him if he wouldn't mind sending them on when he had a spare moment. When they arrived, I glanced at one or two but was too mortified to read any further. In the interests of research for this chapter, I finally braced myself and plunged in to endure sheaths of lame puns, sketchy match reports and whiney carping about my teachers, my friends and my home town.

The letter I wrote to him the day after the Scunthorpe match is a little unusual compared with the others. Normally, I told him the score, the scorers and whether Lincoln had played well or not. I might speculate vaguely on their promotion chances, and then discuss any games I'd seen on TV or had played in. But my report of the Scunthorpe match was strangely detailed, almost as if I was writing in code. Or as if I was desperately trying not to write about something else.

'On Saturday we went to Lincoln v. Scunny,' I scrawled, 'and Scunthorpe managed to score two goals with one shot, whilst Lincoln scored two goals with twenty.' Normally, I'd have left this gross injustice at that and gone on to offer some carefully selected highlights from my school work and my own footballing performance, and some brief semi-jocular insight into my alienation from the world that only served to highlight my superior place in the general scheme of things. But not that day.

'It was the usual story of bad luck after opening with a brilliant header from [Mick] Harford after a fine move,' I went on, in more detail than my dad can possibly have wished to know. 'Scunthorpe pulled one back before half-time [editor's note to 15-year-old self: they didn't "pull one back", they equalised], but David Hughes put Lincoln back ahead with a good volley just before half-time [editor's note to 15-year-old self: this is why you didn't make the grade as a football reporter. It should have been a "cracking" or "blistering" volley. But a "good" volley? How my dad must have wept over leaving Lincolnshire after finding out he'd missed "a good volley" at Sincil Bank.] Then Steve Thompson scored a soft own goal, and after that Lincoln missed a lot of chances.'

So far, so thrilling. But what about the rest of this momentous Saturday? Was I about to tell my dad that I'd taken the first steps towards coming of age? Would there be a similarly detailed account of my grapplings outside Tealby Village Hall? Perhaps something like this:

> It looked like being the usual story of bad luck and not copping off with anyone, when someone told me this lass with ginger hair fancied me. I took her outside to explain that I couldn't possibly cop off with her because she'd only just chucked one of my best mates the day before, and besides, he was staying at my house that weekend.
>
> We sat down on a bench and next thing I know, it's in! I suppose it's all about snaffling up the opportunities when you've got them, and if you don't get into position, then you don't get the chances. When the lass put her tongue down my throat, I responded, and then, not really having much idea what to do next, I peppered her neck with a series of good love-bites that she had to cover with a scarf on Monday morning. She only had time to pull one or two back, but I was able to display these trophies to the lads in the changing room at Rase Park the next morning and they were well excited. I also got a brief bonk on, but it didn't count for anything, and by the time it was all over I'd just about had my fill of her perfume. It was an interesting night, but it all went very quickly. Perhaps if I hadn't been off my head on neat Martini swigged direct from the bottle, I would have appreciated it more.

But no. Here's what I actually wrote: 'After another late-night party last night, Rooey [Neil] and I weren't feeling 100% for this morning's first home match at Rase Park against Nettleham.'

And that was it. *Not feeling 100%.* Nothing about how we lied at the off-licence to get a bottle of Martini, and then when we arrived in Tealby – the token posh village in our area, where the better-off kids had parents who hired out the village hall so that we could shove each other's tongues down our throats – we had hidden the bottle in a nearby stream to keep it cool, and every half hour or so we would duck out of the disco, where alcohol was not allowed, and run down the road, increasingly reeling, to down as much as we could take until finally the bottle was empty. Talk about leaving out the best part of the story.

Something else I can recall about that night is dancing to 'Baggy Trousers' by Madness and remembering this was the second time I'd heard the song that day. The first time had been at Sincil Bank, where it was part of the usual pre-match entertainment – pop hits over the crackly tannoy. As I danced, I was thinking, *Lincoln v. Scunthorpe was an age away. That was back in the mists of time, before I got off with somebody. Ha ha ha, I've done it. I've got off with somebody. Wait till everybody hears about this. I have snogged. I'm a snogger. I bet you I'll be at it all the time now.*

The girl with the long red hair didn't look so good in a blue snorkel parka on Monday morning, and I decided not to go out with her. It's doubtful she would have wanted to in any case. Twice over the coming months, after I'd drunk enough to summon up the courage, I tried to get off with her again at discos, reasoning that where I had been successful once, I'd have a fair chance of being so again. But you know what they say about players going back to their former clubs – it's never the same. She was having none of it, and turned me down both times. Maybe she recognised the smell of alcohol on my breath. And when Monday morning came around and I watched the sober snoggers go through the motions of asexual lip contact at morning break, lunchtime and afternoons too, I was always relieved she'd rejected my less than noble advances. It was two years before I even got close to a girl again.

Football and the Contradictions of Kissing

It's well known that footballers used to shake hands when they scored goals, then trot back to the centre circle manfully suppressing any display of joy. At most, a player was allowed to tousle another teammate's hair. The more money that came into the game, the more expressive and emotional players became when they scored an important goal. During the 1970s, commentators had plenty to say about players kissing each other when they scored goals. I can't recall who these commentators were, but I'm pretty certain that at least one of them was Jimmy Hill, who had come so far in his career as the self-appointed Mr Controversy that the only way he could now be controversial was if he dared *not* to be controversial. The general tone of these discussions was that all this kissing had got out of hand – the implication being (though it was never explicitly expressed) that this behaviour was in some way homosexual.

Anyone who's ever experienced the sexual culture of a professional football team would have to laugh at this notion. Football lads together spend as much time talking about their shagging proficiency as they do about tactics. Kissing a teammate would be no more interpreted as gay behaviour than sinking 16 pints of lager and sleeping with the club barmaid. Paradoxically, if you didn't kiss a teammate, it could be seen as a bit odd. It might seem that you were scared of something, like suddenly being overcome with the desire to *go the whole way*. Yes, even right out there on a muddy field in front of several thousand fans.

Kissing became football's equivalent of rugby players masturbating over a digestive biscuit and then forcing the last one to come to eat the biscuit, topping and all (although I suspect this is more of an urban myth, as I've never met a rugby player who will admit to having taken part in such a ritual. Then again, who would?). Footballers are for some reason more reserved than rugby players, even after 16 pints of lager, so the kiss is a reflection of their masculinity. It's saying, 'I love you so much for scoring that goal I want to elevate you to the status of an object of desire, like a beautiful woman. But it doesn't mean I'm gay.' And just as the mythical rugby players are showing each other what they've got, there's really no hint that when they stand in a circle with their jockstraps down and their todgers out, they want to do anything besides decorate an item of food and humiliate someone into eating it. Right?

I can't speak for kiss-happy footballers, so I'm not really sure why lip contact at the top level became so common in the 1970s. There must have been a single brave initiator, perhaps the kind of hard man like Jackie Charlton or Nobby Stiles whose heterosexuality was apparently beyond question and who performed the act in a moment of joyful spontaneity, and then everyone else thought it was okay. After that, like perms and sideburns, this excess quickly became the fashionable norm, questioned only by those old fuddy-duddies like Hill who were horrified to see anyone on the field perform an act which didn't promote football as an ancient, noble art form.

The nearest I came to being kissed was when I scored the winning goal for my hall of residence football team in the Birmingham University 1983–4 Inter-Departmental Cup semi-final, deep into extra-time. In the bar after the game, our captain, Nige – a huge guy who was the archetypal, boisterous, fart-in-the-changing-room-and-think-it's-the-funniest-event-in-history Total Lad – told me that I had come 'very close' to receiving a kiss from him when I'd scored. He wanted me to know what a privilege this was, and he said it quite openly, so there was no hint that he wanted us to slip off to a pub-toilet cubicle to get to know each other better.

Crucially, though, he hadn't actually kissed me. That's because I was considered by the team to be 'a bit gay'. I didn't join in with their pub drinking games and drop my trousers to the townies when I was drunk. I was considered stand-offish as I tried to muster as much intellectual disdain for their activities as I could dredge up with the help of an aloof posture at the bar and a vocabulary growing ever more pretentious. So our captain had stopped just short of planting a wet one on me. Still, he wanted me to know that he appreciated my goal to the point where I had *almost* been accepted as one of the lads. Ultimately, though, I was still too gay to be kissed by a fellow man.

Of course, nowadays kissing isn't what it used to be. Notorious hatchet men of the '70s like Charlie Cooke have probably filled the role of Jimmy Hill as nostalgic old fart, and look back to the days of wavy curls and puckered lips as a time when delight was expressed sincerely on the spur of the moment. 'We were happy just to be playing the game we loved, and winning was a bonus, and nowadays it's all about the money and the marketing men, isn't it? We didn't get one-tenth of the wages they make today, but we didn't complain. But look at them now, with their five-man choreographed corner-flag routines and their pre-recorded T-shirts with instant messages on the front. They must spend more time at training practising their goal celebrations than they do their bloody free-kicks, I tell you.'

Kissing, meanwhile, has come to mean something more significant. Now players score a goal and they kiss the club badge conspicuously in front of the fans. 'I may be earning 10 times more in a week than you'll earn in a whole year, but I love this club, right?' Oh yeah, he kissed the club badge, he must really mean it. Although I sometimes have the sneaking feeling that they're surreptitiously kissing the sponsor's logo too.

Another common reaction is for married or engaged players to kiss their rings. In the '70s rings were for 'poofters', and if any players had them, they certainly weren't worn on the pitch. Now they have come to mean: 'I am a well-rounded and sensitive individual in a serious long-term relationship. Despite earning way too much cash, I have not forgotten the most important things in my life – love and my family. To them I dedicate this goal.' Ah, how sweet, although it could also be seen as a slap in the face for the fans, by saying, 'Although that makes it 1–0 to us, I didn't score it for you, dear 67,000 fans. I did it for the missus and the wean.'

Finally, you can kiss the trophy, the only criterion being that you must have won it. This is completely above board. A trophy is usually made of metal, and only a sicko would suggest that someone who kisses metal is some kind of freaky fetishist. Mind you, I did once hear a story about a group of rugger players who stood with their trousers down around a silver trophy...

Forgive and Go

Like I said, Neil didn't mind that I'd copped off with the girl who'd just axed him. He was probably already lining up his next snogging partner, and was genuinely pleased for me that I'd officially been seen Kissing in Action. He was just as cheerful the next morning, when he picked me up from the ground to congratulate me on my first goal of the season, as I put Rasen Wanderers ahead with a sliding 20-yard shot. 'What a weekend you're having!' he shouted (though we didn't kiss).

It was easy for him to be so generous. He probably knew better than I did that this was a one-off freak event, and that in the coming year he'd be racking up far more goals and girls than I could ever begin to dream of. That day we went on to lose 1–3, and four days later I broke my arm playing rugby, of all games, when, believing myself now to be capable of anything, I was given the ball during a house match and sprinted for the corner in a bid for even more glory. Si, a broad and bulky member of the first XV, had other ideas and gave chase, before sandwiching me between himself and the turf just short of the try line.

After I returned from hospital that night, Si came round to apologise. What could I do but tell him not to worry about it? (I was just relieved that he hadn't brought along a packet of digestive biscuits.) After all, compared with snogging one of your teammate's ex-birds, unintentionally snapping someone's arm in two was barely a violation of the sporting code.

Kissing through the Ages

Young kids are liberal kissers, offering unconditional pecks and hugs in an uncomplicated manner. Up until the age of about six they'll even kiss kids they just made friends with at the playground, already announcing plans for marriage 20 minutes after they've met (this occasionally also happens to single people in their late 30s). For the next few years after that, early playground romance can often ape its older, slightly more sedate and sophisticated teenage version. While children can often be embarrassed by parental kisses, especially in public, girls of this age in particular seem to have no problem chasing the other sex around and snogging them openly, even against their will.

In the teenage years, broadly speaking, once the initial shyness is overcome then kissing goes public in a big way. You want to be seen, preferably by as many people as possible. Exaggerated suction is a necessary evil.

From the age of 20 onwards, things generally regress until death. Kissing is an embarrassing concept that should be neither seen nor heard except on telly, in books or in the dark of the cinema. Either it's not the done thing any more or you're cheating on your partner, so discretion is of the utmost priority. And when it comes to other people gouging each other's mouths out, you discover that you've become strangely prudent. That's because you've reached the stage of running from everything that reminds you that you're no longer young.

Programme Highlights

'I am quite sure today Scunthorpe will provide a most formidable opposition,' wrote Colin Murphy towards the end of his programme notes, 'and our games against them always seem to start with both sides being very much in contention.'

It was always hard to tell whether Murphy was being deliberately clever or deliberately thick. Was he really pointing out that when the game starts, at 0–0, both teams are on an equal footing? It's similar to when commentators say, in the excitement of a game and with the score standing at 1–1 or 2–2, that 'it couldn't be more equal!' Even the slowest of spectators can pick up on the fact that when the score is level, there is the possibility that either side could take the lead.

Or was Murphy being disingenuous? Was he really saying, 'On paper, it starts at 0–0, but we know we can thump them 4–0 like we did here last season.' After all, he only says that the teams '*seem*' to start in contention. What he really wanted to say was, 'They're shit, just like Scunthorpe teams have been for the past 10 years, and we should be sending them back to their doleful, dying town with their hides whupped.'

Still, as we know now from the riveting letter to my dad, Lincoln couldn't turn that theoretical superiority into goals, and 'our old friends from Scunthorpe', as the Lincoln and District Football Supporters Club calls them in its brief and bland half page, were just as level at the end of the afternoon as they were at the start. How tempted must Scunthorpe manager Ron Ashman have been to point to his posterior at full-time and say to Murphy, 'It *seems* to me that you are in contention to bend down and kiss my arse.'

Vince Grimes

If Charles Dickens had been alive to write about English fourth division football in the 1970s, he could not have invented a more fitting name to perfectly characterise all you needed to know about the subject than the moniker 'Vince Grimes of Scunthorpe United'. If Vince had been around in the 1990s, when the publishing craze for gritty life-at-the-bottom-end football memoirs kicked in, that would have been the perfect title for his book. *Vince Grimes of Scunthorpe United.* Film adaptation by Alan Sillitoe.

But Vince really did exist. According to the programme notes, he 'turned professional with Hull City in May 1972 and later completed 89 league appearances for the Tigers before joining Scunthorpe in 1978. He also had a loan spell with Bradford City.'

Was Grimes ever touted to a southern club? You can imagine scouts from Plymouth or Luton expressing an interest in the doughty midfielder and asking for his name. 'Oh, him? That's Vince Grimes,' a passer-by would inform them. And with a shake of their heads the scouts would mutter something under their breaths and walk away. Vince Grimes was made for the north, and the north was made for Vince Grimes. More specifically, the fading, obscure steel town of Scunthorpe was made for Vince Grimes. It's possible he once contemplated a move to Grimsby, but thought that Grimes of Grimsby was pushing it a bit too far. Even Dickens usually drew the line at such blatant alliteration.

Something Fowl Is Afoot – A Pair of Partridges

You're not going to believe this, but Scunthorpe had a striker called Malcolm Partridge, and the referee that day was Pat Partridge. Malcolm, who had played for Grimsby and was universally derided by the Town fans at my school, had taken the hint and stepped down a division to join the neighbours, the Scunny Triangle of Lincoln, Grimsby and Scunthorpe being a kind of experimental predecessor to globalisation and the Free Trade Agreement, with players moving liberally between the three sides to save them the bother of moving house.

Malcolm's name *didn't* appear on the team sheet that day, however, and I've no idea if he played or not. Partridge isn't the commonest of surnames, and it's possible that he and Pat were related, so Scunthorpe pulled him from the line-up as a sporting gesture. Possible, but highly unlikely. Remembering how my Grimsby-supporting cohorts described and mocked his efforts, it's more likely that he was dropped for being crap.

'Malcolm was the club's top scorer with 13 goals last season and he has netted once this term,' the programme notes said prosaically. His whistling namesake, however, got much more space. Pat Partridge was one of those 'name' referees that you remember because they were on *Match of the Day* a lot. To me, it was quite an honour to have them come to Lincoln, where we took all the big names we could get.

Partridge had reffed the 1976 World Club Cup Final, the 1977 European Cup Winners' Cup Final and the 1978 League Cup Final, and had also officiated at the 1978 World Cup in Argentina and the 1980 European Championships in Italy. And here he was, the arbitrator at humble Sincil Bank for the bread-and-butter local derby. What kind of sophistication could we expect to rub off on us from a man so well travelled and obviously well versed in the ways of the world?

'Married, he is a farmer, interested in gardening and collecting book matches and neck-ties,' relates his biography. In other words, he was the John Major of the refereeing world. You can just imagine his mates asking him, 'Hey, Pat, how was Argentina? Did you have any trouble with the military junta? What's César Luis Menotti like in the flesh?'

'Thank you for enquiring,' the man from Cockfield, County Durham, would reply. 'I picked up a nice beige neck-tie at the airport and a fascinating book match in the hotel bar that says "Hilton, Buenos Aires" on the front. Didn't get to see many gardens, unfortunately.'

But all credit to him, he doesn't merit a mention in the letter to my dad, and they always say that the best refs are the ones you don't notice.

He's Scott to Be Joking

If I hadn't been writing a letter to my dad that evening and recovering from a hangover and all the excitement of kissing a goal and scoring a girl and seeing Pat Partridge in the flesh on the same weekend, I could have gone to the LCFC Social Club to enjoy Dave Scott, billed as a 'vocal personality'. It's not specified under exactly which category of entertainment this falls (is it possible he was plucked from the terraces by a social club talent scout?), although Dave and his colleagues were pushing their demands for better pay at the time.

'Due to the ever-increasing cost of entertainment,' says an URGENT NOTICE, 'it is with regret that your Committee deem it necessary to increase the normal charge for entertainment on Saturdays and Sundays by 10 pence making the concert charge 20 pence.

'This additional charge is in order to maintain the present standard of entertainment.'

I wish now that I had gone to watch Dave Scott to round off the weekend, so that I could report back here on what sort of standards were having to be maintained with a 100 per cent price hike. But, as I wrote to my dad, I was 'absolutely knackered' and in no mood for vocal personalities. And so I signed off my letter with 'all my love'. And five kisses.

5

Violence

Celtic v. Rangers, Scottish Premier League, 3pm, Saturday, 23 August 1980

Sassenaccent

On this day, at Celtic Park, isolated among several thousand silent home fans, my dad and I stood and cheered a last-minute winning goal by Rangers. We couldn't help ourselves. And we survived to tell the tale without a scratch between us.

My dad is a lifelong Rangers fan, and at the time I was keen enough too. They were my 'Scottish club' now that, following my parents' divorce, I was coming to visit him in my perceived homeland several times a year. He had moved back to the area where he grew up to run the veterinary practice in Lanark that was attached to the University of Glasgow. Mostly, I read books and went for walks and constructed idle (or ideal) fantasies about the women I might meet, but never did, while out on these walks. Then, when my dad was off duty, we went to watch football.

Describing Scotland as my homeland is a lie, but it's what I believed at the time. My homeland, if I must have one at all, is England, where I grew up. I talk like an Englishman, even though as a kid my greatest desire was to have a Scottish accent. Especially when I went to Scotland.

We had always spent half-terms and Easter holidays going north to visit my grandparents in Biggar, Lanarkshire, and so for years I had already been taking care to hide my Englishness. There was only one way to do that – shut the fuck up. It wasn't that Scottish kids would beat you up when they heard your voice. In fact, many of them didn't give a shit beyond their initial curiosity. But there was a certain core of wild-eyed tartan youth that would look at you in a funny way that said, 'Just ye wait until we get one-to-one in the tackle.' And I wasn't hard at all; I was tearful, remember. So when I was forced out of the house by my parents ('Away and play fitba in the park'), I prowled around in a constant state of alert. If I saw other kids, I'd hide. If they saw me and wanted to play with my ball, I'd nod and do my best to avert the inevitable. But most Scots are garrulous and instinctively ask you questions.

'Ye English?'

'No.' (Attempted unconvincingly as 'Nae'.)

'Ye've got an English accent.'

'I'm at my gran's, she lives here in Biggar.'

'Aye, hear that? He's fuckin' English.'

Being 'fuckin' English' wasn't meant as an insult, necessarily. It just seemed to be the automatic adjective of choice whenever Scottish people talked about their friends from the south. The English were 'fuckin'' as a matter of course, just like the skies were blue. It didn't matter if I explained that both my parents were Scottish, and so that made me Scottish too (at least that's what my dad had always told me). In their eyes, I was English, and in the end I gave up telling Scottish kids about my Scottish parents and grandparents because they ignored every word I said, all the while hearing more and more of my English pronunciation.

I had a recurring dream when I was young that I moved to Scotland and had to start at a new school. I wasn't accepted by my new classmates until I'd played for the school team and scored a goal. Footballing ability transgresses national boundaries, some well-meaning Fabian Society report on multiculturalism in football would probably state today. It's possible that in the dreams I ended up with a Scottish accent too.

When my parents' marriage broke up, they decided that I'd continue to live with my mum in Lincolnshire so as not to interrupt my schooling (it was about the only thing they managed to agree on). I was more than happy with this, because it meant I never had to walk for the first time across a Scottish school yard with a fuckin' English accent. Yet there was obviously a part of my subconscious which regretted that I'd never had to face up to and overcome this challenge. And be accepted as 'Scottish'.

If I left Market Rasen by train at eight on a Saturday morning, I could make it to Carstairs Junction by two, and from there my dad would pick me up and we had time to reach either Motherwell, Hamilton or Airdrie – Lanarkshire's equivalent of the Scunny Triangle (the axis of wee villes?) – by kick-off. Because we hadn't seen each other for weeks, or usually months, I'd have plenty to tell him, and wasn't always paying that much attention to the game.

One Saturday afternoon, not long after my dad had moved back north, we were at Douglas Park, the former home of Hamilton Academical. I was standing there watching some mediocre lower-division part-time football with a couple of thousand other local folk, chatting with my dad, when a loud voice behind us remarked conspicuously, 'There's a lot a' fuckin' English in the ground today.'

It hardly ranks alongside Hearts fans throwing bananas on the pitch at Mark Walters a few years later, and as long as I was standing next to my dad I didn't feel any sense of physical threat. Perhaps if I'd been a different kind of fuckin' Englishman I would have turned around and said in a clear-cut BBC accent, 'Now listen here, my good man, you wouldn't want the subsidies from Westminster that keep your moribund Scottish economy running to be cut off, would you? So be a good chap and keep your thoughts to yourself, eh?'

It's perhaps just this kind of condescension, however seriously intended, that ensures a large percentage of Scots seem to dislike 'the fuckin' English'. At the time, I didn't care much about the reasons. I just knew that when a lot of people heard my voice it immediately caused them to resent both me and the place where I grew up. It didn't occur to me to ask them that if it was so bad living under the fuckin' English, why didn't they stage a fuckin' revolution?

The Brief Golden Age of the Scottish Premier League

'The scene is set for a first-class Old Firm occasion this afternoon,' began Celtic manager Billy McNeill's programme notes. 'Celtic are top of the Premier League table having full points and Rangers are in second place with three.'

Well, hardly big news for Scotland, especially considering that only two matches had been played. If you look at the Scottish table at any time over the course of the 20th century, you'll find Rangers or Celtic, or both, pretty much in contention for the title. The 1964–5 season, when Kilmarnock won the league, remains the only season in Scottish football history where both teams finished outside the top three.

Yet at the start of 1980, Aberdeen were the defending champions, and in the following six years won it twice more, with Dundee United also taking a title, before the Old Firm (was there ever a more apposite title to characterise the duopolised stitch-up that was Glasgow-dominated Scottish club football prior to Rangers' bankruptcy in 2012?) re-established their tedious domination. Since the mid-1980s the championship trophy has never even remotely looked like leaving town, except perhaps for a day trip to the coast to be exhibited at the Saltcoats branch of the Rangers Supporters Club. At the time of this game, though, Rangers varied between mediocre and garbage, and the Scottish game was all the more interesting for it.

Having been brought up on a diet of almost exclusively Lincolnshire-based third and fourth division football, it's easy to see why I was excited by Scottish football in the early 1980s. Not only did they have teams that still performed respectably in Europe, but they were producing players who were kings in the English and European game, and who also were capable of standing out for the national side. They also had proper crowds; noisy crowds who, unlike my nemesis at Hamilton's Douglas Park, were in the main much more interested in the game than they were in some puny Sassenach with an East Midlands accent.

At Ibrox and Celtic Park, a single stand could have swallowed up the combined crowds at Sincil Bank and Scunthorpe's Old Showground and spat them out again without even pausing for a huff on its cigarette. The stadiums were gargantuan, the football was much racier, and the spectators cursed with a diligence that would have seen my 'useless twats' epithet – yelled as a seven-year-old – either ignored for being too mild for a boy of my age, or drowned out by the men behind me offering similar words of discouragement, but with greater volume, colour and conviction. Even if Frank McGarvey had scored a hat-trick the previous week, it could be quickly forgotten with a single bad touch of the ball that would cause at least one person to stand up and scream, 'Away tae fuck, McGarvey, ye yoosless fuckin' eejit!'

There was a greater sense of frustration at the time among Celtic and Rangers supporters because their teams were being regularly challenged by Alex Ferguson's and Jim McLean's upstart sides. The Old Firm simply weren't used to losing, and the purple-faced, murderous insults aimed at a ball boy for fumbling and squandering two seconds of valuable time were symptomatic of their inability to cope with a temporarily waning empire. For a boy used to hearing the odd weary 'Come on, Lincoln, now', it was never less than thrilling.

Part of that thrill ought to have been the overhanging threat of violence. Truth be told, I don't remember it that way. In all the games I went to in Scotland, I only once saw punches thrown, while standing among Aberdeen fans who had been infiltrated by a few home supporters at Celtic Park in 1986. It was a handful of spotty casuals having a minor bundle, and no one had the chance to get hurt before the police threw them out. In 45 years of watching football, it's the closest I've ever been to a fight.

Car Trouble

To judge by the Celtic v. Rangers match programme, the threat of crime and violence was real. 'Fans everywhere are under close scrutiny these days,' McNeill concluded in his column, 'and while I appeal to Celtic supporters to give the side every encouragement, the need for good behaviour is essential. Terracing trouble could result in sanctions on the club.'

In the 'Behind the Scenes' section of the programme – right next to the touching tale of a visiting fan from Manchester, up for the Danny McGrain testimonial game, who sent his thanks to the person who handed in the giro cheque he'd dropped in the car park – is a dry section of police advice for car owners: 'Secure your vehicle; lock valuables in the boot; never park in a quiet street; fit an anti-theft device.'

There was no need for that, though. Whenever you parked in Glasgow near Hampden, Ibrox or Parkhead, you'd be surrounded by a small crowd of what my dad called 'wee tchoochters' (not sure how you spell that word, so I've written it phonetically) offering a top-class security service for your vehicle. 'Watch yer car for ye, mister?' they would squeak optimistically, the idea being that you would give them a quid or two to stand on guard against car thieves, while you enjoyed the game safe in the knowledge that your very own urchin was protecting your property from the serious crime rings of Glasgow. 'Aye, ye'll get a pound if ye're still here when I get back,' my dad would respond. Which they never were. And his car was never nicked or broken into, which was always a relief to someone like me who was eager to get in the car, turn on the radio and hear what I'd missed at Sincil Bank.

The police advice in 'Behind the Scenes' continued: 'To all fans: don't carry large sums of money or valuables to the match; don't take wallets from your pockets in a crowd; don't carry your wallet in your extreme pockets or back pocket or trousers; in large crowds you are liable to jostling – hold on to your cash.'

So the best thing to do was to bring along only as much cash as you'd need to get into the ground and buy a pie, keeping it scrunched up and held tightly in your fist, only to be prised out of your cold, dead hands in the event of you being lynched by one of the notorious football mobs the media was leading us all to believe dominated every ground in the country. Not that I'm suggesting no one ever had his car stolen or his pocket picked at a football match. It just seems funny that this advice was placed next to the story about the bloke who had his unemployment cheque retrieved and sent back to him.

Don't Go Back to Millwall

Apart from the sawn-off Scottish scallies who blew kisses to each other at Celtic Park in the incident described above, and who were probably more concerned with keeping their logo-stitched sky-blue jumpers from getting crease marks, here are my other encounters with hooliganism in the several hundred games I've been to down the years:

Lincoln v. Peterborough, September 1977: my short Monday morning of hooliganism. There was a kid in my year who was a Peterborough United fan. I've no idea why. He didn't play football, and he didn't wear anything to identify himself as a Peterborough fan. It was just known. I'd been to the game on the Saturday afternoon, and Lincoln had lost 1–0, miserably. I was 12 years old, and on the Monday morning I took it into my head to avenge Lincoln's defeat. I went up to the Peterborough fan in the school corridor and said, 'You're a Peterborough fan, aren't you?' 'Yes,' he replied. Perhaps he thought I was going to congratulate him on his team's fully deserved victory. But I didn't. Instead, I said to him, 'This is for Saturday,' and hit him on the chin. Not with any conviction. It was just a jab. But it caught him full on and caused him some pain, and his eyes welled up with tears. He looked at me, hurt and uncomprehending. Until then, there had never been as much as a malicious word between the two of us. He just wasn't the sort of kid anyone would have a problem with, and he certainly wasn't the sort of kid who was ever going to hit me back. If he had been, I would have been too cowardly to hit him in the first place.

The Peterborough fan rubbed his chin and just about held back the tears. I turned and walked away to my next class, feeling deeply ashamed. I never apologised to him. I never told anyone what I'd done. I went to school with him for the next six years and he never once mentioned it. We were never close, but after we'd done our A levels he had to resit. When I brought my old school books back at the start of the following year, though, he greeted me like an old friend, and when I think about that now it makes me feel more ashamed than ever before.

It's the only time in my life I've struck anyone in the name of football, and it's still once too often.

Lincoln v. Southend, November 1980. My mate Kev, a Grimsby fan, came to this top-of-the-table fourth division encounter and wore a red Liverpool scarf so he wouldn't stand out. Unfortunately, he did stand out – to a bunch of Southend fans who spotted him waiting by my mum's car to get a lift back to Market Rasen, and chased him and roughed him up down a side street. But he was more bothered at having been mistaken for a Lincoln fan, and having his scarf nicked, than with getting to casualty for a check-up.

Lincoln v. Millwall, September 1981. The visiting charmers from South London began to throw stones across the long terrace (the 'Bank' at Sincil), one of which hit the metal crush barrier I was standing at. A couple of yards higher and further and it could, potentially, have blinded me or knocked me out, or even killed me, I suppose. I moved to stand behind the goal instead. During the game there were violent outbreaks in the away section. An old bloke standing next to me stared at me in amazement because I was still watching the game and refusing to even look in the direction of the violence.

At this time, I usually went to Saturday games with my mum, but for midweek fixtures I'd take the train from Market Rasen. The last train from Lincoln to Rasen left about an hour after the final whistle, so there was nothing else to do but wait and read. Or swap stories with the Market Rasen branch of the Lincoln City Casual Thug Ensemble (the Inter-Village Firm?), who took the same train.

This consisted of around half a dozen kids from my school, some in my year but most a couple of years younger. We all knew each other by name. Some of them I'd been to Sunday school with when I was a toddler. Their ringleader was a friendly but volatile lad of my age with whom I'd been playing football and cricket for years. He was interested in Lincoln City, but his loyalties swayed towards Blundell Park and the City Ground when Grimsby and Forest were doing better. Regardless of results, he and his morose cohorts claimed to be much more interested in fighting than football.

Strangely enough, they never had a bruise or a cut between them, despite their posturing. I sat and listened as they ran through which group of terrified opposition fans they'd chased to which corner of the ground. I never saw any of this with my own eyes, so I had to take their word for it. Often they would sneer at someone who was in their posse, but who wasn't there to defend himself that night, and who had purportedly been all front, only to run off 'shittin' 'imself' when the moment of confrontation had finally come.

I was never invited to join the gang as I was clearly made of the wrong stuff. When the train came, they'd go and sit in a different compartment, occasionally striding up and down the two-carriage train to assert their territorial rights to the five other passengers hopelessly staring out of the windows into the Lincolnshire night.

'The Onion', the Wolves, autumn 1983. 'The Onion' was a fellow student at Birmingham University who was also a drunkard, a Wolves fan and a member of the Socialist Workers Party, approximately in that order. I ran into him one night during my first year, on my way home after last orders. He was staggering around in the middle of the road in Edgbaston, singing football songs. I must have said something because he wobbled up to me and demanded to know which team I supported. 'Just tell us, I won't hit you or anything,' he promised generously. 'Albion Rovers,' I said, being an 18-year-old smart-arse. 'Wot, West Bromwich Albion?' 'No,' I said. 'Albion Rovers. Scottish Division Three.' 'You taking the piss?' he asked. And then he swung out at me, several times, but was so plastered that he was some feet away from connecting. I left him in the middle of the road, flailing at thin air and swearing at the stars. I overheard some people talking about him in the Student Union a few weeks later. I told them my story, which was remarkably similar to theirs. That's how I found out he was called 'The Onion', which physically made some sense. I can't remember his real name, but he must rank as the worst football hooligan of his era.

Scunthorpe v. Lincoln, December 1986. This Boxing Day clash was the last-ever game I went to at the ramshackle but legendary Old Showground before it was replaced with a flat-pack identikit stadium on the outskirts of town. I stood with a friend, a Scunthorpe fan (we didn't fight), watching a brawl between two sets of opposing supporters in the top level of the cantilever stand opposite. Maybe it was prearranged, because there was no way cops or stewards could get to them up there, and with the advent of closely policed segregation, 'taking the opposition's end' was now a part of hooliganism's history (or mythology – never saw it happen either).

After a minute or two, the fight fizzled out, as if they weren't quite sure what to do without the cops intervening. Or perhaps it was one of those pivotal moments in the annals of football thuggery, when they all collectively realised: 'Shit, what are we doing? Why am I hitting this bloke just because he supports a different football team to me? What's the point? These are our Lincolnshire brethren. We're all human beings, let's sit down and just watch the game.' Which is exactly what they did. By the time the police made it up to the stand, they had no clue who to arrest.

Millwall v. Manchester City, January 1990. I went with Drew, a Man City-supporting friend, to this Monday-night FA Cup replay at The Den. The place literally hummed with the threat of violence – a non-stop monotone that gradually spread around the home support and was kept up for at least half an hour. There was a certain sonic beauty to it that left you enthralled. I had never heard an entire home support 'sing' so persistently. At the same time, it felt like some sort of ritualised, hypnotic group chant that preceded a hunt and a slaughter. After extra-time we were kept in the ground for another half hour, with nothing to do but stare at the floodlight pylon which had obscured our view of the game. Then we were kept for another half hour in a dark alley next to the ground, while what sounded like a full-scale riot took place in the adjacent street. 'If we let you out, they'll kill you,' promised a grim policeman. Eventually, we were escorted to New Cross Gate Tube for a direct train to King's Cross. I never went back.

This is my point about football violence: I'm not in any sense denying that it frequently took place, and that for years it was a serious problem which put people off going to games. But if you didn't want to fight, it wasn't that difficult to avoid. I didn't much fancy The Den, so I didn't go back. When I lived in London I usually went to Orient instead. There was no 'hum', but I never felt like someone was going to kick me in the teeth either.

But even Millwall's reputation for violence was founded on the hilarious BBC *Panorama* episode in the '70s that made out a small bunch of Herberts to be the kingpins of a dangerous wave of thuggery sweeping through the nation's stadiums. In a Channel 4 follow-up documentary almost two decades later, numerous Millwall fans testified that no one at the club had taken these idiots seriously. When they saw themselves portrayed as hard men on national television, they started to believe their own fiction.

All of this isn't to say that innocent bystanders didn't get caught up in violence. Drew stopped going to games for years because he was randomly thumped by a passing Liverpool fan near King's Cross station, a gratuitous punch that left him with a Rio Ferdinand-style upper lip that could only be cured by an operation. He was nowhere near a football ground at the time, and wasn't wearing anything to identify him as a football supporter.

This, in a way, backs up my point. As a male teenager in 1980s Britain, I felt the same threat of violence walking down the street as I did in a football ground. At the football, I never came close to being involved in a fight, but in the same village hall where I snogged the red-headed girl on the day of the Lincoln v. Scunthorpe game I was head-butted by a drunk member of the Inter-Village Firm – a kid whose house I used to go to when I was six years old so we could play together with Matchbox cars. I was forever being warned at discos and pubs that I was going to get my head kicked in, and it was nothing to do with me supporting Lincoln; it was because young men like an excuse to fight, and if they can pick on a skinny kid with a big gob, then they will have every justification to lamp him.

There was a lot of discussion in the 1980s about football violence being 'society's problem'. As a football fan, all I cared about was how the perception of violence was ruining the game. But 'the game' finally took the problem on board after the Bradford, Heysel and Hillsborough disasters and made football stadiums safe places to watch sport, even if the result was a significant loss of atmosphere. At that time, the notion that the majority of fans were hooligans was fabricated by the same people who now bring you the idea of 'football fans as obsessives' (the successors to that *Panorama* documentary).

In the spring of 2005 the excellent *Soccer America* magazine published a piece by Mike Woitalla on the extremes of the rivalry between the US and Mexican national teams. Every time the two met in Mexico, Woitalla wrote, the US media printed the same stories about intimidation by the 'fanatical' Mexican supporters, including various objects and bags of urine being thrown at the US players.

Woitalla asked his fellow journalists whether they had ever seen bags of urine thrown at US players. Neither a single journalist nor the US Soccer Federation could confirm any actual incident over the previous 20 years where bags of urine had been thrown at US players or anyone else. Woitalla told me that the journalists had confided to him privately that the only way they could get their editors to give prominence to football stories was to emphasise the violence and the myths of the 'bags of urine'.

It's the way journalism works in all fields – playing up a salient angle to lure in readers, regardless of the truth. The truth about football fans in the 1980s is that millions of them went to games and didn't get in a fight. That includes Millwall. We enjoyed what we saw. We didn't talk about or think about thugs for games at a time. And at Parkhead, my dad and I stood up in front of thousands of Celtic supporters and cheered a goal by Rangers, and no one touched us. No one even threatened us. They may well have been hating us at that very second, but what concerned them more was this: they had just gone 2–1 down at home in the final minute. To them, the most important thing of all was *the game*.

Hooligones

One birthday my sister gave me *The Football Factory* by John King. There's a long tradition in my family, and doubtless in many others too, of buying books with the word 'football' in the title for the perceived fan. It started as a kid, with *Shoot!* annuals from well-meaning great-aunts that I barely even flicked through (too many words), and ended in my forties, when my German in-laws caught on that not every single book with the word '*Fußball*' on its cover was necessarily of huge interest to me (that guide to the upcoming 2002 World Cup wasn't much use six months after the tournament had finished). Anyway, *The Football Factory* was one of the worst books – football or otherwise – that I've ever read, but people can be sensitive about presents. When my sister asked me what I thought of it, I said I'd really enjoyed it. The following year she bought me *Headhunters*, by the same author.

The first-ever football hooligan book I can remember reading was *Steaming In* by Colin Ward. I thought it was okay, and it must have sold well because there followed a wave of copycat hooligan porn (publishers always run with the crowd), with John King and the Brimson brothers[1] at the forefront, and all of them saying broadly the same thing – until you've experienced 'the rush' of running towards, or away from, a set of opposing football supporters, you will never understand what drives a hooligan. Around this time, *When Saturday Comes* magazine parodied the phenomenon by running a high-octane but clearly over-the-top extract from an 'as yet unpublished hooligan novel', and found themselves fielding enquiries from publishers wanting the non-existent author's contact details.

Missing from this flooded genre was the book that said or did anything other than glorify the author and his posse's heroic battles.

1. I once wrote a scathing online review of a Dougie Brimson book, and within three hours I had an email from him ('A friend sent me the link' – sure, like you don't have a Google alert set up for your own name) claiming he was really pleased because it was all good publicity, etc. He signed off with the chipper phrase 'job jobbed', which I've never quite been able to erase from my consciousness.

Where was the one self-aware memoir that acknowledged its posse's part in destroying the game as a working-class spectacle thanks to their selfish, senseless, gratuitous desire to claim that they were apparently 'harder' than a group of young men from another town? Maybe there was one but publishers turned it down due to the lack of an obvious market. Who needs nuance when it's Us v. Them?

My own take on this posturing drivel is that these are the people who came closest to ruining the game I love, and for no good political reason. Thanks to the thugs, it wasn't worth the bother any more for thousands of fans, and attendances sank year after year. Thanks to the media, police and the public perception that all fans were hooligans, we ended up with the unconscionable tragedy of Hillsborough and its iniquitous aftermath, and stadiums that are now safe but sterile, and way out of the price range of millions of people who used to go and watch games. Yet these writers portrayed the whole thing as though it was an almost unstoppable, natural phenomenon – all part of youthful high jinks and a bit of a laugh, but also an act of rebellion against the state and authority in general. Then the retired hooligans sat down at their laptops, forging new identities for themselves as the thinking man's thug, proclaiming that they were too old for that stuff now, while appearing all over the media as 'experts' on football violence.

My solution to the problem of hooligan literature? Don't buy the book. It's the only language publishers understand.

The 'Englishman' at Parkhead

The reason we had tickets in the Celtic support was that we had come to a European Cup Winners' Cup preliminary round first-leg tie the previous Wednesday, when Celtic had beaten DVTK of Hungary 6–0. Although we were Rangers fans, we were happy enough to watch a game wherever one was on, whatever competition (it was my first-ever European tie – something else we didn't get much of at Sincil Bank), and so we frequently came to Parkhead regardless of who Celtic were playing. And because my dad was always worried that even the most unattractive fixtures would sell out, he liked to get tickets in advance, if at all possible. After the DVTK game, it made sense to buy tickets for the Rangers match the following Saturday, knowing that it was likely to be a capacity crowd.

It was clear that we would be sitting with the home fans, and we behaved ourselves throughout the afternoon. When Celtic went 1–0 up, we didn't react. When it looked like Celtic had gone 2–0 up, we didn't react either, but then the goal was spuriously disallowed for offside, despite the fact the player in an offside position could hardly be said to have been interfering with the 25-yard shot that comprehensively beat Peter McCloy. Rangers equalised in the second half through Jim Bett, but again we sat still, not even moving as our fellow Blues fans danced wildly 100 yards away.

In the last minute of the game, Rangers' Alex Miller swung his left foot at a throw-in from a colleague around 30 yards from goal, in a position that looked anything but dangerous. The ball flew a barely credible path into the top far corner of the Celtic goal, and both my dad and I couldn't help it – we were up on our feet, cheering furiously without restraint. After maybe just two seconds, it occurred to me that not everyone else around us was as excited at this amazing late twist of events, then I remembered where we were. It must have struck my dad at the same time, as we both sat down suddenly, as if we could pretend this had not just happened.

No one looked at us. They were staring ahead, or downwards, as if we were all in church and the two of us had broken protocol and stood to cheer and applaud the vicar's sermon. The thousands of jubilant Rangers fans at the other end of the stadium were bad enough, but to have these two dancing goons in their midst was almost more than they could bear, and the only thing to do was hope that we'd quickly shut up. Which we did, and maybe that granted us some leeway. No one told us to fuck off or threatened to kick us in. At the same time, no one offered us a hearty smile and a congratulatory, 'Aye, fair result, right enough.'

If we had been on the terraces (which is purely hypothetical as my dad didn't like standing – if we hadn't got seats, we'd probably have gone to the other Glasgow derby that day: Queen's Park v. Clyde), we would have been torn apart. But violence is not so easy up in the seats. There's a reason why football's authorities think seats are safer. It's because they are. It's not so much a crowd as several rows of ordered individuals. While I support safe standing areas at all levels of the game, and would personally far rather stand than sit, I'm not entirely opposed to what the defunct teenage football mag *Match Weekly* once memorably referred to as 'the sissy seating stand'.

On the way out, we got mixed in with joyous Rangers fans and were able to laugh and smile at our ease. A taxi carrying two Celtic fans negotiated its way through the celebrating away supporters. They smiled nervously as endless hands thumped the car roof. But in victory you can afford to be generous, and eventually the vehicle was afforded safe passage.

Rivalry and 'Passion'

So my dad, a Rangers fan, married my mum, whose own dad was a Celtic fan. This was a potentially explosive situation. Might my grandfather have considered disowning his own daughter for such an act of infidelity? At the very least, there must have been dynamite discussions over family dinners about who were the true kings of Scottish football. Should Jimmy Johnstone be in the Scotland team ahead of Willie Johnston? Was Jock Stein part of a secret Hun conspiracy to undermine the enemy from within?

As it was, football may have been mentioned in passing, but there was never any kind of argument. My granddad didn't talk much. My dad's theory was that my granddad sat there saying nothing in the hope that people would think he was wise, but I think he was just a very shy man (except, I'm told, in his younger days, when he was on stage performing dynamically in local amateur dramatics). When I went to visit him on my own in later years, and my garrulous grandma was in the kitchen making tea and cake, there would be a long, awkward silence. I never had a clue what to talk to him about except for football, and so the conversation would go something like this:

Me: 'We went to the Old Firm game on Saturday.'

Granddad (nodding): 'Aye.'

Me: 'It was a bit lairy. Dad and I were sitting with the Celtic fans.'

Granddad: 'Aye.'

Me: 'It was an amazing game. Miller scored the winner in the last minute and…'

Granddad: 'Aye, I saw it on the telly.'

The longest sentence you could get out of him was always the one that killed the conversation. You couldn't tell if he was pissed off at the result or utterly indifferent. It would have made life, and my visits, more interesting if just once he'd leaned forwards and said with a twisted smile, 'Aye, but we'll fuckin' hammer ye Hun bastards next time.' But it just wasn't there. I think he cared far more about the imminent cup of tea my gran was about to bring through on a tray with a plate of shortbread.

You wonder for how many other thousands of fans it isn't really there either. Of course, the Rangers–Celtic rivalry goes back decades and has huge history, and it's all founded on religious bigotry and the Union Jack v. the Irish tricolour, and there have been pitched battles and fights and stabbings and great games for as long as anyone can remember. Except that when the teams formed in the late 19th century, there was no rivalry at all, religious or otherwise, and it's thought that the name 'the Old Firm' stems from the friendly way they had of referring to their early clashes.

You can read all about this kind of rivalry in one of those big glossy football magazines in the US or Britain, where a fan-turned-reporter sails into a city, goes to a derby game and comes out the other side declaring what a big deal it was, and how both sides hate each other, and how the most important thing in the lives of these fans is to beat the city rival. The reporter never stays on to see how the city functions on the 363 days of the year when there is no local derby. Is it civil war or civil society? So although there are obvious no-go areas in the city for both sets of fans on match days, millions of Glaswegians work and live alongside each other every day of their lives. How do they manage this without killing each other? Is it just possible that for the majority of the city's inhabitants, Rangers v. Celtic is not really a matter of life and death, it's just a sporting event that happens a few times per year?

If the Vatican City disappeared into a hole, the Catholic Church collapsed into splintered, powerless oblivion and Celtic Football Club disbanded and locked its doors for good, there would be no group of people more upset than the fans of Rangers FC, despite the brainless, bloodthirsty sectarian songs chanted by a minority of twats. They might celebrate for a night, until they looked around and got bored. No one to taunt. No one to compete with. No fear, no tension, no scapegoats. Slagging off Edinburgh just wouldn't feel the same. Rangers and Celtic really do love and need each other more than they'd ever be prepared to admit.[2]

It's the US v. Mexico 'bag of urine' syndrome. The hatred and the rivalry are more imagined than real. Most people have lives to be getting on with, and only the headcases make the headlines. This doesn't stop your below-average journalist from writing up the same old scare story to keep the myth floating for another week. But Rangers and Celtic are just one part of Glasgow's identity. A significant reflection of its identity, that's true, but in themselves not as important as journalists and the clubs themselves perhaps like to think.

I once got chatting to a young Glaswegian in a Birmingham launderette. 'Who do you support, Rangers or Celtic?' I asked. 'Support?' he said wearily. 'Ah support ma legs, and they support me.'

Programme Highlights

Celtic's new-look match programme had, according to the programme itself, received the approval of fans. It wasn't just about Celtic and Scottish football, it covered the European game. There's an article by Brian Glanville on the continent's best *liberos*, for example. Other manly areas of interest include motorcycles (there's a riveting piece on the comparative performances of various brake systems in wet con-

2. See Kristof Vanhoutte's paper 'The Importance of Trivial Oppositions: The Narcissism of Minor Differences of Derby-Team Fans', presented at the University of Basel, 30 June 2016.

ditions) and convertible cars ('Car Makers Go for Topless Look' by Jeremy Walton. Phwwwoooaaaargh!). With all the ads for cigarettes and lager, it looks like a 'serious' porn mag, only without the pictures of naked women.

'The programme does carry English topics,' says the magazine apologetically, 'but we believe that Celtic fans take a wide view of the football scene and that the English game as well as happenings in Europe and other parts of the world are of interest to them.' Right. As long as we beat the fuckin' Hun first.

And finally, in the 'Behind the Scenes' section of the programme that brought you all those warnings about car thieves and pickpockets, comes news of 'a new service for Celtic fans... a souvenir shop'.

Those dots in mid-sentence tell you that the club sounds almost embarrassed about this, as though 'souvenirs' are a bit non-football, being associated with shopping and, therefore, women (of which there were very few at either Parkhead or Ibrox in the early 1980s). 'The premises are on the ground floor of the Pools Office opposite the main stand, and are open Monday to Friday from 10.30am to 3.30pm and most Saturdays. Take a look in... it's an ideal spot for some early Christmas shopping.'

There, they said it. Shopping. And they mentioned Christmas shopping in August, even earlier than Woolworths, for Christ's sake. But at least those midweek opening times will allow you to send the wifey down to buy a 'souvenir' for the bairn's Christmas. And the thought of selling a poor-quality replica shirt for 10 times its actual value had yet to enter anyone's entrepreneurial head.

Worst football-related ad: 'Bank of Scotland helps you *manage* your money.' Geddit?

Reasonably clever football-related ad – Deep Heat menthol muscle cream: 'Put the heat on right from the start of the game.' It was the 1980s now, and those ads were starting to get sophisticated.

Most baffling ad claim: 'Rent A Skip... and relax.' Presumably by turning it into an impromptu cocktail lounge and inviting all your friends over, both Rangers *and* Celtic supporters.

6

Despair

Aberdeen v. Celtic, Scottish Cup Final, 3pm, Saturday, 19 May 1984, Hampden Park, Glasgow

Unwanted Attention

Four years later and I still hadn't learned my lesson. The Rangers fan with the English accent was back among the Celtic fans.

Sometime in the second half, I think, of the 1984 Scottish Cup Final, with Aberdeen leading 1–0 – thanks to a goal from Eric Black – Paul McStay scored the equaliser for Celtic. Before I could react, the complete stranger standing next to me picked me up in his arms, whooping deliriously. We both began to jump madly up and down on the Hampden terraces, one arm each pumping the air. I hope that I sounded convincing. I hope that I *felt* convincing, and that my body wasn't giving off the limp vibe of a reluctant wife fulfilling her partner's conjugal needs. What I really felt like, though, was as if I'd been forced at gunpoint to dance the cancan on my mother's grave.

This was a game I should not have been at. I had little interest in its outcome. I'd already been to Scotland twice in the previous two months: once for my Easter visit to my dad, and the previous weekend for my grandfather's funeral. I had no money, and I was in the middle of sitting my end-of-first-year exams at Birmingham University. Yet somehow I ended up at the Scottish Cup Final.

I must have had a bag with me, although I don't remember if I stored it in a locker at the train station. If I did have the bag with me in the ground, and if the Celtic fan, all covered in green and white, had got suspicious – because I wasn't wearing any green and white and was probably wearing jeans and a T-shirt, and while I was shouting 'Wahaaaaaaaaay!' in spurious delight at the Celtic goal he might have noticed that I shouted it with the tinge of an English accent – and opened it up, then the book he would have discovered was *A Short History of the German Language*. He could have waved it around at his fellow Celtic fans and said, 'Look, lads, this yin here's a fuckin' stoodent.' And when they'd all turned around to stare I could have smiled and said in my best university Queen's English, 'And not just a student, but a fan of the good old Rangers Football Club too. What do you make of that, my fellow men of the city of Glasgow? An English-born bluenose right here in your midst!'

I wasn't alone at the game. I was with a bloke called Kevin, who was a bona fide Scot and a bona fide Celtic fan. He'd done all the talking since we'd arrived on the overnight coach. We'd been to the Scottish FA to get tickets, and he'd asked me to take a picture of him on the steps with SFA chairman Ernie Walker. They grinned and shook hands. It was a nice day, at least, and so the picture came out well.

Aberdeen had beaten Kilmarnock, Clyde and the two Dundee sides to get to Hampden. Celtic had overcome the might of Berwick, East Fife (6–0 – well done, lads!), Motherwell (6–0 again – God, how exciting is Scottish football with all those goals?) and St Mirren. Here is my own personal road to the Scottish Cup Final:

A couple of days earlier, I'd been sitting in my room in the hateful hall of residence where I'd spent the most miserable year of my life, surrounded by my student peers, who were too determined to have a good time for my liking. There was a bank of phones in each wing of the hall, and optimistic parents would occasionally call in the hope that someone would pick up and have nothing better to do than trawl the long corridors of the five-floor building to knock on Jemima's door and tell her that Mummy would like a word. The only time anyone had called me all year had been earlier that month, when my sister had phoned to say our granddad had died.

On this night, back in an age when it seemed like having a phone was a luxury, and not necessarily one that you'd want when you'd just left home, and when people managed to communicate and make arrangements by word of mouth and written notes, someone had made the effort to knock on my door and shout, 'Phone call for you.' I wandered down to the phones, thinking, 'Who's died now?' On the line was Tim Bastard, in a pub in Norwich, where he was at the end of his first year, having enrolled on something like Media, Film, American and Anything Else We Can Get Away with Studies.

I hadn't heard a lot from him all year because he'd fallen in love with a girl from our school the previous summer, and moved in with her right after our A levels. In that year, they had both discovered sex, and I think they'd more or less been at it and nothing else for the previous nine months. At one time they even became engaged, but fortunately they thought better of it. Who did they think they were, getting engaged at 18? Our parents? Anyway, besides a couple of letters and some sightings back in our home town when he'd been quickly whisked off for in-law duties, as well as a weekend visit to Norwich when we'd all had an early night (at their behest), I hadn't seen or heard that much of him compared with the almost daily contact of the previous eight years. So I was thrilled that he'd made the effort to phone me when there was such a small chance of actually tracking me down.

'Hey, Plendy, do you want to go to the Scottish Cup Final this weekend?'

He didn't need to ask me twice. What a fantastic, Kerouacian, free-jazz idea! Kerouac and free jazz were our pointers towards a libertarian cultural lifestyle at the time, even though it was a lifestyle we failed to live up to on any level. But hey, now it was happening! Never mind the live-in girlfriend, Tim was breaking out and phoning his old mate so that we could spend a couple of days of high-octane boozing, watching football and talking about old times. This was a prototype stag weekend before stag weekends were even thought of, and yet it wasn't a stag weekend at all.

'Fuckin' 'ell, yeah, great idea!' I almost yelled back down the phone.

'Great,' he said. 'You remember Kevin, that Scottish bloke you met when you came here a few months back? The Celtic fan?'

'Erm, yeah.'

'Well, he's going up for it this weekend and he's looking for someone to go with. I'll put him on.'

I often wondered afterwards if it was a stitch-up in revenge for one or two humiliating but distant incidents at school, but I think it was just Tim, pissed in the pub, thinking he'd come up with a great idea. He's come up with millions of great ideas in pubs down the years, and none of them has withstood the test of sobriety, if they were even remembered at all come dawn's rational light.

Kevin came on the line. He told me that he was going to Glasgow by overnight coach from Norwich, and that it stopped at a certain place in Birmingham at midnight on Friday for a pick-up. We'd go to the game and then on to his gran's in Falkirk to stay Saturday night.

'Yeah,' I said weakly. 'I'll see you Friday, at midnight.' Just me and Kevin, obviously.

And so, 24 and a bit hours later, there I was, a few minutes before midnight, staggering around the streets of Birmingham with six pints of beer sloshing around my stomach, 35 quid in my pocket, my overnight bag, and unable to find the bus stop. I stopped a taxi, but the driver told me I was only 100 yards away from where I wanted to be. It all seemed too unlikely that a coach would just stop by some office buildings around midnight and pick people up to go on to Glasgow. I didn't believe it was going to happen. A feeling of relief began to wash over me. I'd just say I'd got drunk and missed the bus, which I had a feeling was about to come true until I managed to follow the taxi driver's simple directions and walked around a corner, and there were a few human beings standing at the kerb-side, looking bored and desolate, huddled like they were just the kind of people who would take an all-night coach ride to Glasgow. The things you don't know about. *Hey, next season I can do this every weekend.*

I joined the mooching gaggle. The bus was late. It was like waiting for the school bus on those wintry rural Lincolnshire mornings when you were allowed to go home if the bus hadn't arrived by a certain time. I'd done that once during the Winter of My Parents' Discontent, the abysmal 1978–9 season. After timing it to the second, I skipped away from the bus stop and was walking back up to my house when the bus sloshed past a few dozen yards away, and I made no effort to flag it down. After all, it had technically arrived after the cut-off point. With both parents at work, I spent the morning taking the dog for a walk through the woods (probably further than it would have been to walk to school), and when my dad came home at lunchtime I made the mistake of showing my face, and he gave me a proper bollocking. It was only years later that I wondered if he used to meet his girlfriend there, because his reaction was way out of proportion for the crime of a missed day at school. Or maybe he was just concerned that the whole bad 1978–9 season thing was turning me into a truant and a miscreant who was neglecting his education in order to do deviant stuff like staying at home and taking the dog for a long walk.

Back in Birmingham, the coach came half an hour late. I couldn't find Kevin, but it was dark and a lot of people were sleeping, so I decided it would be best just to take a seat. I settled down for a long night of developing a headache and wandering backwards and forwards to the bog to piss out the six pints of beer. I couldn't sleep, so I thought about turning on the overhead light to try and read *A Short History of the German Language*. The thought of disturbing the bulk of human mass asleep next to me, however, made me think twice, so instead I spent the night wishing that I wasn't on a coach heading towards Glasgow just so that I could watch the Scottish Cup Final with a bloke I barely knew.

My final hope was that I'd make it to Glasgow and there'd be no sign of Kevin. I'd have some breakfast, look round the record shops, then get the train back to Birmingham. I'd sleep on the train and be back in time for some revision and an early night. It would be good for my body and my soul.

Programme Highlights: To Your Health!

It's funny that people say 'To your health' when they toast you with an alcoholic drink. It's said sincerely, or at least that's what I always thought. Perhaps I've been missing the joke all these years. 'To your health…' followed by the unspoken 'Ha ha ha, this stuff's gonna kill you, you know, because your grandfather was an alcoholic, and he set himself and his flat on fire when he was pissed, and so was your great-aunt, and those are just the ones we know about, sonny – it's a disease that a lot of people hide. Your family included.'

The opening message in the programme for the 1984 Scottish Cup Final was written by Stanley Mitchell, the director of the Scottish Health Education Group, the cup's sponsor that year. After the usual guff about a 'thrilling and fitting climax' to the competition, and 'a hard-won place in the Final', he got down to his agenda. Stanley's a health nut, fans!

'I believe that both team managers would be the first to agree that achievement rarely comes without effort, and that you have to work hard in order to generate success,' he opines. Did this bastard know that I was bunking off revising for my 'History of the German Language' exam? If not, his warning was uncannily prescient. But learning wasn't really his main concern.

'And these basic truths apply to all of us,' he went on, 'whether we're looking to improve our sporting abilities or simply to succeed in what we do.'

Oh stop, Stanley, your wisdom is killing me. Who could possibly concentrate on the game once they'd read these philosophical guiding principles? But wait, there's more: 'One of the most useful areas in which we can all recognise scope for achievement lies in the setting of our own personal health goals. In other words, in looking to make sure that we live, eat, and exercise sensibly.

'It may take a little effort and training. And it will mean tackling regular exercise, refereeing your alcohol intake and blowing the whistle on cigarettes.'

What a genius! He has an audience of thousands of drunk, overweight, tobacco-addicted football fans, and Sir Stanley *scores* with a great triple metaphor to get their attention.

By the time Kevin and I got to Hampden that day, I doubt I was even fit enough to read Mr Mitchell's patronising advice without it wobbling before my eyes and distorting into a combination of several other languages entirely. He could have written 'Ian Plenderleith, you've drunk too much and you're in Glasgow, when you should be sober and back in Birmingham revising for that important exam,' and I probably wouldn't have registered it. Because all I could think was, *What the fuck am I doing here? What the FUCK am I doing here?* Not even for the archetypal Tuesday-night fixture at home to Halifax on a wet winter's night in Lincoln had I experienced this level of doubt about walking through a turnstile. This was football, and given the chance, I always wanted to go to football. Just not with a bloke like Kevin.

On the surface, it looked like we'd enjoyed a straightforward pre-match morning. Such was the demand for overnight travel between Norwich and Glasgow that there'd been two coaches, and Kevin had been on the one behind me. We met, and we went for breakfast. We walked around Glasgow in the morning spring sunshine. We went to the SFA for tickets, as I mentioned before, and then we had a couple of pre-match pints before the game.

During all this time, I'd been listening to Kevin, being too tired to talk myself. Kevin was a young man of opinion. He was two years older than me, but we shared the same birthday. We had Scottish parents. We both supported football teams from Glasgow. It turned out that was all we had in common.

'Look at the fuckin' tits on that, eh? Ah'd give a few bob to be puttin' ma meat and two veg somewhere warm and wet up her right now, eh?'

Yeah, I suppose so. Maybe once or twice you can ignore it. But relentlessly, over the course of several hours, interspersed only with observations about how Thatcher had to smash Scargill and the miners, and all the other extreme right-wing positions on the issues of gender, race and sexuality that you can imagine? And all posed as rhetorical questions, starting with the words 'Do ye no think that...?' For example, 'Do ye no think that there are too many [expletive racist term] bands in the charts these days?' Yeah, absolutely, Kev. Far too many. A brilliant and important point. They're taking over. Soon you won't be able to see the fuckin' charts at night, eh?

Nowadays, if I meet someone like Kevin, then I'll leave the room rather than listen to this old crap any more, and it's surprising how often you can still hear it if you're in the wrong place at the wrong time. Unless I've had the right amount of alcohol – enough to make me argumentative but not enough to make me weary and cynical (about three to four drinks) – then I'll leave the futile fightback to younger minds. At the time, though, I still believed it was possible to change people like Kevin. Yet that day I more or less gave him free rein to spout off. Weary and hungover and in a shit mood, I could not be arsed to take issue with someone who was already so sure that he knew what was wrong with the world: too many blacks and commies, and not enough women ready to go down on his dick.

Actually, I could empathise with the last problem, even though I would never let on. At the time, I was a scrupulous male feminist who would upbraid sexist comments from almost any quarter (provided I wasn't hungover and sleep-deprived). I can no longer truthfully say whether this was because I believed in equality at all costs, or because I wanted to impress a certain type of woman with impeccable New Man credentials and get them into bed. If it was the latter, I had so far been largely unsuccessful.

Despair and Virginity

It would have been better for me if I'd been born into a strict religious culture where retaining your virginity until after marriage represented as important a landmark in your life as losing it did to skinny, spot-pocked teenagers in 1980s Lincolnshire. I would have been good at that – holding on to my virginity. No, I *was* good at it. I was genius at it. I couldn't get rid of the fucking thing, no matter how hard I tried. All efforts were stymied by my clumsiness, cluelessness and inarticulacy in the face of any woman who looked for a couple of seconds as though she might, for whatever reason, be interested in me.

I can blame the conditions – the perceived lack of suitable women who were available, for example, or our very good feminist English teacher, who taught me and my classmates all that was correct about not treating women as sex objects (fat chance of that happening). I could claim that my mum being in the Labour Party, therefore exposing me to even more people who thought this way, while at the same time having the *Guardian* delivered every day, were all factors behind my failure to have some experienced girl take me by the hand and give me a healthy seeing-to. The problem, though, was me. I was fussy, arrogant, awkward, uptight and relentlessly romantic, all at the same time. My heart was telling me that I needed to find the perfect girl, and that this love would lift us to a higher plane whereby sex was almost incidental, although at the same time natural and beautiful. My body, meanwhile, was telling me all day long that I needed to shag. Anyone would do. Just once, to get me started.

When the two collided, it led to Despair. I was nearly 19 years old and finding neither love nor sex. It was mainly for this reason that I was standing on the terraces at the 1984 Scottish Cup Final, thinking, *What the FUCK am I doing here?* It wasn't necessarily to do with my hangover or my fatigue or Kevin wittering on about fanny, or even the encroaching 'History of the German Language' exam. What I needed to be doing was spending more time looking for love. And/or sex. And Hampden Park, with 58,900 Celtic and Aberdeen fans, was possibly the last place on earth I was going to find it. Kevin's gran's house in Falkirk later that night, I rightly suspected, would also offer up few possibilities. Another day passes in virginity's luckless wasteland...

Dear Diary...

I'm sorry to say that I kept a diary around this time, and I'm afraid you're going to have to read some excerpts. Here's what I wrote on 15 May, four days before the final, aged 18 and three-quarters:

> Sick of work [!?], sick of Birmingham, sick of people, the only refuge an empty evening library. I immediately stop to be a real person when I start thinking about being a bleeding shepherd on some faraway Scottish isle, [the] one that I love to keep me company, relaxing, releasing seed, writing, experimenting with a synthesiser and a four-track studio ha!

I'm not sure if 'releasing seed' was a reference to sex or to cultivating my own crops as part of a vision of nutritional self-sufficiency in case the sheep, my writing and my musical experimentation failed to bring in enough to feed both me and my loved one. But you can broadly see what I was hankering for.

When I returned from Scotland, the entry for 21 May barely mentions the game, although there's reference to (get this for drama) the 'alcohol-ridden streets of Glasgow, everywhere drunks stagger and mutter and shout and beg, the pubs full of men, tatty and worn could apply to both of them, throwing back the vein-eroding liquor'. Wow, that's so evocative. Glasgow is full of drunks. Who'd have thought? Though, of course, that all changed once Stanley Mitchell's programme notes had circulated among the city's drinkers and dropouts.

All through my first year at Birmingham I had been hopelessly in love with a girl on my course, but I hadn't told anyone, least of all her. On 23 May I saw her and talked to her, and this event is chronicled and hailed as though we'd spent three blissful weeks in bed together.

'Intoxicated,' it begins, because I'd been reading too much German *Sturm und Drang* poetry. 'Today presents several images to souvenir.' (I apologise for the continually tortured prose, which reflects a young man attempting to find a style, all the while over-conscious that after his young, tragic and heroic death there would be several literary historians eager to scramble through his journals.) 'First, the quite easy history exam, which included last second takeaway glances from her [the object of love is never mentioned by name, lest the diary fall into the wrong hands]. Then the steps in the Union. She approaches, me cool [yeah, sure]... concentrating on her more than anything [what, more than on the imminent triumph of Thatcherism and the crushing of the trade union movement? Shame on you!]. Christ, I've been to Scotland twice since I last saw you, *amour de ma vie* [oh, please]. Next is drinking in *The Green Man*, amid this morass of alcohol Spurs win a cup on penalties [that'd be the UEFA Cup – sports ed.], Hermann and Tony [non-virgin friends] both chat whilst my thoughts stroll away to lands of love...'

Well, that's enough. I was drunk and 18, okay? The next day it was back to sober moping, as the entry for 24 May starts, 'The reality we search for, phantasise [*sic*] over, is the unreality we've seen all too often in films.' I go on at length to point out that reality is – guess what – dull, and that nothing ever happens to me. Meaning, *sex* never happens to me. Clearly, I didn't bump into my unrequited love on 24 May. Not that I'd have done anything about it if I had, except write it up in my diary later while gazing out the window.

It's curious that the Spurs game, even with all the drink-induced navel-gazing, the self-pity and the visions of an Arcadian pastoral landscape soaked in soppy, idealised love, gets a mention. Without the diary's help, I can remember that night only in as much as I can remember I was in a pub in Harborne, Birmingham, with Tony and Hermann watching Spurs win the UEFA Cup. I find it hard to believe that I was thinking more about my unrequited love than I was about the extra-time and penalty shootout showing on the TV behind the bar because I don't associate that event, this drink-up, with anything other than the game. I have to rely on my diary to tell me what I was apparently feeling that night.

It's the same with the Scottish Cup Final. I can recall the date no problem. It was right after my granddad's funeral, and right in the middle of my first-year exams. I can remember nothing about the actual game besides the scoreline and the reaction of the Celtic fan next to me when Paul McStay equalised. The events on the field, while doubtless significant to many people at the time, are just so many kicks and headers, around which various things were happening (or failing to happen) in my life.

Levels of Despair in a Football Fan

On the Day: this is a transitory state of Despair that can last as little as half a second. A particular player may misplace a pass to an opponent. It so happens that the fans don't think this player is good enough to be in the team. It so happens that the team is trailing and doesn't look like scoring. The team may be eight points clear at the top in early October, but that doesn't matter in the here and now. People swear and clutch their heads in their hands or raise their arms to the sky, all because one unfortunate player makes one small mistake. A second later, he may win the ball back with a crunching tackle and then play a pass into space. Instantly, all is forgiven, and the momentary aberration is erased from memory.

At the End of the Game (1): as mentioned above, many fans' memories have the capacity of a small sardine, and it's no different when a single game has been lost. Let's take the same scenario, with the team eight points clear at the top in October. Then they lose their first game of the season, and the 'chasing pack' is suddenly a little closer. Despite the good run of results, this is the end already. We've blown it. It was a fluke run. There have to be changes; there were too many players out there today who are just not cut out for first-team football. A few people will already be calling for the manager's head, because there's always someone calling for the manager's head, and you hear them loudest after a defeat, the Great Wise Men of Hindsight. All that has gone before becomes invalidated.

At the End of the Game (2): this time, the team has lost for the fifth successive game, maybe more. This longer-term Despair has settled in, and is actually much more bearable for most fans than the sudden defeat following a good run. When you're used to Despair, you have better mechanisms – such as a perpetual pessimism blackened with gallows humour – for dealing with it. Despairing fans will either call for the entire team to be transferred and the board and manager to be sacked, or they start to atrophy, becoming accustomed to failure and expecting nothing better than misery. There are some fans, and I have to admit I'm one of them, who perversely enjoy following this kind of team more than any other. How else do so many perennially unsuccessful sides survive at the lower ends of English professional football? They owe it to the inherent joys of Despair.

It's a similar psychological process you can see at work in my diaries from the spring of 1984. It's arguable that my inability to get laid was subconsciously intentional. I preferred to mooch about listening to The Smiths, dreaming of perfect love and moaning to my diary about how tough the world was than actually getting out there and saying to some girl (or *the* girl), 'Do you fancy meeting me in The Green Man for a drink tonight?'

At the End of the Season: this is the cruellest form of Despair for any football fan, when you just miss out at the final hurdle, or when you're relegated on the last day of the season through some freak combination of results and a last-minute goal. This happened to Lincoln in 1986–7. It was the first season that there was direct relegation from the Football League to the Conference. It was also the first time I had ever known Lincoln to be in last place of the fourth division, and they didn't hit that spot until the final day of the season, in the final minute, when Burnley scored at Orient. It's the only time in my life I've drunk Special Brew, because to me it tastes like industrial cleaner, but that day I went out and bought two cans and made myself drink them in the bath while contemplating this, that and the other (you'll be relieved to know the virginity was gone by then, so I had more pressing matters to mull, such as the future of Lincoln City Football Club in the depths of the Northern Premier League in front of 300 fans).

Obviously, it's worse for some fans than others. When your team's not involved, you can't help but enjoy the camera shots of youngsters at the end of the cup final defeat with tears smudging their little painted faces (what do you mean, it's just me who enjoys that?), or grown men sitting there with their heads bowed like it really matters. There are always a few, though, standing around who suddenly see themselves on the big screen and break into a grin and start waving. I love these fans best of all. But the editor cuts away from them instantly because that's not the proper story. The commentator's been rapping on about 'heartbreak', and all of a sudden you get some happily grinning buffoon jumping up and down and waving like he hasn't just experienced the most crushing event of his life – a 2–0 loss to Southend in the Division Four play-off final.

I was too self-absorbed to notice any Despair among the Celtic fans that day when they finally lost 2–1, to a Mark McGhee goal in extra-time. If you support a team like Celtic, there's sure to be another trophy along in a few months' time. I don't recall Kevin being that gutted, and I can't remember if we hung about to see Aberdeen get the trophy or if we rushed off to get the train to Falkirk. Kevin was probably wishing, like me, that I hadn't come along, because I kept whining that I didn't want to go out drinking in Falkirk that night. I had to stay in and revise and read *A Short History of the German Language*, and I didn't have any money left, and there were no Midlands Bank cashpoints in Scotland. And that's what happened. I read my book upstairs in the spare room, while Kev went on the piss with his cousin, and his gran watched telly (I liked his gran – when we were watching the news, she told Kevin to shut up because he was talking shite about the miners' strike). My one and only chance in life to get drunk in Falkirk and I squandered it. Now *that's* enough to make you despair.

7

Hope

Scotland v. Yugoslavia, International Challenge Match, 8pm, Wednesday, 12 September 1984, Hampden Park, Glasgow

Living with Great-Aunt Hope from Fife

If Despair is football's depressive cousin who is always on the verge of quitting the game and finding something better to do, then Hope is its deceptively kind great-aunt, ready with a smile and a cup of tea to tell you that things can only get better. Hope is crueller than Despair, because her euphonic words so often turn out to be illusory, and the depths we chart after the false raising of our expectations are much more difficult to bear than mere everyday pessimism. Yet without Hope we wouldn't even be in the stadium. Without Hope we wouldn't even be alive. Hope is a feel-good drug with a crashing come-down effect, but we're all addicted. The only cure for Hope is to kill yourself.

Hope helped me buy into the idea that one day I would live to see Scotland lift the World Cup. Need I say any more?

I watched Scotland in the 1974 and 1978 World Cup finals, carrying Britain's Hope. I remain unconvinced that any more than a handful of Englishmen were behind us. Many said they wanted us to win, but then they turned around and laughed when we were eliminated. Yet you know they'd have been claiming reflected glory had we been a success, pointing out how many of these players performed in their *English* league. These were deceitful part-time travellers, and ever since I've adopted a similar attitude to the England team out of puerile revenge (support them while they're winning, then laugh when they lose). My English friends, who are not petty enough to remember the 1970s, or who have very selective football memories, find this as deeply annoying as I find it rewarding.

Scotland fielded world-class players in these tournaments. The fact that they qualified for a 16-team tournament tells you how good they were, and it's going to be a long, long time, if ever, before they come that close again to winning a major international honour. Either that, or we'll have to reinstate the Home Championship, but even that would be well out of their range right now. Of course, in '74 and '78 they didn't come *close* to winning, as such, due to a variety of factors that Scotsmen will tell you ranged from bad luck to more bad luck. That they didn't win enough games or score enough goals comes into it too. The point is that millions of Scots *genuinely* believed they were going to become world champions, and at last we could shut the English up from going on about nineteen sixty-bloody-six. Scottish Hope has never been so ascendant as in the months preceding these finals. She stood high, beaming and passing out her little happy pills for free, and we all swallowed them and beamed too, and no one even thought about grassing her up to the polis.

I was similarly afflicted at the 1982 finals, although the 4–1 thumping by Brazil (after David Narey cruelly pumped up Auntie Hope with his spectacularly fluky long-range toe-poke to put us 1–0 ahead) had perhaps for the first time made me aware of Scotland's true world ranking. I was babysitting that night, and my employers – my PE teacher Dick Brewis (see 'Kissing' chapter) and his wife – came home to find me slumped in their armchair staring stupidly at the screen, flag on the floor, replica shirt stained with catatonic dribble, their dog hankering to be let out for a piss, while I sat oblivious to its howls and scratchings at the door. Dick knew the game well, and he knew it well enough to have foreseen before he went out for the evening that we'd get hammered. He consoled me in an avuncular manner, with the air of a man who has lived long enough to know how often results don't turn out the way you want them to. As far as I can remember, he didn't profess to support any particular team – a policy rooted in common sense and sanity, even if it hardly marked him out as a fan.

After 1982, Scotland was still producing good young players to add to an already strong squad. The gifted Celtic striker Charlie Nicholas began scoring goals for fun, and I witnessed him doing it several times before his fateful transfer to Arsenal and the coaching whims of Don Howe and Terry O'Neill (who once famously played him at full-back). Aberdeen were producing flair attackers like Peter Weir and Eric Black, whom, as well as seeing them score in the 1984 Scottish Cup final, I witnessed putting a hat-trick past Celtic at Parkhead. Up front, Davie Cooper and Mo Johnston would be shoo-ins for today's lacklustre team, if they deigned to play at all. Midfielders Paul McStay and Jim Bett were on the cusp of long international careers, while also at his peak was all-round battler and goal-scorer John Wark, who (nostalgic old fart alert) was probably as good as the entire current Scottish midfield put together. Experienced, sovereign players like Kenny Dalglish (one of the few players I've ever allowed myself to idolise), Graeme Souness, Willie Miller, Richard Gough, Alex McLeish and Alan Hansen formed the backbone of a squad that makes today's line-up look as shallow and weak as my analysis at the time – we're a plucky wee nation and we're good enough to win the World Cup! The idea that other countries had players who were either equally good or much better apparently never occurred to me.

I have long since given up Hope that Scotland will even qualify for the 32-team finals, let alone win them. Even if we qualify, we'd stink the tournament out playing for draws or sneaky 1–0 wins. There seems to be no prospect in sight of Celtic, Aberdeen, Hearts and Rangers producing a rash of talented young Scots who will become our golden generation. The reason this won't happen can be explained by Jocky Jockson, a flinty man with thin, hard features nursing a glass of malt whisky at the dark wood bar of the Prickly Thistle: 'It's because they dinnae send young men doon the mines any more. They're ae too busy playin' yon computer games to go outside in the cauld and play fitba.'[1]

In 1984 I was 19 years old. Almost exactly four months after the Scottish Cup Final of Despair, I was back in the same stadium, but

1. Yes, you're correct, this is just my old fart's opinion cunningly disguised as the fictional Jocky Jockson.

I was in a different mood. I was with my dad and my mate Neil (see 'Kissing' chapter), not some raving neo-fascist Celtic fan. I was watching Scotland, not some partisan, internecine club affair where complete strangers held you tight and threw you in the air. In the meantime, I'd been to Israel to work on a kibbutz for two months. I wouldn't say that I'd enjoyed it exactly, but the experience had been enough to reinvigorate me when I returned home and make me look forward to my second year at university. I would be moving out of the hall of residence and living in a flat – 'in the real world', as my imminent flatmate Tony and I dogmatically phrased it at the time. The new football season was about to start, and a new World Cup qualifying campaign was about to get under way.

Prior to playing Spain and Iceland at home in the qualifiers later that autumn, Jock Stein had arranged this warm-up friendly against Yugoslavia, who had qualified for the previous summer's European Championships but lost all three games and finished bottom of their group. Still, they had scored twice against the hosts and eventual winners France in a 3–2 defeat, so they couldn't be that bad, the programme noted. Scotland manager Jock Stein described them as 'a team of talent and initiative' coming to Hampden Park 'with some new faces and determined to get a victory'.

'We could have chosen easier opponents for our World Cup curtain-raiser but what would we have gained? *I wanted to test our strength against a quality side* [Jock's italics].'

Stein asked his players not to treat the game as a friendly, but as a proving ground for their suitability to be selected for the forthcoming qualifiers. Well, he must have been happy that they scored six goals. Or was he? What if the easy win left him thinking that the Slavs were nothing like as good as he'd thought? Did this mean that his players were good enough to beat Spain, or not? What if the 'Slav international team bosses', as they are referred to in the programme – presumably the team was run as a communist collective – had told their players to treat their game as a kick-around, and that the main reason they were over in Scotland was for a day's shopping in Edinburgh? In fact, now that I think about it, I'm pretty sure I saw Darko Pančev in a tartan and traditional Scottish knitwear shop on Princes Street the next day.

Pančev, who came on at half-time when the score was 3–1, along with a new goalie, is the only player I recognise now from the away team's line-up. A young Dragan Stojković, who'd scored a penalty against France at Euro '84, had been unable to travel because of 'army commitments'. Who knows how he would have shaped the game? Or Jock Stein's selection plans? Or my hopes?

Although it's not possible to assess the worth of the Yugoslav team at this time without some serious archive research, it's worth noting that while they were an inconsistent team, this was a country that a decade or so later broke up into Serbia and Montenegro, Croatia, Slovenia, Bosnia-Herzegovina and Macedonia. That's five teams. Against one of those five teams, Slovenia, Scotland could only draw 0–0 in 2004. Four years later they lost 1–0 to another, Macedonia. On this night, they beat the whole, unified Slav entity 6–1.

Yes, I saw Scotland win 6–1. It wasn't against San Marino or Gibraltar; it was against Yugoslavia, a proper football nation. We were brilliant. We outplayed them. From where I was sitting, it was clear: we would win the 1986 World Cup in Mexico.

Hope on a Rope

Sometimes I think that US sports have done things right by excluding relegation and promotion. It's true that sports are run on cravenly capitalistic principles, but at least everyone knows that. If a franchise fails, it's sold to another city. This rightly offends the sensibilities of small-town English supporters steeped in over a century of tradition, with a ground that is as much a part of the community as the church, the post office and the grocery shop. It horrifies us that the crude Yanks have this safety net against failure. At the same time, smaller towns with smaller teams have no chance of getting ideas above their station. A Minor League baseball team will always be Minor League. They can win the Minor League but they will never win the Major League. That way, no one's ever too disappointed.

The problem with supporting a team like Lincoln City is that, in theory, they could climb up the divisions and win the Premier League and then the Champions League too. It won't happen, but it could. For years I thought that this was one of the strongest characteristics of our league system. Now I'm no longer so sure. I wonder if it would be better to put some sort of official clamp on Lincoln: 'You can get promoted to Division Three ["League 1"], but you will never get out of there no matter how hard you try. You couldn't before [at least not since 1952] because you weren't good enough, and you can't now because we're banning you from the top two divisions. It's for your own good.'

Now the top teams would love to be guaranteed no relegation, and they've been talking about it for years. We purists, the guardians of the game's morals, are horrified at their greed and the idea of such a stitch-up. We point to Wigan Athletic, promoted in 2005 to the Premier League for the first time in their history and a non-league team when I first started following the game in the 1970s. On the other hand, advocates of a no-relegation clause can point to Barnsley and Bradford City, who enjoyed one and two seasons each in the Premier League respectively, but were nearly ruined by debt in the ensuing years. They got beaten 6–0 a lot too.

No doubt many of their fans would say they don't care, because they were there at least, and the seasons threw up multitudes of great stories and unforgettable games (Barnsley's 1–0 victory at Anfield, for example), and they wouldn't trade those years for anything because they made a change from playing Grimsby and Port Vale. But was it worth the near bankruptcy of the club and the stringent cutbacks that have followed? Was it worth losing 6–0 at home to Man United for that?

At the end of the 1981–2 season, Lincoln missed out on promotion to the old Division Two (the current Championship) by one point, the closest they've come to such heights in all the years I've supported them. I had no notion back then that promotion would have been anything but a good thing. I hoped that their excellent team of the time would stay together and they'd go on to make that final step to the top flight, followed by heady European nights at Sincil Bank. I can honestly say that I thought about this a lot, the glorious scenarios developing in my imagination like they were actually going to happen. My dad tolerantly, but dismissively, called me a dreamer whenever I went on about this, and about Scotland winning the World Cup. It's a wonder he wasn't tempted to slap me. Instead, he let me find out for myself, in footballing terms, about 'the real world' I was so keen to experience by moving out of student accommodation and into a flat of my own. Slowly but surely.

From 2003 to 2007 Lincoln made the Division Four ('League 2') play-offs on five successive occasions, and each time they failed, twice in the final. Older and possibly wiser, I consoled myself by saying that for a small club run on a tight budget, a top-seven finish in the fourth tier was the best they could hope for, and that winning more games than they lost was the best thing to keep the fans happy enough to come and watch. If they went up and got hammered, then it would be like 1978–9 all over again – bottom of the division, with crowds down and no money coming in. But by doing well in League 2/Division Four, but just not well enough, Lincoln could survive. And the crowds would keep coming, in the hope of something better, little realising that it is not in Lincoln's destiny to do any better. Stick with what you know. Rochdale, Oxford and Orient – again.

Yet even as I watched them beat Macclesfield on their way to the play-off final in May 2005, I was at it again. If they beat Southend in the final they'd be in League 1. That's just one successful promotion away from the Championship. And that's just below the Premier League. It's frightening how your thoughts can meander off into the realm of ridiculous fantasy while you're watching Lincoln play Macclesfield. It's frightening, because no matter how many times you've been fooled by passively cruel aunt Hope, she'll always stitch you up again.

Rather than your aunt, perhaps Hope is more like the partner who your friends all know is way out of your league, and with whom you're perpetually getting back together after yet another dramatic break-up. Hope is the slinky seductress, all curves and up-front sexuality, causing you to forget what you've found out to your cost countless times before. Once she's got her hands on you, Hope will leave you penniless and bereft, feeling cheap and used and, worst of all, stupid for having been so gullible, despite the bitter experiences of the past. You're a loser, and your team are losers, you fucking loser. It will always be this way. Oh look, there goes Hope, that seemingly lovely lass who stiffed you good and rotten last year. Yes, I know she has a new dress on, and it looks pretty good on her... Wait, come back, where are you going, come back, you fucking idiot, STOP FOLLOWING HOPE! Leave her alone!

Utopia Joking, Mate

There's a piece of lined A4 paper inserted into my diary for 1984–5. It's undated, and it looks like the second or third page of a monologue. Despite there being no date, I can tell it was written around that time, and not just because it's inside the diary for that year. It's the Arcadian vision again. I wasn't writing about football, but I might as well have been.

> Then there's the 'true' love fantasies, nothing to do with physical desire, oh no, this is deeper, deeper, it's always the same person, a girl I know, purity personified, beautiful, charming in the social circles, and [she] worships me. It's during the holidays and I'm on a train journey, then amazing surprise it's her, she [is] astonished too and don't we just talk talk talk, and it gets so deep don't we just feel we really know each other now, eyes connect, fall fall fall into each other's arms, she wearing white cotton and from then on it's holidays together, living together, every fuckin' thing together and we're oh so blissfully fulfilled, sitting arm in arm on summer evenings beneath a tree on lush green grass watching the tranquil river roll by.

Meanwhile, on the other side of the river, a dual ticker-tape parade is marching down to the shore. Lincoln City's players are holding aloft the Championship trophy, surrounded by adoring fans and waiters serving prawn canapés and champagne, while behind them comes the Scottish squad, holding aloft the World Cup as jubilant red-headed tartan females in very short kilts wave over to us, smiling. 'Go over and have a good time,' whispers my girl in white cotton. 'I'll still be here waiting when you come back.'

I'm no longer sure who the girl in white cotton was, because my unattainable objects of desire tended to change quite frequently, and as usual, in my paranoia, I named no names. But even Lord Hope of Utopia was beginning to see the darkness by now.

'The reality,' I continued:

> Someone told me the other night that she 'shags around'. At the time I was halfway up the stairs to drunkenness, but still my insides started a wrestling match. She 'shags around'. True love fantasies axed since then.

Aw. (Although I should have been grateful it wasn't me she'd shagged around with and then given the axe.) Your team lost. They weren't as good as you thought. They were one point short of promotion. They were one or two goals short of making the final stages. Behind those ticker-tape parades on the other side of the river was a mean little fan dressed in a Barcelona shirt, shouting, 'Wake up, you idiot, you're in a dream!'

Even back then I was starting to realise that was the way I liked it. Just as when people ask me, 'How are you?' and I reply, 'Miserable, which suits me just fine,' back then I knew that being unfulfilled was sometimes the safest place to be. You don't go bankrupt there. You don't get hurt. And so in a rare moment of insight for my teenage self, apart from the alcohol-driven whining and self-pity, I wrote:

> ... I really love being the melancholy lover-boy, like the knights of the Middle Ages writing verse for the unobtainable noble lady. Lying back in bed, staring at the ceiling, oh woe such misery, but such sweet misery, I never try to stop it recurring.

Brazil outclassed us 4–1. In front of the whole world. But we've some good young players coming through. Perhaps at Mexico '86 we'll do better…

Revolution, Paradise and Scottish Football Glory

I feel privileged to have witnessed Scotland scoring six goals in one game, I really do. It was the first time Scotland had scored six times against an opponent since beating Finland 6–0 in September 1976. The next time came over 30 years later, when they hammered mighty Gibraltar (more of a misunderstanding than a country) 6–1 at Hampden in March 2015 in a European Championships qualifier. Just to prove how much better they were than a small stretch of rock with a border point, Scotland won 6–0 in the return match a few months later. I really like to think that nowhere in the country did this give rise to the hope, even among the smallest and most naïve of followers, that this meant Scotland were bound for glory at Euro 2016.

However, at the same time, the 6–1 defeat of Yugoslavia was the worst thing that could possibly have happened to me. It refuelled my head with ludicrous delusions of glory, and cranked up my Hope to the kind of preposterous level you might associate with a gaping eight-year-old. It wasn't just Hope, it was one step beyond – Belief.

I was filling a gap. It's a cliché that everyone needs to believe in something. I had been an atheist since the age of nine, following the last-minute own goal in my first game (see 'Tears' chapter), and I had been struggling with socialism since I was 16. This was partly because, through my parents' membership of the Labour Party, I had encountered most of my teachers in a social(ist) setting, and felt the need to argue with them from a less leftist angle, even though I did my share of leafleting and proselytising come election time (which may explain Labour's continued poor showing in Lincolnshire to this day). Then, at university, the barking righteousness of the newspaper-selling cranks on the hard left demanding revolution NOW! was no more alluring than going to a pub in front of which stood half a dozen skinheads with a pack of howling, slathering guard dogs held on a taut leash. No way was I going to get laid if I was a member of the Spartacist Revolutionary Front. (My friend Tony, a Labour stalwart from Burtonwood, is fond of telling the story of a girl he met on his first weekend at university who asked him to explain the difference between the House of Commons and the House of Lords. The following week he saw her outside the Student Union selling *Socialist Worker*.)

I mistrusted the Spartacist Revolutionary Front, and the Labour Party too, now that I think about it, because I had read a German play in our A-level class which centred on the concept of doubt. My battered copy of Siegfried Lenz's *Die Zeit der Schuldlosen* (which translates literally as 'The Age of the Guiltless') had become a sort of sceptic's bible, and I could quote huge stretches of its dialogue – although this wasn't much use in arguments as hardly anyone I knew spoke German, so I tended to try and improvise on the spot while people lost interest. This play led me to believe that all political, religious and philosophical belief systems could be undermined with a few well-thought-out questions, and that no single tenet of thought was worth believing in exclusively. It all seemed so obvious to me, but not everyone had the pleasure of a liberal arts education. Not that this makes any difference – out of seven people in my French class, one was a convinced Jehovah's Witness, and two were Billy Graham acolytes. André Gide didn't stand a chance.

Die Zeit der Schuldlosen doesn't have much of a plot. Nine apparently innocent men are arrested by the ruling totalitarian regime and placed in a prison cell with a dissident political prisoner. The authorities inform the men that they will be free to go the following day should the political prisoner somehow die during the night. The core of the play centres around the discussion of whether the man – the kind of energetic doctrinaire who used to sell inky leftist newspapers outside the Student Union – should die, who should do the deed, and whether or not any or all of the nine men could be considered complicit in the prisoner's death should he be dead come morning. Among the nine men is a character called Der Konsul who offers sneering commentaries on all the other characters' flimsy justifications for doing away with the prisoner in order to regain their freedom.

Birmingham University boasted its share of both hectoring leftist factions and religious nuts peddling fiery rhetoric about eternal roastings. The mass of students, though, no longer cared much about the outside world compared with the post-'68 generation, and the boorish right-wing thugs of the rugby club, the compulsively exhibitionist footballers (though it didn't mean they were gay, or perverts) and a multitude of other pointless excuses for a piss-up – such as Croquet Soc. and Liberal Soc. – made up the numbers and largely kept the educated off the streets of Birmingham and out of the way of 'the real world'. Meanwhile, I had retained the words of my guru long after the final exam, and appointed myself as something of a *Konsul*, a tiresome über-cynic who looked down at everyone and everything from a lofty intellectual height. I'll spare you any further entries from my diary, not least because they're dreadful, but this sense of myself as a superior being who at the age of 19 has already seen and heard it all before pervades the text, especially when I'm drunk and trying to cover up for the fact that I don't have a girlfriend.

And all the time I was hiding a secret. At least the idealists were coming out with their ridiculous Hope of imminent revolution and roaring it out to passers-by in front of the Student Union building. At least the Bible-thumpers were praising God on high and trying to share with the world what they believed to be true – if you take Jesus into your life, you'll enjoy the bonus of a rather nice eternal stint in Paradise. At least they had the integrity to act on their convictions. But me? Do you think that every lunchtime I ran down to the Union clutching a pile of hastily printed, typo-ridden, stapled-together leaflets proclaiming in block caps 'SCOTLAND TO WIN NEXT WORLD CUP'? Was I sermonising on the sturdiness of Miller and McLeish at the back, the studied calm of Souness in midfield (when he wasn't going in studs first, thigh high) and the emerging genius of Nicholas up front? 'Read all about it in the "Forwards to Mexico!" special edition! McStay to down Brazilians with second-half hat-trick. Super Mo Johnston to destroy the Germans!'

Not a bit of it. The *Konsul* in me was making cheap jibes from the sidelines at all those who still had something to live for. And all the time I was concealing my equally incredible notions of a future fantasy. Red Revolution. Eternal Paradise. Scotland winning the World Cup. Which one of these visions was the most utopian?

Idea for a Short Scottish World Cup-Themed Play about Doubt, Responsibility and Collective Guilt

In *The Age of the Clueless*, nine apparently innocent men are arrested by the Scottish footballing authorities and placed in a cell with a fan who firmly believes that Scotland are going to win the World Cup. In order to halt the spread of delusional Hope across the country, forcing the SFA to develop a decent youth system and a single league structure throughout the Scottish game, and to break the strangulating monopoly of the Old Firm, the nine men are told that they can walk free once the optimistic fan has 'passed away'...

After a two-minute discussion about the need to get down the pub before last orders, and a brief scuffle in the dark, the nine men walk free. The falling curtain is inscribed with the words: 'The Death of Scottish Football'.

Don't Tell Yanks There's No Hope

In many ways, I'm grateful to the current Scottish team for being so inept. Despite the odd flush of unfounded, irrational hope, it's clear that several years are going to pass before it can qualify for a major tournament again. With all those new nations emerging from the old Soviet Union and Eastern Europe, most of whom are better than us already, success for the Scotland football team is one hope I can realistically dispense with. I can think about other stuff instead, because there is surely only a finite amount of time in your life that you can waste on such a ludicrous proposition. Let go and move on. We were never much good to start with, and now we're garbage.

In late 2003 I was interviewed by John Haydon of the *Washington Times* for his weekly soccer column (my dad, who takes a strange delight in the fact that other people, just like him, are getting old too, loved the headline referring to me as a 'veteran writer'). I answered various questions about the state of Major League Soccer and how I thought its standards compared with Europe, drawing generous parallels between the best US clubs and the more mediocre strugglers in the English Premier League. Then he asked when I thought the US would win the World Cup, and I replied, 'They won't.'

'Never?' he responded.

'Well, they have about as much chance as Scotland,' I said flippantly, and forgot about it.[2]

When the piece appeared, however, it turned out I'd touched a raw nerve. I'd dissed American Hope, in a country where optimism is a way of life. You should never say never, responded the critics via a lively and widely read football message board. Worse still, I had foolishly compared the US's chances with those of Scotland, who by then had slipped several dozen places behind the US in the world rankings. The reputation I had tentatively built up through my columns as a supporter of US soccer took a severe battering.

The US is a relatively virginal football country. Its fans have every right to believe they might one day win the World Cup. And drawing a parallel between the US and Scotland was downright stupid. Scotland's days as a footballing power are over, and the mines that fostered such a rich tradition of players and managers are long closed. The US has millions of players and country-wide training facilities. It can only get better. If I were a young US fan, I'd be looking at just a few of the results that the US has pulled off over the past few years and thinking: *If these guys all play their best game at the right time, there's a chance we could win the World Cup.*

And they'd be right. They weren't far off in 2002, going out unluckily to Germany in the quarter-finals after victories over Mexico and Portugal. In 2009 they reached the final of the Confederations Cup by beating Spain, who hadn't lost a game for two years. In 2015 they won away against the German world champions, and deservedly so. Maybe it's time for me to take a Pledge of Allegiance. To Hope!

2. As I put this book through a final edit, both Scotland and the US have just failed to qualify for the 2018 World Cup.

Programme Highlights

'We have got a good squad who will go flat out to qualify for the World Cup,' wrote Alex McLeish in one of the programme's 'Starspots'. 'Certainly for me, it would be a bitter disappointment if the lads failed to make it to Mexico. Failure is unthinkable.'

It's telling that he doesn't mention his hopes for what Scotland will achieve once they make it to Mexico, although in fairness he was probably taking it one step at a time. For the record, Scotland *did* qualify for Mexico '86, managing one goal and one point in their three group games, including a 0–0 draw against a Uruguay team reduced to ten men in the first minute.

Match referee Keith Hackett of Sheffield was another of England's 'big name' refs. Off the field, though, he was 'a sales director with a firm which specialises in garage doors'. You have to be happy for him that he had his refereeing as an existential bolster while making small talk at parties:

Partygoer (to Mr Keith Hackett of Sheffield): 'And what do you do?'

Mr Keith Hackett of Sheffield (quickly at first): 'Sellgaragedoors, but I'm also a Football League referee, and only last year I was senior linesman to Mr George Courtney of Spennymoor at the semi-final stage of the European Championships in France. You know, Paris is so very beautiful in the early summer…'

Partygoer (interrupting Mr Keith Hackett of Sheffield): 'Can you come and take a look at my garage door? It keeps getting stuck, and I think we may need a new one.'

8

Change

Arminia Bielefeld v. Eintracht Braunschweig, German Second Division, 3.30pm, Sunday, 22 September 1985

Frisch Start

One of the best books I've ever read was by the Swiss novelist Max Frisch, called *Stiller.*[1] The protagonist, the Mr Stiller of the title, walks wordlessly away from his family one day because he's had enough of life's tedious repetition and his wife wittering on, and so he emigrates to America, where he reinvents himself as Mr White – you know, as in a blank page, starting all over again. In America nobody knows him, so he can not only start a new life, he can become a completely different person too. After a while he returns home, and in response to everyone who says, 'Ah, Stiller, where the hell have you been?' he replies, 'I'm not Stiller. My name is White.' Despite everyone's insistence that he is indeed Stiller and they *know* him, he sticks to his guns, preferring the person he has had the chance to become, unrestricted by Switzerland's socially, and his own personally, oppressive environment.

When I arrived in Germany in the autumn of 1985 to spend a year

1. I liked it so much that I also referred to it in my book *Rock 'n' Roll Soccer: The Short Life and Fast Times of the North American Soccer League*, by way of explaining the allure of the US to young British players in the 1970s. It's a good book, and I think you should buy it. No, not *Stiller* (Max Frisch is dead and he doesn't need the royalties, though you should read it anyway), I mean *Rock 'n' Roll Soccer*. Damn, my self-marketing skills are hot and polished, aren't they?

at the University of Bielefeld, I hadn't been to the country since a one-night layover in Bavaria on the way back from a holiday in Austria when I was four years old. I'd meant to study French at university, but my exam results were all mixed up, so I decided to study German instead. Almost every year when I was young we had gone on holiday to France, and I'd been learning the language since I was seven. I had only been learning German since I was 14, and knew very little about the country or the people. I was terrified.

I didn't know anyone in Bielefeld, or in the rest of Germany either. A friend on my course, Helen, had given me the name and address of a friend of hers in the city, but the idea of knocking on a female stranger's door and attempting to communicate with her in a foreign language was almost as alien to me as approaching a woman in a nightclub. I did seek the address out one day, and stood in front of the doorbell, and after some hesitation I did manage to ring it. When no one answered within five seconds, I scarpered, so then I could tell Helen I'd tried but no one had been at home. This might have had something to do with the fact that I went round there on a weekday, in the middle of the morning, when I knew it was least likely there would be anyone there.

So when I arrived by train early on a mid-September Monday morning, after a sleep-deprived overnight coach and ferry journey from Nottingham to Dortmund (a cheap ticket booked through a travel company I found in the back pages of the *NME*), the first thing I did was to buy a map of the city and look up where the youth hostel was. It was about four miles out of the town's centre, but rather than dare to ask anyone which tram to take (because they'd all start jumping up and down, laughing and shouting to passers-by, 'Did you hear zis guy trying to speak German? Ha ha ha!'), I walked all the way, half-pinned to the pavement by the weight of the cheap and crappy rucksack I'd bought from the Army and Navy Store in Lincoln, which was filled with nothing but clothes, my Walkman, about a dozen cassettes and a Collins German–English dictionary.

Aside from being chronically lonely, homesick, helpless, hungry, alienated, muted, paranoid, tired and running on a strict budget, I was almost shitting myself with excitement. I was 20 years old, and I had no one to answer to. No one here had any expectations of me. I had no cares, obligations or responsibilities other than to obtain, at some distant point in the future, a couple of certificates testifying that I had attended some classes at the university. The whole year before me was a blank page, and I could write on it what the hell I liked. I could do what the hell I liked. I could be who the hell I wanted. Once I'd got over being homesick, lonely and paranoid.

On my walk out to the youth hostel, I was so sensitive to my new environment that I kept looking around, sure that people were staring at this foreigner who had come to town with his weirdly shaped green rucksack, though as there was a British Army barracks on the edge of town, they probably just thought I was another hungover squaddie gone AWOL. One time I looked over my shoulder I saw a car was coming towards me. It was travelling fast on the wrong side of the road, and was about to ride up on to the pavement and knock me down. I jumped and let out a stifled cry of alarm.

The car passed me by. It wasn't travelling on the wrong side of the road at all. It was travelling on the right side. A woman walking about 10 yards behind me burst out laughing. So it wasn't true what they said about the Germans having no sense of humour.

The Things We Brits Think about the Germans

In 1994 I was preparing to move to Germany for a second time, this time to take a job in Frankfurt. I'd been working in London for eight years, and playing for a football team in the Southern Olympian League. When I told some of my teammates I would no longer be playing because I was moving to Germany, they said, 'Oh, that sounds interesting. Well, what with a unified Europe and the forthcoming single currency, I suppose we can expect increased mobility among working people in a more ethnically fluid and tolerant continent. And think of the fantastic cultural landscape you'll be exposed to in the land of Beethoven, Heine and Hesse. Best of luck!'

Or perhaps I'm remembering this wrongly, and what they actually said was, 'Ha ha ha! Germany! What are you, a fucking Nazi or something, Plendy? Will you be wearing a pair of jackboots when you're over there?! Ha ha ha!' Well, it was only 49 years after World War II had ended, and I'm sure that on a German football pitch somewhere that same day a young lad called Hans was telling his teammates that this would be his last game as he was moving to a new job in London, and they were all saying, 'Ha ha ha! England! Are you going to invade Africa and India as soon as you get there and either kill or enslave the natives, and then exploit all of its natural resources? Have you got a job crushing trade union rights and destroying the country's industrial base? Will you be shooting deserters after a desultory trial and jailing conscientious objectors? Eh? EH? Ha ha ha!'

The conversation with my hilarious teammates reminded me of the time a few years earlier when I'd told my mum's next-door neighbour that, having completed my degree, I was about to move down to London to look for work. We were standing watching the Middle Rasen village team I'd played for a few years before, and clearly there's something about standing on the side of a football pitch that brings out a philosophical streak in grown men. 'Wot the fook do yer want to go and move down to London for?' asked my neighbour, genuinely disgusted. 'It's a fookin' shit'ole, that place. You want to get a job in Lincoln, Ian. Why don't you stay up 'ere?'

Given that this was the same man who had once expressed amazement at my mum going to see friends in Bradford one weekend because the city was 'full of' dark-skinned people (he was less subtle in his description, like many men of a certain generation), I was doubtful about following his advice. It's odd that people don't like the people they know moving off to strange places they know nothing about, but about which they still have an opinion anyway. Of course, the good thing about the strange places is that these same people, the ones with the big opinions, are unlikely to follow in your footsteps. Too many dark-skinned people or Nazis, see?

There was some sort of national poll in the UK in the 1990s, in which students were asked to name the three most famous Germans they could think of. Jürgen Klinsmann was very high up, having recently moved to Tottenham and become something of a darling for taking the piss out of his own reputation as a diving German bastard.

The other two biggies were Hitler and Mozart. Who, unfortunately for prejudice fans, were Austrian. Nowadays, most young people in Britain quite like the Germans, largely on the basis of having visited the place and met some of its people.

I didn't know what to expect from Germans when I came to Bielefeld back in 1985, and of course most of the people I met were fellow students. Still, they were unlike the students I knew in England. They liked to drink, but only because they liked to drink, not because they wanted to fall over and vomit and then go on about it for a week. Their tongues didn't hang out overtly when a member of the opposite sex walked past, and they didn't brag or lie about how many women they'd slept with. They could talk about politics without posturing, and they enjoyed music because they actually liked it, not because they slavishly followed the doctrines of the *NME* and the *John Peel Show* (I was a chronic victim). They were accepting and tolerant of this nervously drunken musical fascist in their midst, bemused at his feral idiocies and determinedly nocturnal habits, like they had some sort of sociological study object they were keeping and observing in a loosely controlled environment. Encouraged by the lack of judgement, peacockery, damning stares and implied readiness for violence, I began to come out of myself. Instead of standing quietly in the corner and leaving early with a dark cloud of British misery seeping into my ears, I took the revolutionary step of starting to enjoy life. It was about five years late, but that was just the way things had to be back then. In Margaret Thatcher's England, the only people conspicuously enjoying themselves were the entitled twats spilling champagne on to each other's cummerbunds. Going to a nightclub meant an exorbitant entrance fee, intimidating hard-man security, more cash for the cloakroom, lots and lots more cash for shite lager, crap chart music that was too loud to talk over, and blokes ready to fight on pretexts that included: looking in their direction; looking in their girlfriend's direction; looking like a pretty boy; looking like a student. My flatmate Tony would drag me along whenever one of his mates was visiting from Warrington. If they were having a good time, they hid it well. The default nightclub expression in the pre-rave era was a scowl or a leer. I couldn't perfect either, so I moaned instead, and at some point in the evening Tony would ask me, quite reasonably, 'Why don't you fuck off home?'

In Bielefeld, they had a Bhaggy disco. That's exactly what it sounds like – a disco run by the Bhagwan religious sect. I've no idea why they ran cheap discos across Germany, they just did, and sadly they're long since gone. It cost five Deutschmarks to get in, maybe less, and that included two drinks. Everyone looked relaxed. There were no twats. No one dressed up, no one stared at you, you could dance however the hell you wanted, and the music was presentable – stuff like The Cure, New Order and Simple Minds. The more commercial end of indie pop, but never Kajafuckinggoogoo. It's the only time in my life I've said with any sincerity and enthusiasm, 'Hey, let's go to the disco tonight!'

The other thing about the Germans – they liked their football, right enough. But in keeping with their seemingly relaxed attitude to everything, at that time they didn't seem to care much about it.

Youth Hostile

This game took place on a Sunday afternoon at 3.30pm, which was an alien kick-off time and day to me. In the mid-1970s Lincoln played a couple of times on Sunday afternoons (see 'Cursing' chapter), but when I went home after the match I felt really down because it was school the next day and I had to go to bed early, although my body was telling me it was Saturday. It was in a post-match state, looking forward to *Starsky and Hutch* or *Kojak* and, if I could swing it, *Match of the Day*. But no, even though I had been to Sincil Bank and should, by rights, have been enjoying that mental shutdown Saturday-night vegetative state in front of cop-centric US television, there was no escaping homework and being sent off to bed at eight.

Bielefeld v. Eintracht Braunschweig took place six days after I'd arrived in the country. I was still living in the youth hostel, until I could take over a student room at the end of the month. In three days I had barely talked to a single human being, apart from an unfeasibly hairy American called Gian-Paolo from New York (who spoke effortlessly fluent German, and in the coming weeks was kind enough to rescue me from a hundred conversations in which I was floundering). I was terrified to talk German, and when anyone spoke to me I couldn't understand what they were saying. The only other people in the youth hostel were a bunch of school kids who seemed to think I was the funniest person on earth. The morning of my arrival, after walking from the train station and thinking I was about to be killed by a car on the 'wrong' side of the road, I had walked up through the woods and around a corner to the youth hostel's main entrance, sweating and stressed. And there was my welcoming party – a huge party of German school kids, seemingly with nothing better to do than sit outside and wait for my arrival. When they saw me, they spontaneously burst out into a chorus of laughter. I went even redder in the face and beetled past them into reception.

My greatest companion in Germany so far had been a copy of a magazine called *Neue Revue*, a few issues of which were lying around my eight-bed dormitory. I'm still not sure what market this magazine is aimed at – its contents included TV listings, recipes, celebrity gossip and some pictures of women with their baps out. This last section was of particular comfort as I lay in bed at night, thankfully not asked to share accommodation with the squealing pre-teens who were getting such a kick out of the awkward comic figure in their midst. After my sole roommate Gian-Paolo had moved out of the youth hostel and into a flat in town, I was able to appreciate the liberated norms of northern Europe, where soft porn was freely available in what was traditionally the wholesome, fresh-air environment of the youth hostel. (Not that soft porn can't be wholesome, but I digress.)

By the time Sunday arrived I had wandered around town half a dozen times and was bored out of my skull. I had also managed to work out where the trams went and how not to buy a ticket – ticket checks were rare and perfunctory, and I rode the whole year for free, to the shame of my now law-abiding, respectable, middle-aged persona, with a single ticket in my pocket, ready to 'cancel' it at any second should an inspector come on board. I had staked out the university and taken a language entrance exam, which qualified me to take a second language entrance exam three weeks later, which in turn would allow me to stay in Bielefeld for a year, mainly drinking. If you can just get past the bureaucracy, every institution has its rewards.

I had also worked out from the local paper that Arminia Bielefeld were playing at home on Sunday afternoon, at 3.30pm, and I had located the Alm stadium on my already dog-eared city map. Sundays in Germany are dead because almost everything is closed, and it was much, much worse back then. Only the newsagent at the train station was open, and the nearby kebab shop where I spent a lot of time and Deutschmarks in those hungry first weeks. It's not a religious thing particularly. Germans, with good reason, just like to do nothing on Sundays. And as I discovered from the match programme, at that time they weren't at all keen on playing second division football on the Lord's designated day.

Programme Highlights

As talking points go, it's not the most thrilling, but it illustrates a certain Germanic ability to moan about an issue with a dogged tenacity that makes us Brits look like beaming Jesus-rays of sunshine.[2] Grumpy programme-notes editor Hans Büttner was peeved at the inconvenience of Sunday-afternoon kick-offs, and pointed out that Sundays 'for years have been the day for amateur football in the eastern Westphalia area'. Mind you, he was clearly a guy you couldn't win with either way. The upcoming Saturday-afternoon game with Aachen was no good either, because 'that's the day Boris Becker will be playing against Russia on TV', he whined, 'which will certainly stop a lot of people coming to the Alm'. Testimony indeed to Bielefeld's pulling power.

In an interview for the programme, Bielefeld trainer Gerd Roggensack (what a missed opportunity for tabloid headline writers that he never came to unsuccessfully manage in England) took up the theme as well, while his opposite number, Willibert Kremer, was in

2. A headline in the *Süddeutsche Zeitung* in the summer of 2016 read: 'Germans have never been so well off, yet we're complaining more than ever.' So nothing's changed in that regard.

no-holds-barred, table-thumping mood when he declared, 'Sunday games are a catastrophe!' Although he didn't exactly say why. Perhaps that was the day his mum had the whole family over for pot roast and sauerkraut, and this week he was going to miss out.

Kremer had decided to make the best of the unusual kick-off time by developing a master plan so that he could come away with 'at least a point to keep in touch with the leaders. We'll be coming to Bielefeld on Saturday already and staying at the Novotel!' Unfortunately, this chain-hotel accommodation trickery didn't help prevent what he had correctly forecast as a 'catastrophe'. Bielefeld beat Braunschweig 7–1.

I think the problem was that, like myself, his team had nothing better to do than walk around the pedestrian zone in Bielefeld all Sunday morning, staring into the shop windows and waiting for kick-off. Maybe, like me, they'd nipped up to the station for a kebab and it was lying heavy in their stomachs. Bored, and stuffed with Turkish food, they got crushed. Or perhaps they were pampered just a little too much in the Novotel. They needed a night at the spartan youth hostel with me and the snickering school kids to sharpen them up.

Efficiency, Rules, Etc.

That afternoon Bielefeld were an efficient, well-organised machine who played in knee-high jackboots... ha, just kidding. They walked all over Braunschweig from start to finish, that much I can remember, going some way to quelling my disappointment that, after I had applied to study here, they had been relegated from the Bundesliga. A friend who'd spent 12 months in Germany two years earlier had described them as 'a Coventry City'-style team, which I had taken to mean that they would still be in the highest division, immune to relegation, as the Sky Blues were back then. Nonetheless, if they were going to tear teams apart every week on their way back up, that would be fine by me.

I was impressed by the set-up. The pre-match beer and bratwurst ritual struck me as a thoroughly honourable way to prepare for watching a football match, compared with the British habit of tanking up on six pints of lager in the pub beforehand and being too wrecked to have any idea what was going on out on the pitch in between frequent trips to the bog to puke or piss. This seemed much more civilised. It's true that the team played well that day, but the spectators seemed to encourage rather than abuse their own players, muttering a mournful '*Schade!*' ('Shame!') when a home player made a mistake. This corresponded more to the stoical yet fair attitude of my dad, who had annoyed me for years when I was young by applauding well-worked goals scored *against* Lincoln.

Most of all, I loved the ground, and the feeling that for the first time since I'd crossed the border, I understood something that was going on and that I was in sync with the people around me. There's a goal. Wahaaay!

'On Sunday I popped along to see Bielefeld play,' I wrote home a few days later, although for some reason I didn't mention the hours of hanging around bored and the intense loneliness I'd been feeling all week. I think kids are terrified of telling their parents they're bored, ever, because the first few times they try it at the age of four they get yelled at, or clipped around the ear, or made to do a chore. Parents, including me, hate to hear their kids say they're bored because it means they have to do something about it, which we do: we yell, to stop them saying they're bored. As for not telling my dad I was lonely as hell, I suppose I just didn't want him to worry or think that his 20-year-old son was a social inadequate.

'... and in front of 8,000, mercilessly tore apart the opposition 7–1 and went top of the German second division,' my exciting match report continued. 'The referee was a bit dodgy [that would be "Retzmann (Hamburg)". The programme gives no further details, no hobbies, not even a first name, presumably because fans were not expected to call him by it] as he gave three penalties, but the home crowd only seemed to object to the one awarded to the opposition (which admittedly was the most fantastic dive of the three).' A bit of internet research reveals why Friedrich 'Fiete' Retzmann handed out penalties in both directions so liberally. During a second division, top-of-the-table game between Hessen Kassel and Waldhof Mannheim two years earlier, he'd refused the home team (Kassel) a penalty and given one to Mannheim, who'd converted it. The game ended 1–1, and at the end an incensed 21-year-old Kassel fan jumped the security fence and head-butted Retzmann. The club got away with a fine.[3]

In the letter I also mentioned watching West Germany play Sweden in a World Cup qualifier in Stockholm on the youth hostel's compact TV the night before, the 'fifty or so screaming school brats who never stop stomping and shouting' (previous week's letter) having gone back to more secure institutions. I stuck to another dull match precis rather than describe an incident that started me thinking that not all German stereotypes were completely inaccurate. Bedtime in the youth hostel was 9.45pm. I knew that, and I was alone in the dining room watching the game as the young man in charge cleaned and closed up around me. But I assumed that he would let me watch the game to the end and tell me to turn the light off afterwards on my way up to bed. I was, after all, just about the only resident, so I was hardly likely to start a wild party by myself, especially not with a copy of *Neue Revue* waiting by my bed.

'It's 9.45, we have to turn the TV off now,' said the earnest young man politely. Germany should export some of its earnest young men to places like Britain, where we have a surplus of wacky pissheads who think they're funny, but they're not. You know, to achieve a single European balance of some measure.

'The game'll be over soon,' I said reassuringly. 'Don't worry, I'll turn it off before I go upstairs.'

The young man bit his lip anxiously. You could see he was genuinely perplexed. The rules stated that the TV had to be turned off at 9.45, and here was someone, some problem youth hosteller, who wanted to watch it for another 10 minutes.

'But the rules clearly state...'

It was a long debate that almost took us to full-time before I could convince him. Perhaps the reputation of British football fans preceded me. No sooner would he leave than I would fish out six cans of lager, kick in the TV screen and proceed to wreck the place, despite the fact

3. In 2000 Retzmann collapsed and died suddenly from a lung embolism while out walking with his wife, aged just 54.

I had been residing there peacefully now for nine long, tedious days. But just as in two world wars, British common sense prevailed. Or rather, my stubborn insistence prevailed, because there was no way I was going to miss the end of the game. When there was football to be watched, I watched it, despite my complete lack of German or Swedish blood ties.

Watching the highlights on YouTube, I probably missed the wonderful commentary moment all those years ago, either because I was arguing with the youth hostel manager or because my German wasn't good enough. As the final minute started, with Germany 2–1 up and the team needing both points to secure their qualification for Mexico '86, the ball was far away from the German goal, and the away side had a throw-in at the halfway line. ZDF commentator Eberhard Figgemeier began to opine, 'Well, we're in the last minute, ladies and gentlemen, and I think we must safely assume now, I think we are *allowed* to assume now, that Franz Beckenbauer's team has once and for all qualified for Mexico, after three poor defeats in a row with no goals scored and six conceded… And here's the new man, 2–2!'[4] During those few seconds, Germany took the throw-in, lost possession, the Swedes made three passes forwards, and the substitute Mats Magnusson, who'd come on a minute before, ran through on goal from the right and scored with his first and only touch of the game. The referee allowed the restart and then blew immediately for full-time.

So the German team that night had no more staying power than the youth hostel manager faced with an unexpected British football saddo. Magnusson's one-touch cameo thoroughly vindicated my insistence on seeing the game through to the end. The youth hostel manager had fucked off by then, though, so I didn't get to tell him, 'I told you

4. Figgemeier had become a commentating legend the year before when covering a German Cup semi-final between Bayern Munich and Schalke 04 that had ended in a 6–6 draw. In his euphoria at the end of the game he announced bafflingly, 'What this game has done for football cannot be repaired!' He also jumped the gun that night too. When Dieter Hoeneß put Bayern 6–5 ahead, he yelled, 'That's the decisive goal! That must be it!' One imagines a disappointed girlfriend called something like Ulrike smoking a cigarette while lying next to Eberhard, who is red-faced and apologetic and saying, 'It'll be better next time.'

so!' or to teach him the simple lesson that you should never give up. Not on the game, and not on life, *mein lieber Freund.*

Fußball: Just Once a Week

Given that I was young, free and single, it's interesting to recall how little football I watched over the course of the year when I compare it with the number of games I watch now. I followed Arminia Bielefeld for the season I was there, and probably went to around a dozen home games as their promotion drive to the Bundesliga finally faltered. Occasionally, I would wander into a bar at six on a Saturday evening and catch the Bundesliga highlights programme, but I didn't have much idea of who was playing or what the league standings were. I didn't buy a single copy of the alarmingly comprehensive football weekly, *Kicker*, and I didn't check up on the results of the other games in the division unless I happened to buy a newspaper. I remember skipping the 5–1 home victory over Freiburg because it was too cold.

I need the record books to tell me that Bayern pipped Bremen to the championship on goal difference that season, and that the men from Munich hammered Stuttgart 5–2 in the German Cup Final. I was in Berlin that weekend, but it never occurred to me to go to the Olympiastadion to see the game. A girl on my corridor had a tiny black-and-white television set, and now and then she'd let me watch European games in her room if she was going out for the evening, but she wasn't my type and I stopped asking for the favour so that I didn't feel obligated to her in any way, especially as all that I had to offer her in return was a loan of the new Fall LP. There was also a TV in the basement to the hall of residence, but you had to get the key off someone, and that someone was never in their room. Most evenings I was either out or sitting in my room reading and listening to music.

This was the season in England when Manchester United won their first 10 games, reportedly playing glorious football under Ron Atkinson, but no one ever saw the footage because of a TV rights dispute. Imagine that – for months there was no television coverage of top-flight football, and we all lived to tell the tale. No doubt marketing executives shudder at the thought of all that lost hype and wasted income, but I prefer to see it as a golden age when all the games were played at 3pm on a Saturday afternoon and my participation involved reading the match report in the *Observer* the next day, for which I made a special weekly pilgrimage to Bielefeld's train station.

I wonder what has changed in me. Now, at an age when I should be doing something more useful, I live in Germany and subscribe to *Kicker*, which comes out twice a week. I go to watch Eintracht Frankfurt or FSV Frankfurt or Kickers Offenbach whenever they're at home and I'm not refereeing. I watch the Bundesliga highlights every week and subscribe to a pay-TV channel called Sky (no idea who owns it) and watch two or three games a week live. Back in 1985 the only German team I vaguely cared about was Arminia Bielefeld, and the only teams I'd heard of aside from the famous names of Bayern, Schalke, Cologne and Borussia Mönchengladbach were the ones that came to play at the Alm stadium. I can't believe that I spent a year just over an hour's train ride away from the Ruhrpott and failed to go and watch Dortmund, Schalke and Düsseldorf.

At the same time, I'm convinced that I'm no more a fan of the game now than I was back then. I can still remember dancing wildly around my room to the goals when I picked up a distant signal from BBC Scotland with the commentary from the World Cup play-off game against Australia. Every Saturday afternoon I listened in to the English results coming in on the British Forces Broadcasting Service radio station, and as I mentioned before, splashing out six Deutschmarks on the *Observer* was a major weekly indulgence. But the game was better compartmentalised in my life at this time. Some of my Saturday and some of my Sunday was spent thinking and reading about football, and apart from the odd European game, that was it. Now I feel mistily nostalgic for the times when several days could pass without a game or the compulsion to find out an unknown score, and I worry that I've been as much a victim of the all-pervading hype as the next fan.

Outside Left

Here are three stories that to some degree reflect the attitude to football among Germans at the time, all from the 1986 World Cup:

(1) *Scotland 1 – West Germany 2.* I had been stoked up for this one ever since the draw had been made months before. My dad had sent me a Scotland scarf that I'd waved around at my fellow players in the team I'd started playing for in the city league, Die Wilde Liga ('The Wild League'), which was affiliated to a local anarcho-Marxist newspaper (every major German city had one) and whose tables – there were two divisions – were printed under the headline 'Links Außen' ('Outside Left', but which you could also loosely translate as 'Leftists at Play'). My teammates all smiled tolerantly when I announced what a hiding their national side was in for. They assumed that this was jocular bravado.

I went to watch the game at my German friend Michael's place, as the only Scotsman among several natives and Gian-Paolo, who was cheerfully indifferent to sport in any form. When Gordon Strachan put Scotland 1–0 ahead, I began to leap around the room, yelling and shouting and intimidating and gloating and generally acting like the sort of wanker whose team has gone 1–0 up against superior opponents and who doesn't realise that this is the sort of team against which it's a mistake to go 1–0 up too early. My hosts smiled tolerantly. This was West Germany. There was no way that West Germany were going to lose to Scotland at the World Cup.

Sure enough, just five minutes later they equalised through Rudi Völler. I sat back and waited for the deluge, the violently returned insults, the thoroughly deserved taunts, all delivered 10-fold because there were 10 of them and only one of me. I looked to my friends, slumped in their chairs, nursing beers. 'So, it's 1–1,' somebody might have said, though I can't swear to it. It could just have been a fly, buzzing in the summer night. I checked the screen and the action replay to make sure the goal had really counted. I looked back at the Germans. Still, nothing.

Perhaps they're waiting for the winner, I thought. Indeed, they *were* waiting for the winner, because they knew far better than I did that the winner was a matter of when, not if. Sure enough, Klaus Allofs made it 2–1 in the 50th minute. Again, no reaction. Perhaps they were waiting for the final whistle. During the rest of the game, as I swore at Maurice Malpas, Eamonn Bannon (what the hell was he doing in the Scotland team?) and Roy Aitken, many of those around me began to fall asleep *while watching their national team at the World Cup*. Once it had all finished with the inevitable Scottish defeat, all someone said to me was, '*Schade*, I thought Scotland deserved a draw at least.' A long-nosed anarchist called Kai, who had introduced me to the team in the Wilde Liga, said kindly, 'You're still the only Scotsman I've seen who can play football.' Michael doesn't even remember the evening, let alone who was playing or what the score was.[5]

Fucking 'ell, Fritz, could you not at least laugh in a cruel, vindictive manner? Could you not at least say, 'So, you dickhead, all that dancing around when you went 1–0 up was for nothing, huh?' Or just punch me in the head? Or strap me down in a dentist's chair, grab some sharp-looking implements, shine a light in my face and say, 'For you, Jock, ze Vorld Cup is over, ha ha ha ha ha'?

I walked home through the deserted streets of Bielefeld (no one was out celebrating a victory over Scotland), stunned less by the defeat than by the manner in which I had got away with it.

(2) *Mexico 0 – West Germany 0* (West Germany won 4–1 on penalties). Two weeks later, I gathered with my mates from In Flagrante, our team in the Wilde Liga, to watch the Mexico v. West Germany quarter-final at the house of Thorsten, our captain. This was a less studenty crowd, with several of the players having actual jobs, and we were meeting to commemorate a successful season in which I think we finished top or second in our division. They gave me a football

5. When I asked him 30 years later, his response was an exasperated, 'For Christ's sake, why the fuck would I remember something like that?'

autographed by the team to take home to England. With the game being a straight knockout, it was a much more emotional evening than the Scotland game, and there was much shouting, up to and during the penalty shootout.

Not that everyone was cheering for their home nation. This being a mixture of various kinds of radical, there were a number of players who, for anti-nationalistic reasons, wanted their own country to lose. The post-match discussion swiftly abandoned analysis of Karl-Heinz Rummenigge's inability to last the full 90 minutes and turned to a lively back and forth about a demonstration some of the players had gone to at the Wackersdorf nuclear power plant, in southern Germany, in the wake of the Chernobyl disaster in the Soviet Union. As far as I could make out through my beer-hazed head, it was a debate about whether or not violence was a legitimate means to overthrow the state, and almost ended in fisticuffs as one of our strikers, a huge Trotskyite called Detmar, squared up to the aforementioned Kai, who that week was seeing the world through the texts of the French anarchist Proudhon. Fortunately, Thorsten, as captain, goalkeeper and, it seemed to me, social democrat, stood between the two and calmed the situation down.

So, when it came to football, a lot of Germans didn't much care if they won or lost, and would even actively cheer on the opposition. But when it came to politics, they didn't mind a fight. Surely, though, this would all change for the World Cup Final.

(3) *Argentina 3 – West Germany 2.* If you read about my hopes in the earlier chapter of the same name, you'll know that the 1986 World Cup Final was the one where I'd been expecting Scotland to lift the trophy. I'd even been thinking this after we lost to Denmark and Germany, because if we beat Uruguay in the third game, we'd be third and through to the last 16, and after that anything was possible. Uruguay, with a reputation for hard play, had a defender red-carded in the very first minute, but even with a man advantage Scotland couldn't score, and back home we went, as was our habit. I watched the highlights of that game alone in the flat of Gian-Paolo, whose presence in the youth hostel at the start of the year had prevented me

from fully enjoying *Neue Revue* for a couple of nights. I wandered into the kitchen, where he and several Germans were busy not giving a shit about West Germany's 2–0 loss to Denmark, which we'd watched earlier. 'Scotland are out,' I said solemnly. They all burst out laughing, like my national team was some kind of joke. 'We couldn't beat a team that was down to 10 men for 89 minutes.' They laughed some more. I stopped talking about Scotland and got drunk instead.

So, unbelievably, another final without Scotland. Instead, it was Argentina v. West Germany. I was in a hotel in the university town of Göttingen with my mum, who had come over by car to fetch home all my things and take a tour of those nice little German towns, like Goslar, Hamelin, Hildesheim and Marburg, with lots of quaint squares and old houses with wooden beams. It had gone well up until that very afternoon, when we had got lost on a walk in the Harz mountains and couldn't find my mum's car. At one point she burst into tears and blurted out, 'I'm never going to see my wee car again!' My main concern was – big surprise – getting to Göttingen and checking into our hotel in time for the final.

Once I realised we'd accidentally started following the walk with the red filled-in triangle instead of the walk with the red-sided, blank-in-the-middle triangle, we finally found our way back to the right path and my mum underwent an emotional reunion with her Ford Fiesta. Then she made me buy her a huge ice cream for putting her through such a trauma, but we still made it to Göttingen in time to settle down in the hotel lounge with around 50 other guests, mainly Germans of all ages.

It was eerily quiet. I thought that the natives were simply too tense to speak. I tried to imagine what it must be like when your country is playing in the World Cup Final. How would I be feeling right now if this were Scotland? Running backwards and forwards to the bog in between plying myself with copious quantities of soft drugs and gibbering excitedly, I was fairly sure, given that's how I watch Scotland even when they're playing Latvia in a friendly. But here, no one was moving, neither to the bog nor the bar. They were just watching as though it was the regular Sunday-night episode of *Lindenstraße,* the long-running German weekly soap institution. *Ho-hum, here we go again, every four years another World Cup Final.*

There was no reaction when Argentina went 2–0 up, just as there was no reaction when Rummenigge pulled one back in the 74th minute. Then, when Völler equalised six minutes later, there was one shout of 'Whooooah!' and that came from me, but it sort of died out by the third 'o' because I felt self-conscious making a noise. It wasn't that I wanted West Germany to win, not at all, but I was at least a little sucked into the drama of a late comeback in the World Cup Final, even though I had to keep reminding myself, *This is the fucking World Cup Final!*

And then, despite the comeback, Harald Schumacher's reluctance to come off his line (unlike four years earlier, when he smashed into France's Patrick Battiston and ended his career) meant that Argentina's Jorge Burruchaga scored the winner five minutes from time. *Schade.*

Schumacher admitted to the German press a day or two later that 'I played like an ass.' He needn't have worried about it too much, if the reactions of the hotel guests in Göttingen were anything to go by. They stood up at the final whistle and trooped out, without tears or curses or any sign of pain and suffering. After all, there's bound to be another final along in four years. Probably against Argentina again. And we'll probably win it next time.

My mum and I watched Diego Maradona lift the trophy, then stepped into a local bar for a drink. The only other person in the bar was a drunk German fan in full regalia, who homed in on us and immediately began to rant about the match. 'I don't like this place, let's go somewhere else,' said my mum, who speaks no German but was getting the general gist. Göttingen is hardly renowned as a footballing hotbed, but our ranting friend was the only evidence we saw all night that someone in the town actually gave a rat's arse about West Germany's defeat.

What, No Ref?

If Albert Camus had been living in North Rhine-Westphalia in 1986, he might have written, 'All that I have learned about morality and obligations to men I have learned from the Wilde Liga in Bielefeld.' The league existed without registration forms, goal nets were a rarity, there were no pitch markings and, best of all, there were no referees. The players reffed the matches. During the whole season I played there I didn't see a single dispute over a free-kick or an offside.

It's a common misconception that anarchists don't believe in rules. In fact, anarchists are the purest democrats because they believe in a majority consensus, only without leadership. That's not to say we sat down in the middle of the pitch as a collective and calmly debated each foul. The decisions were reached instinctively, because most players know when they have fouled someone. Without a referee to curse in a knee-jerk way, players tended to hold up their hands when someone called 'Foul!' Then the opponent would place his hand on the ball and take the free-kick.

It was the most enjoyable league I've ever played in, despite my misgivings at first that, without proper markings, this wasn't proper football. Soon I noticed that it didn't matter. If the ball went out too far, the players would stop, someone would retrieve it, and then when it looked approximately like it was in play again, we'd start to run anew. Even though we had a couple of donkeys on our team, no one cursed them, and afterwards no one bitched about the other players. Until the political debate after the Germany–Mexico game, it was all sweetness and harmony.

I think it would be a fantastic psychological experiment to stage an important professional match without referees. Would it end up in a 22-man brawl, or would the players, like the kickers of the Wilde Liga, learn to adapt to their new circumstances and reach sensible consensus decisions in a split second? Say, for example, a tricky forward takes a tumble in the penalty area under light pressure from his marker. 'Dive, no question, play on,' a few players would mumble, and play would continue. The defender would know it, and the diver too. Next time he'd probably just stay on his feet.

It's instructive to watch kids play and organise a game without adult supervision, because it works exactly the same way. Picking the teams might be a bit chaotic, but soon they just get on with it. All they want to do is play, and they still have a genuinely sincere feel for what is fair and what is not. That is, until 'professional' coaches inculcate them with the idea that winning is much more important than being honest.

Mr White Checks Out of Town

Back in Birmingham for the final year of my course, people wanted to know what had happened to me. It was a diplomatic way of asking, 'How come you're not *quite* such an uptight, cynical, miserable, self-absorbed pain in the arse any more?'

It might have been the anarchist football league, the attentive German women, the relaxed and tolerant friends I made, or the fact that I had so much time and space to look at myself and take stock, but the year out of England was by far the best thing that could have happened to me at that time of my life. A year now flashes past at a fearsome pace. Back then, it just went on and on, from bar to Bhaggy disco, with a few stops at the library and a thousand casual coffees in between. I still feel immensely privileged to have been a student at a time when the government paid for everything, on a course that allowed me the leisure to learn a language at my own pace, in an environment more shaped by beer taps and football fields than it was by seminars and lectures.

With no referees around, it's remarkable what you can find out about yourself and the world around you.

9

Love and Birmingham

Birmingham City v. Crystal Palace, Barclays League Division Two, Saturday, 5 September 1987

Football and Love

My time in Birmingham as a student, and thereafter on the dole and as a shop assistant, were my most neutral, loveless years as a football fan. In three and a half years, I perhaps went to no more than around 25–30 games. In the end, at long last, I was finally preoccupied with the kind of love that didn't involve being curled up at night with a Lincoln City scarf tied around my groin.

It seems a denigration of the concept of love to throw it around in the same sentence as football. Sure, you can say, 'I love the game', and perhaps in relation to your love of squirrels or strawberry Angel Delight, it's true. Yet when we say we love football, most of us mean that football is one of our favourite sports or pastimes.

In the opening line to *Fever Pitch*, Nick Hornby says he fell in love with football in the same way he later fell in love with women, but I think it's wrong to equate the two. Human beings who do not give or receive enough love will be unhappy and will suffer. Human beings who do not get enough football will not, really. They might miss it, like they miss custard creams if they don't have one for a while, but it's only a want, not a need. Fans don't kill themselves over the summer because there are no games. The comparisons are facile, and usually stem from the same domain of fallow journalistic inspiration that labels supporters as passionate fanatics. Eintracht Frankfurt's club song has a line in it that goes, '*Der Eine liebt sein Mädchen, der andere liebt den Sport,*' which translates as, 'One man loves his woman, the other loves his sport.' But guess what? It's meant to be a joke, not something we discuss in earnest.

I've felt bad during an impending defeat and I've felt bad after one, but I tend to feel much worse if I'm already down about some football-unrelated matter (love, for example). Ottmar Hitzfeld, the former Borussia Dortmund and Bayern Munich coach, once said that he gets depressed for two or three days after a defeat. But he was the well-compensated coach carrying the responsibility for the defeat, not to mention the disappointment of hundreds of thousands of fans. He has a right to be depressed about losing at football, even if that does reflect a skewed and illogical sense of priorities.

One of the things that I missed about Britain after leaving in 1994 was the Saturday-afternoon or midweek evening ritual of going to a game. You could say that I *love* my pre-match pint, a perusal of the programme and the feeling of coming together with several thousand other people to watch a communal sporting event. I *love* to visit a ground I haven't been to before. When I'm back home, I'll do my best to see three or four games in a short period of time, usually one or two weeks. Compared with my friends, for whom football is also a favourite pastime, I *love* to do this to a far greater degree than anyone else I know. Nonetheless, for the past 20-plus years, on a day-to-day basis, I've largely been able to function without it, even when I lived in the US, where Major League Soccer and college soccer (not to mention baseball) were barely adequate replacements.

It's possible that I'm just not a proper fan and that I've been missing out for all these years. It could be that there are millions of *passionate* football-lovers who go to bed in their replica shirts, hugging their scarves and lying awake thinking about their team, when they last saw each other and what they did, counting down the hours to the next time they'll see each other, on Saturday at 3pm. They cry over a defeat, and during football's interminable absence over the summer. It's unbearable. But when they win they are happy for days! On their bedside table is a framed photograph of the lads. They gaze at the photo wistfully, reaching out to caress the individual faces, calling each player by their pet names – Dobbin, Slammer, Wingnut, Chopper and El Loco. The relationship only ends with the obtaining of an actual girlfriend, who after love's uncritical opening phase puts a stop to such nonsense. As someone once said, it's hard to be in a marriage with three parties (or to shag someone on a Leeds United duvet cover).

These lovelorn fans must write to the club when things are going badly:

> Dear Torquay United FC
>
> I've been thinking for a while now that things aren't right between us. Every week I show up at the appointed place and time, just like you tell me to. You always turn up, but you're not always there – lately you've seemed kind of absent. I keep to my side of the deal, doing what you asked by putting in time, money and rousing terrace chants for 90 minutes, but there's no response. Last Saturday, for example, you lost 0–3 to Braintree, and then left the pitch without even waving goodbye.
>
> I've thought about this a lot at work this week. I even ran to the toilet crying on several occasions. I think my colleagues understood, though it's raised one or two eyebrows. Anyway, that's not your concern, I know (especially as you seem indifferent to any kind of suffering on my part). And even when I endlessly weep and curse you and swear that next Saturday I won't be joining the bus at Plainmoor at seven in the morning for the trip up to Guiseley, I know that it would only take a new signing from you and I'd be back again. Even a goalless away draw would, at this stage, offer me some hope that things are maybe working, that we have a future. And though my friends are calling me a fool for continuing to believe in you (they are so smug and complacent in their successful long-term partnerships with Manchester United and Chelsea, but what's a relationship without sacrifice? How can they love their teams in a long-distance relationship when the only contact is through a sterile screen?), I know that one day things

> can come right between us. If you only show that you can put in 100 per cent commitment, I know we can make this work...

If there are fans that write letters like that to their football clubs, then yes, I accept that it is possible to *love* a team, and to *love* the game. And I am just an unfeeling bastard, sometimes getting a kick out of football, sometimes shunning it completely, but most of all going through the motions, watching games because they're on and because that's what I do. I *am* a football fan.

Upon Being in Birmingham

It's often said that America is the country where you can most easily disappear, just like Max Frisch's Mr White (see last chapter, previous books, etc.). I think that if you want to disappear somewhere in Britain, then the best place would be Birmingham. It's huge, largely anonymous, and no one would think of looking for you there. Who in their right mind would go to live in Birmingham?[1]

I love to return to places where I used to live to see how they've changed and wallow in memories. Since I left Birmingham in early 1988, I've been back twice. Both were work trips, and both were within the three years after I'd left the city permanently. The second one only involved staying at a hotel near the airport for a night before myself, several other journalists and the representatives of a company that made hooks for scaffolding on oil rigs took a plane to somewhere in Scandinavia. We were then housed in a lodge by a lake, where we did healthy Scandinavian activities like chopping wood, playing table tennis outdoors, and making love to each other in the sauna while the company's senior management stood there naked and thrashed us with silver birch branches,[2] all with the aim of making us write nice

1. In case this remark infuriates anyone from Birmingham, it's not meant seriously. And anyway, I prefer unspectacular cities (see Bielefeld).

2. One of these three activities may not have happened.

things about hooks for scaffolding on oil rigs. It's the strange, convoluted way that trade journalism works.

In almost all the places I've lived, I've developed an affinity, if not outright support, for a team in that city. Aside from the core, hewn-on-my-heart, etc. support for Lincoln City, I count among my loyalties differing grades of affection for Arminia Bielefeld, Eintracht Frankfurt, FSV Frankfurt, FC Zürich and D.C. United. When I lived in Walthamstow, in East London, I more or less supported and cheered for Leyton Orient for five years, although for some reason that attachment didn't last. When I return to watch them now, as I usually do when I'm in London, I spectate with the cold-headedness of the neutral, finding it hard to believe that I've paid more than 20 quid to watch this crap.

Birmingham, somehow, was different. I went mostly to Aston Villa games, and three times to West Brom when I lived a couple of miles from The Hawthorns for a year, and then on a handful of occasions to Birmingham City too, but one time was only to see how ex-Lincoln striker Mick Harford was getting on. I always meant to make the trip out to Walsall and Wolves, but even when Lincoln were playing at Moulineux at the end of the 1987 season, I didn't get my act together. Wolves were nearly top, and Lincoln were nearly bottom, and I had no money. We lost 3–0, and I remember thinking, 'That was a good decision.'

In three and a half years in the city, I felt no pull to any team in particular. I saw some memorable games, like Aston Villa losing 2–6 to Arsenal, when Tony Woodcock scored five (and me so desperately wanting Charlie Nicholas to score for Arsenal, but all he could do was miss a goal from 2 yards out as Woodcock tapped in chance after chance); another defeat to Liverpool, when Ian Rush scored a hat-trick; and a 2–2 draw with Southampton, when Joe Jordan, whose number 12 Leeds tags I might still own, scored two typically gutsy diving headers for the visitors. The three games I saw at West Brom in the 1984–5 season were all remarkable too. They beat Notts Forest 4–1 by taking on Clough at his own game – playing attractive football with the ball kept on the ground; there was a 0–5 hammering by Liverpool at their easy best (many home fans on the terrace were applauding the visitors by the end – a counter to the stereotype of 1980s football grounds as spuming cauldrons of hate); and then a 5–1 dispatching of West Ham that recalled the Forest game and had the home fans around me talking about winning the title the next season (when they went down to Division Two).[3]

Yet I didn't *fancy* any of the teams in Birmingham. There was nothing about the stadiums or the fans or the players that really clicked with me. I can't explain why, or how this might have worked at other teams I went to watch. Perhaps it was because I was a student, and students are passers-through. But then again, I was a student in Bielefeld and spent much less time there than I did in Birmingham, and 30 years later I still get vaguely worked up about Arminia Bielefeld's results. I've even been to see them away in places like Cologne, Chemnitz and Offenbach.

I stayed on in Birmingham after I graduated to try and get a job, because I genuinely liked the city. I wanted to be a journalist, so I wrote to the fiercely right-wing and virtually unreadable[4] *Birmingham Evening Mail* and told them that their coverage of popular music was catastrophic. Fortunately, I would be prepared to join their salaried staff and turn that particular area of cultural interest around for them. They didn't accept my exciting proposition to start writing about indie bands that played above pubs in Sparkbrook and Kings Norton, but promised to keep my application on file. So, that was Birmingham's entire print media exhausted. Should I wait around for them to take my application off file and get in touch? Did they have people who went through old CVs and pulled one out, saying, 'Wait a minute, how did we miss this unemployed graduate with absolutely no experience who wants to tell the masses of the Midlands how stupid they were to miss The Membranes' astonishing set last night at

3. Gav, a West Ham fan and fellow aspiring hack, came with me to this game. On the way, we got on the top deck of a bus and found several West Brom fans sitting at the back. Gav, a Londoner, shouted out loudly in an exaggerated Brum accent, 'Cum on, yow Baggays!' and I thought we were dead. They didn't stir. They were either pacifists or they thought he meant it.

4. The template for local newspapers everywhere. Why is this? I follow the *Lincolnshire Echo*'s Twitter feed, and even in the space of 140/280 characters it succeeds in being rampantly conservative and virtually unreadable.

The Knackered Chicken in Balsall Heath?' Or was it advisable to leave town and look for work elsewhere, 'elsewhere' meaning only London?

But although I liked Birmingham a lot, I never found much to swoon about. It was an underrated, unknown place, and on afternoons when I should perhaps have been out courting women, or something, I instead used my WMPTE travel pass to get on a bus and go to some hitherto unexplored part of the city or the Black Country. I liked to wander alongside canals, daydreaming. I once rode round the whole 11C bus route that passed close to my flat. I went to places like Dudley, Stourbridge, Castle Bromwich and Halesowen, just to take a look. I'd have a cup of coffee and look for records in second-hand charity shops. My mate Drew would sometimes come along on Wednesday afternoons. We were fascinated by a bus that stated its destination as Bangham Pit via Weoley Castle. Was there really a pit and a castle worth taking a look at? We didn't find a pit (though there's a reservoir nearby), but there are some Norman manor house ruins at Weoley Castle. According to *The Spectator*, in 2015 it was – with 5,205 visitors – England's 'least visited tourist attraction'. Much more importantly, I think it was somewhere around Weoley Castle that I picked up 23 Skidoo's *Seven Songs* for a quid in a shop raising cash for abandoned cats, a miracle happening that I afterwards talked about way too often to a less than fascinated world.

It might be said that I was making the best of what there was. With little money, but an unlimited bus pass, the entertainment options were already narrow, and it was not as if the city had its own historic quarters, majestic river, charming coastland or imposing lake around which some kind of social or cultural life had evolved and sustained itself. What Birmingham had was the Bull Ring in the centre of the city, an early kind of shopping mall with no interesting shops (that is, no second-hand book or record shops – there are no other interesting shops), which was surrounded by major road arteries. To be frank, if you didn't like football and bus rides, and charity shops in the suburbs, there wasn't a whole lot going on besides the staples of English life – drinking and falling over.

This was illustrated one night in The Junction, a fine old pub in

Harborne that used to stage skittle nights, and which has doubtless long since been ruined by some piss-head brewery's wet-brained idea of commercial hospitality. I sat there watching a huge man in his fifties at the bar drinking his way out of reality over the course of an evening, until finally his six-feet-six frame staggered to its feet and slowly tottered over to the glass door that led to the toilets. He stopped on the other side of the door, and there was a pre-tsunami calm for a couple of seconds before he crashed back in and fell smack across the faded wooden floor like an axed redwood tree, a faint smile on his face. This smile remained in place as various people attempted to move him, and eventually he was able to sit up and crawl out on to the street, where we passed him a few minutes later in the gutter.

Whenever I think of this incident, I think, 'That was Birmingham.' Maybe it was because of Steve Whitton.

COMMITMENT!

Remember what my fictional love-struck Torquay fan wanted from his team? At Birmingham City around the start of the 1987–8 season, the fans were getting it in buckets, according to the *Blues News* match programme for the home game with Crystal Palace. A caption to a centrespread photograph from the 2–0 win over Aston Villa states, 'Here's one of the reasons this season's Blues are looking so much better, COMMITMENT!'

That word had a special significance to me. As music editor on the university's ragged bi-weekly newspaper, *Redbrick*, I'd once received an immaculately typed review of a U2 concert by a writer who admitted early on in the piece that she was a 'committed Christian', and that was why she loved Bono so much. Bono was also committed. To Christianity and to making music. The word 'commitment' and its relation to Christianity became the running theme of the review, repeated so often that, to my shame, I read the review out loud for cheap laughs in a less than complimentary mimic (I'd never met the author) to the other wannabe hacks who were in the office that lunchtime. We didn't run the review because I was only interested in hatchet jobs or reviews of Mighty Mighty playing to three dozen sullen indie-poppers at The Donkey's Cock in Bangham Pit.

I was repelled by this idea of commitment. I was a swashbuckling young romantic. The only definition of commitment that appealed to me was undying devotion to the woman I loved. Commitment to religion, politics or a corporation was a spiritual sellout. Commitment to a football team was just absurd. At this time, I didn't care that I had no money, no job, no direction, and that I was heavily overdrawn and living off a paltry dole cheque. I was in love. We were living together, cooking cheap vegetarian meals and borrowing books and records from the library, and if we weren't watching television at night, we were making a pint stretch for three hours down the pub. We had spent the summer taking long, meaningful walks across the city and beyond. Almost everyone I knew had left Birmingham after graduating to start jobs. Beyond the non-existent post of indie-pop editor at the *Birmingham Evening Mail*, I'd applied for only one other job, which we'll get to in a moment.

This refusal to commit perhaps applied to me still being in Birmingham. Although I'd decided to stay, it was out of laziness as much as anything else. Or a belief that the world would come to me and barter for my as yet undiscovered talents. I had vague plans to start either my own magazine or a soup kitchen, ideas which never got beyond the stage of preliminary discussion. I thought that if I had the idea, then someone else would gratefully come in with all the money and the infrastructure necessary to make it happen. I'd provide the intellect, while they took care of the commitment.

'When Aston Villa put on the pressure,' continued the match programme, 'look how the three City front-runners joined the defence to break down the attack. Whitton and Kennedy out-jump Villa's midfield men Keown and Sims to clear, while Rees joins Godden on the line.'

Steve Whitton was indeed the sort of striker who would give you commitment. He ran and ran, fully committed, coming back to defend, sweating the full 90, giving it 110 per cent. He was strong and bulky, so that when he fell to the ground, he crashed down like… an axed redwood tree. He wasn't much of a pure footballer and he didn't score many goals (114 in over 500 games). So when the huff-and-puff sloggers of Birmingham came up against a young and skilful Crystal Palace team, commitment just wasn't enough. They lost 0–6.

A band called I, Ludicrous from South London had just released a cult post-punk novelty song called 'Preposterous Tales in the Life of Ken McKenzie', telling how Ken, egged on by his mates down the pub, relates a number of stories he claims to be true, but which his mates know are bullshit, like having seen the Sex Pistols at the 100 Club, or having eaten six Mars Bars in half an hour. He also claims, 'And I once saw the Palace score four goals away from home.' Aaaah come on, Ken, say his mates, that's *preposterous*.

What, only four? I once saw them score six. Honest.

Birmingham v. That London, 1

Blues News only had one columnist, Tom Ross of local radio station BRMB, a shamelessly bad commercial broadcaster that burdened its listeners with bland music, mindless DJs, endless condescending local-interest news stories, and phone-in shows that attracted the usual fulminating bigots with time on their hands. Late on Sunday evenings they transmitted a call-in show for people with personal problems, presented by a sepia-voiced man called Michael, whose main advice to listeners was either to get themselves to a doctor or pray as hard as they could. 'God loves you, pigeon,' was his standard sign-off to one regular pensioner who phoned in just to list her catalogue of ailments and the latest misfortunes of her serially dysfunctional family. It was cult listening among smart-arsed students, one of whom was almost certainly the caller who phoned in one night and hurriedly announced in an exaggerated Brum accent, 'Moikel, oy've got a big yellow spot on the end of moy willie.'[5] Michael advised him to get straight to a doctor and cut him off for the next caller before we could hear any more details.

Anyway, Tom Ross appeared twice in the *Blues News*. His first

5. Now I think about it, it was probably Gav.

piece was a portrait of Birmingham's midfielder Vince Overson. 'Vince, known as "Pick-Axe" in the dressing room, is a likeable character who is always likely to wind you up about anything!' Ross reveals. It turns out that this 'wind-up' involved Overson telling Ross that his two dogs were 'savages'. Why, are they Rottweilers or pit bulls? No, it turns out they're Jack Russell terriers!!!! It's precisely this kind of incisive wit that has seen Birmingham anointed as Europe's stand-up comedy centre over the past few decades.

Ah, that would be a typically snide London view of Birmingham, a topic that Ross addresses in his second epic article for the match programme. The previous weekend, Birmingham had apparently staged a Super Prix, 'a magnificent advert for Britain's Second City', according to Ross. The Formula 3000 race 'left you with no alternative but to be proud of the City's achievement... of the way it was organised... of the professional way it was run by the racing authorities.'

What more could the average Brummie ask for than to have souped-up, high-powered cars racing around the city's streets for eight hours on a Sunday afternoon? For Ross, it wasn't enough that the event was an apparent success in itself; he wanted coverage in the media too, so that Brum could bid for a future Formula One Grand Prix. But here's the problem: the media is all based in That London, and 'once again the Second City was let down by the London Media Machine' (a huge mechanical contraption powered hydraulically by the Thames and located somewhere out on the Isle of Dogs – the same machine that was churning out crap articles about football hooligans).

'It appears that unless the event is taking place in London, then it does not count or, more worryingly, matter,' Ross continued. 'It's a fact that the Capital City is too full of its own importance.' (Few would dispute this, I have to admit.) They'd also ignored the recent City v. Villa derby (the only one of 'plenty of examples' he cites). All he wants is for Birmingham 'not to be treated like country cousins by those who have no respect or interest in anything that goes on North of Watford'. Finally, he resorts to capital letters: 'ALL WE ARE SAYING IS GIVE BRUM A CHANCE.'

It has the ring of desperation. The city makes a calm and reasoned appeal for attention, and That London down there south of Watford doesn't give a shit. Birmingham then outlines its case, and still they won't listen. So then it screams out a plea to London's retreating back. PLEASE GIVE US A CHANCE!

The article is a perfect articulation of Birmingham's inferiority complex and the sad geographical reality that it lies too close to London for anyone outside the city to take much notice of it. It should just shut up, enjoy the fact that it has cheaper housing, lots of compellingly depressing canals, a nice central location and, erm... the Bull Ring.[6] Let London be London. Who needs all that hassle and glamour? To repeat the words of my old next-door neighbour in rural Lincolnshire, 'It's a fookin' shit'ole, that place.'

Birmingham v. That London, 2 (or Steve Whitton v. Ian Wright)

It was unfortunate for Ross that his piece appeared in the match programme for the game when Birmingham lost to a London side by six goals to nil. And the difference between the two sides was perfectly illustrated in the differences between their two main strikers. Birmingham had lumbering Steve Whitton, strong but unwieldy, hardworking but unspectacular. Not a hogger of the limelight, and not a scorer of memorable goals (at least not any that I can remember).

Palace boasted a young forward named Ian Wright. The 'Today's Visitors' section of the programme tags him as 'a promising prospect'. He and Mark Bright put on something of a show, dribbling nonchalantly through the static Brum defence and setting up goal after goal. We all stayed until the end, and the home crowd began to enjoy the afternoon in that gallows humour state of mind you attain upon realising that your cause is hopeless and the only way to take a severe hiding is with a grim smile and a certain measure of appreciation, at the same time wondering exactly what kind of novelty score the other side is going to finally rack up. There was even a general hissing of

6. Since I lived there, the 1960s Bull Ring shopping centre has been replaced by a new one, the Bullring (one word – subtle rebranding). I haven't seen it, but this can only be a good thing.

disapproval one time after a single bonehead started to make monkey noises when Wright was on the ball.

It was like watching a gifted schoolboy waltz past opponents who are way below his level, and you know that he's about to go on to greater things. Palace came from south of Watford and showed us the sophisticated kind of football that was currently being played down there in London. I wonder if at 0–4 Tom Ross stood up in the executive box, turned to the Palace directors and shouted, 'Come on, GIVE US A CHANCE!'

Brum Love

Birmingham is one of those cities where you live, but later you can't really explain why. I remember plenty of things that happened to me there, such as being attacked by a gang of scooter-loving skinheads after a remark I made supposedly 'taking the piss out of scooters' was unintentionally overheard. Or being swung at outside a city-centre nightclub by someone who claimed to play for Walsall. Earlier, inside the club, as he'd tried to chat up my future girlfriend, I'd met his claims with scepticism. A remark I made along the lines of 'Yeah, and my name's Zico' was intentionally heard, and met with the rejoinder 'I hear Zico had a fat lip last week' – actually, one of the funniest things anyone's ever said to me. He wasn't laughing, though, and left the club enraged, waiting hours for me outside. By the time he started flailing at me, he was too drunk to connect (see 'The Onion' in the 'Violence' chapter – at this time, swinging and missing seems to have been endemic in football-related West Midlands violence).

One night I stood paralytic and watched as locals invited themselves into a student party and set about smashing up the house and shouting, 'Just remember, we hate you student wankers!' There were numerous other more mundane but not especially happy incidents. But the city itself doesn't impose its character on you, either as a resident or a visitor. It had tons of excellent cheap Balti restaurants near Balsall Heath, and Moseley was vaguely trendy, and Edgbaston was posh, and Harborne was good for a pub crawl. But nothing to make you pine for it while you were away and make returning a matter of urgency. It's hard to pin down why exactly, except to point to a conglomeration of things that the city doesn't have rather than the things it does. You can easily see why Tom Ross was reduced to begging for some attention in capital letters.

Still, as mentioned, by accident or design it was the city where I ended up being properly in love for the first time and living with a woman and going through the inevitable ups and downs that come with the territory. Fortunately for you, I'm not going to quote any of the diary extracts, but it was clearly more real and intense than anything I'd been through emotionally up until that point. Or at least anything that hadn't involved navel-gazing and feeling sorry for myself.

When Birmingham played Crystal Palace we'd been living together for nine months, but my girlfriend was about to move to Brighton to study for an MA, and I'd decided to stay in Birmingham and try to find work. Although we'd been cohabiting for almost a year, we maybe thought it was still too soon for one to be following the other around the country. In the following two years until we broke up, we didn't even live in the same city, let alone the same house.

In hindsight, I should maybe have followed her south, at least as far as London. Instead, I pissed about in Birmingham for another six months, selling cheap plastic personal stereos in a branch of Dixons over the festive season and fighting to extract my housing benefit from the DHSS (as was), while falling further into debt. The wages were so low that they barely cancelled out my dole cheque, and made getting my rent back three times more complicated. The job was so miserable that every morning when I turned the corner into the pedestrian shopping zone, I fervently and sincerely prayed that the shop had burned down overnight.

This was the last game I saw in Birmingham, and I should have interpreted Ian Wright's clear message better. London's where it's hip and swinging, babe.

Sounds of Music

There's a brief item in the programme's news section about how 'Pop Superstar' Jeff Lynne 'is still an avid Blues supporter and takes in every game he can while he's in the country'. Jeff had been to the last three home games, it reported unexcitedly. There's a picture of Jeff, with his unchanged trademark 1970s perm, beard and shades, sitting in the stand.

Eight years earlier, as an avid ELO fan, this would have greatly excited me, although as a newly graduated indie-pop cynic in 1987, I probably sneered at the item while feeling a vague flush of shame at the thought of my old copies of *Out of the Blue* and *Discovery* safely stashed away from the hipster police in a cupboard back at my mum's house. ELO was as uncool as Birmingham, and it seemed only right that such a derivative, commercial outfit would hail from the Midlands.[7]

This book might just as easily have been written around the bands I liked at various times, marking the stages of my life. Aged eight I was into the gaudy glam of Gary Glitter, Sweet and Slade. Aged 13 I thought that Wings and ELO were, beyond any shadow of any doubt, the best that pop had to offer.[8] Aged 16, I had started to disown them and listen to anything that was on Rough Trade and Factory, disparaging all else as contrived fodder for ripped-off suckers. And so on. But I don't think the formula would have worked without fitting too many preconceived ideas into a tight-fitting authorial straitjacket.

Here's the difference between music and football. So many of our most salient memories are associated with particular songs, just as so many of my significant 'life events' are stationed fortuitously along-

7. In 2016 I bought *ELO: The Classic Albums Collection*, a lovely boxed set of all 11 ELO albums. *Out of the Blue* and *A New World Record* especially are still played with a greater regularity than I'd care to admit.

8. I also liked The Stranglers, Ian Dury and Buzzcocks, but as it was my sister who owned their records I wasn't allowed to like them devotedly because she'd got there first. She had naming rights, meaning that she was allowed to write their logos on her exercise-book covers and any other available surfaces, and I wasn't.

side certain football matches. While most of us have different individual songs and matches that correspond to our specific memories, you can always replay the song years later if you want to trigger off a little nostalgia late at night while settling into an armchair with a whisky and a glow of longing for a seemingly better past. The song is a fixed recording that will convey the same sounds to the listener at all times, in any place, even if the emotions it sets off vary for each listener.

A football match, by contrast, is a one-off event. When I go back to Sincil Bank, the ground looks nothing like it did in the 1970s, having been completely rebuilt. Even if it hadn't, it would be impossible to recreate the atmosphere and feel of any game that took place 30–40 years ago. Aside from the programme, the only thing you have to rely on are your memories. Who scored that day? Who was playing? The memories, save perhaps for a single outstanding incident or two, are dim and fading further into rank unreliability.

The song may be the central part of a story, and a memory, the tune that causes you to cry because you remember how you kissed a girl to it, or made love to it, or broke up to it, or it was playing on the car radio just as you looked across at a woman you loved and the sun was angled across her face in a particular way and she looked so beautiful (and then she turned around and said, 'We have to talk…'). Whereas the football game, as I've been arguing all along, is just background.

On this day, I know that Palace scored six and that both Ian Wright and Mark Bright had blinders. But I can't remember any specific goals or incidents from the game, and I certainly can't remember anything that Palace defenders Gary Stebbing and Gavin Nebbeling did. Until I looked at the line-ups on the programme's back page, their very existence had slipped from my mind. Stebbing and Nebbeling were no Wright and Bright.

I know, however, that while I was watching this game, I was excited that my life could be about to change. The only job I'd applied for all summer was with the *Rough Guide* travel publishers, at that time a very small undertaking that wanted to produce its first book on Germany. They were looking for a team of German-speaking writers who were free to travel and accept nominal wages, while taking advantage of a government grant that was available at the time to unemployed people starting their own business (the 'Enterprise Allowance', I think, happily exploited by almost every slacker I knew who went to a dole office and presented themselves as something like CEO of an Avant-Garde Improvisational Jazz Collective). It would be hard work and poorly paid, but it was exactly the kind of area where eager college-leavers could wedge their foot in the door at the start of an imagined long and illustrious writing career. I had just been interviewed for one of the three posts available, and thought it had gone well. I was expecting to hear back from them any day, and much as I tried to steel myself against disappointment, I couldn't help but race ahead to how I was going to spend the next year travelling around Germany, seeing old friends and sleeping on floors and in hostels, while researching the kind of book that would surely set me up for a rewarding and healthy life of travel and writing.

The book was going to include communist East Germany (GDR) too. Nagging me at the back of my head was the thought that I had forgotten to tell the two young men interviewing me that I had spent a week in East Germany, and that I had written a long paper on East German youth subculture, and that I had done a course on East German socialist realist literature. I still don't know why; I probably just forgot in my eagerness to tell them how much I didn't mind working for slave wages and sleeping on floors. I thought about phoning them after the interview to tell them this, but I didn't want to be too much bother. And so I received a letter the following week saying that they'd thought long and hard about giving me one of the jobs, but they felt I didn't have enough knowledge or experience of East Germany. Did I call them back to tell them what I should have told them the previous week, just in case someone else had turned down their offer? No, I sank into despair instead. I was going to be staying in Birmingham, unemployed, because I hadn't applied for any other jobs.

But wait, there *was* another career opportunity. I had sent a couple of live concert reviews to the music weekly *Sounds*, and although they hadn't used them, they'd called up to say they were looking for someone in Birmingham to send regular articles, and so could I go to a few more concerts and send them stuff? I reviewed Chumbawamba live at the Mermaid Pub in Sparkhill, and eagerly ran to the newsagent's every Thursday to see if they'd printed it, but they didn't. Then, when my girlfriend moved to Brighton, I moved to a new flat, where there was no phone. I didn't have the money to have one installed, nor, somehow, the enterprise to get one installed. What use is a music journalist in Birmingham to a magazine in London if he doesn't have a phone? Discouraged by the non-appearance of my Chumbawamba review, I just gave up, exactly at the time when I should have had a phone put in and been going out to concerts five nights a week, bombarding the live desk with so many stunning reviews that they'd be impressed by my industry, enthusiasm and florid prose and take me on.

Ten years later, I was self-googling (as we all do now and then while looking for some kind of affirmation that we have had an impact on the world) when I found a snippet from my review on the Chumbawamba website, in a section compiling reviews in which they'd been slagged off by the music press. It turned out *Sounds* had used my review after all, but three months later. If I hadn't given up looking in the newsagent's every Thursday, it might have given me the necessary incentive to follow up. And even though I discovered – in 2004, when I finally tracked down the issue on eBay, 17 years after its appearance – that they'd cut out the middle section of the review and obviously used it as a space-filler in a quiet week around Christmas, it would have meant a proper article in a professionally produced magazine, which would have changed the course of my life. If I'd seen the piece printed two months before I left for London, I might have stayed in Birmingham after all. I might have used the money I earned from selling plastic electronic garbage in Dixons on having a phone installed. Today, I could be the owner of millions of free CDs and be boring all my friends with tales of what Jack White's really like when you meet him in the flesh. Meanwhile, I'm glad *Sounds* ended up going bust. The bastards never paid me for the review, and at that time I could really have used the cash, even if it had only been 10 quid. Oh, and the reviews editor advised me to 'write like Mat Snow'. Bollocks to that.

In the late summer of 1987 I was busy making the kind of mistakes that would cause me some regret and pain over the following 10 years, and which undeniably altered the course of where I went and worked, and who I met. I didn't make that call to the *Rough Guide*. I gave up too easily on *Sounds*, failing to go the extra few quid on my overdraft for a telephone. Idiot.

I walked home from Birmingham v. Crystal Palace, thinking, 'Wow, 0–6. That's an unusual scoreline, and I reckon Mark Bright and Ian Wright are names to watch out for in the next few years, and I wonder if I'll get a letter from the *Rough Guide* on Monday and what'll we do if I get the job with my girlfriend being in Brighton and me being in Germany for a year and busy on the book she's bound to meet another bloke on her course some big intellectual type and I'll be left in the lurch and I should just go to Brighton and move in with her so I don't lose her but that's maybe not very feminist of me to think like that I'd be putting too much pressure on her I'm being too needy and it'd be too claustrophobic and I'd be putting her off her studies, but let's wait and see first if I get a letter from the *Rough Guide* on Monday and what'll we do if I get the job...'

Watching from the Crowd

So part of me had wanted to be a travel writer and visit tons of fascinating places, but I ended up staying at home. The only travelling I did in the coming years was when I went on holiday, like everyone else. I almost landed a job on a travel news magazine five years later, but after an interview and two trial days, I missed the final cut after the candidates had been narrowed down from 85 to two. Well, someone had to be the loser.

When living in Switzerland several years later, I landed some freelance work for the US travel publisher Fodor's, updating their annual guide. It turned out that travel-writing was mainly checking facts, walking from hotel to hotel and posing the same questions. The pay was negligible. One insane hotelier in Zürich screamed at me because the previous year's guide, which I'd had nothing to do with, had described her hotel as 'not central' (it wasn't). In Sion I was chased down the street from a virtual fleapit by another nutcase after a misunderstanding over the bill. I'd agreed with the co-owner that my stay would be 'sponsored' by the hotel (i.e. free). The co-owner wasn't around the next morning as I first checked, then ran out. So the job wasn't that glamorous after all.

Another part of me had wanted to be a music journalist and meet all these crazy, incredibly creative musicians and tell the world my tastes, which I believed to be intrinsically superior to the rest of mankind's (see 'Success' chapter). But I couldn't have been *that* motivated to be a music journalist, because I didn't go to the trouble and minor debt of getting a phone installed. So I continued to buy the music press and to listen to music and enjoy it and tell everyone I knew what they should be listening to, but once more I was the passive consumer, a small and insignificant part of the crowd (despite what I liked to think).

Like millions of other starry-eyed, self-deluded boys, I dreamed of playing professional football, but the furthest I got was to play for the Lincolnshire Schoolboys B team and the Birmingham University Third XI. By the time I was 22, I had a degree in German instead, and the day I watched Birmingham City versus Crystal Palace I was on the outside, with the majority, looking in at the players who had made it. Even then, there were a lot of mostly forgotten names on the team sheet. Who but a few diehard Brum fans can remember Brian Roberts, Tommy Williams, Tony Rees and Steve Wigley? Who but the live-alone editor of the *Die-Hard Eagles* fanzine can recall the particular skills that Stebbing and Nebbeling had to offer? Though maybe they became a double act years later on the Palace Podcast.

Even among all these men who were talented and devoted enough to make a living out of booting a ball across a stretch of flat grass, there were nearlies and nobodies. To be truly outstanding you had to play like Ian Wright and Mark Bright did that day. Bright went on to have a reasonably successful career at Palace and Sheffield Wednesday; Wright played for England and broke Cliff Bastin's goal-scoring record for Arsenal. And I, along with almost all of the rest of you, stood passively in the crowd, just watching and admiring, maybe just a little bit 'inexplicably and uncritically' in love, to use Hornby's phrase from that first line in *Fever Pitch*, in which he draws the parallel between falling in love with football and falling in love with women. Or more likely, we were thinking, *Why the fuck don't we have any players like that in Birmingham?*

10

Death

Leyton Orient v. Wrexham, Division Four Play-Off Final, Second Leg, Saturday, 3 June 1989

When we see Chelsea or Manchester City walking away with the Premier League because they have used their owners' millions to buy an unbeatable team, and when we observe the same teams every year winning the major leagues in Europe because they have all the best players, and they have all the best players because they made so much cash from the Champions League, and so the cycle repeats itself year after tedious year, then some of us are inclined, somewhat dramatically, to describe this predictability brought on by the game's all-engulfing commercialisation as the Death of Football.

It's strange that we are using this exaggerated term when the game is thriving more than at any other time since the period following the end of World War II. Attendances are way up and brand-new stadiums have been built, and they are continuing to be built and extended and modified. Crowd violence, in Britain at least, has been marginalised, and there are hundreds of games to choose from on TV, and hundreds of (mainly low-paid or no-paid) jobs for football writers, as reflected in the unnecessarily extensive coverage of every last kick and huff, both on the field and off. Never mind that the market has been saturated by the product (as the charlatan consultants and PR pinheads might say), the game is alive with riches, big names and… the struggle for survival among all those teams in the lower leagues who missed out on the windfall, or former Premier League teams, mainly from Yorkshire, who overspent massively and then dropped down a division or two and spent the next several years fighting off bankruptcy or advances from potential owners with dubious motives. Or, put another way, fighting to stay alive, to avoid death.

But that's just the polemic of a small-town fan, and it's been said often enough before, especially by me. The reason I bring up the term 'death' in this context is to point up how quickly we forget. Yes, it's a huge shame when a football club is threatened by bankruptcy because of greedy and unscrupulous owners, or by unsustainable excess in the transfer market, but surprisingly few teams go under in the end, and there have emerged, through supporters' trusts, ways that fans can save their team, if they care enough (and they usually do). But the death of a football club, while lamentable, is abstract compared with the deaths of people who went out one day to enjoy a football match and never returned.

Death on Saturday Afternoon

Seven weeks before this game, which saw Orient gain promotion to Division Three, I had been in the same ground watching them play Torquay United, on 15 April. Orient were pushing for a play-off place. It was a fine spring afternoon, and I'd persuaded my two flatmates, Tim Bastard and Dukey – the future eternal pretender to the title of London's Rudest Cabbie – to come along. Normally, they had better things to do, but that day was just one of those glorious days you have in your youth, when nobody has any commitments to girlfriends or family or paperwork, and all you have on your plan is a couple of lunchtime pints and a game of football. For many men of both my and previous generations, there are few more satisfying ways to spend a day of leisure.

It was around the time when fans were waving various inflatable objects, a cult that started with Grimsby Town followers waving blown-up haddocks. It had triggered a trend whereby you could wave either something that symbolised your team or was in some way unusual and original, or you could wave what the hell you wanted. I had an inflatable penguin because at the time I had a fetish about the birds and collected them in any format. God knows why. Girls found it cute, so that was at least one advantage.

So this inflatable penguin and all the other inflatables around me were symbols of a new attitude among football fans. Since the disasters at Heysel and Bradford four years earlier, overt hooliganism had been on the decline, and people were starting to go back to games. Orient were within walking distance of our flat in Walthamstow (in those days we thought nothing of a 2-mile walk, but if it was raining or I was pushed for time, I'd take the bus), and so we strolled along, chatting, stopping for a drink on the way.

Orient won the game 3–1, and their striker Mark Cooper fluffed the easiest open goal I've ever seen in my life, but there was more joviality than despair at the miss. It was one of those opportunities that are too easy – right in front of goal, with no obstacle, the goalkeeper stranded – but somehow he either scuffed it wide or blasted it over. I just remember the general laughter mixed with incredulity.

Orient also brought on a sub named Mark Smalley, who was from Lincolnshire. He'd once dismissed me in an U13 cricket match, and Tim and I had played against him in Sunday football leagues at U15 and U16 levels. He wasn't that outstanding a football player in his teens, at least not that we noticed. So it was cool to watch him come on in a professional game and think what might have been if we'd kept in step with him. It was cool to know you'd once played against him and hadn't been overshadowed by his talents. At least not as far as we remembered. Again, it was all part of the afternoon's casual chat, and I wouldn't even recall that he'd played that day if I hadn't looked at the old programme, which triggered off repressed memories of the afternoon.

On the way out of the ground Tim – a quasi-Norwich fan since living in the city for five years – asked a bloke with a radio if he knew the score in the FA Cup semi-final between Norwich and Everton. The bloke started to incoherently tell us what had been happening in the other semi-final at Hillsborough, between Liverpool and Nottingham Forest. Tim said, out of shock, 'You're joking?' and the bloke fair exploded at him, like we really had accused him of making it all up, and we walked away, not wanting to ignite a fight over nothing.

Then we went straight into West London to meet a couple of other people and get hammered, which had been part of our plan for the day, and we almost forgot about the news because all we knew about it was from the ranty bloke with the radio,[1] and I had entered into a long, tired and emotional political argument with Tim's cousin, an up-and-coming estate agent, who had provoked me by saying out of nowhere, 'Your trouble is that you're the kind of person who doesn't appreciate why someone would want to pay sixty thousand pounds for a new car.' This had ended with me dry-humping a sports car that had stopped in front of us at a red light in Trafalgar Square. The driver had jumped out to confront me, and several helpful passers-by had gathered in expectation of a fight, with one asking me if I had 'a problem'.

That all ended when the lights turned green, the driver hopped back into his wankmobile and everyone else dispersed in disappointment. It was well past midnight by then, so we went to wait for the night bus, bought the Sunday papers and quickly sobered up into a state of being utterly stupefied.

Right at that moment you think no one will ever play or watch football again, and that no one will ever be able to cheer a goal, or be competitive, or start a fight or even an argument about whose team is best. It was one of those events where you can't imagine anything ever being the same again. It wasn't just the tragedy of the deaths and the awful way that people died, although these were deeply shocking in their own right. To put it selfishly, it was the fact that this had happened in a football stadium. The recognition of someone else's death always hits harder when you think, *That could have been me or any one of the several dozen people I know who go to watch football.*

It's one of the reasons why a journalist's obsession with the number of deaths at any given fire, explosion or fight strikes me as hitting the wrong tone. Rationally, you can say that the number of people who died in road accidents or from cancer on 15 April 1989 was far higher than the number of people who died at Hillsborough that day, so in the greater scheme of things, it wasn't that big a deal. Emotionally, the comparison doesn't make any sense. Cancer and road fatalities are part

1. It was easy to avoid the news in the pre-internet age.

of death's equation, factored in beforehand, if you like. They happen every day and they're shocking when they touch you personally, but you don't read the road-death stats every night and fall into a numbed depression. The number of deaths at Hillsborough could have been one-tenth as big and it would still have been deeply shocking to any fan, and would still have been a landmark event for football in the UK.

Time to Move On. Goal!

Only seven weeks later, I was back at Brisbane Road, cheering as the same Mark Cooper who had fluffed the open goal against Torquay scored a superb winner in the play-off final against Wrexham. Looking back, I have difficulty facing up to the truth that the two events took place so quickly one after the other. Yet I cannot deny that with the scores at 1–1 on the day, and 1–1 overall (Orient having drawn the first leg in Wrexham 0–0), I jumped up and down, cheering like an idiot, when the Cooper we'd all laughed at on the day of the Hillsborough tragedy smashed a first-time cross from the right wing past Wrexham goalkeeper Mike Salmon (the record-holder for the number of Welsh newspaper headlines that contain the word 'leaping'). The score stayed 2–1, and Orient went on to win the final promotion spot.

I wasn't even a proper Orient fan, but I still gave the impression that this was a huge moment for me. Dukey, who came to maybe less than half as many matches at Brisbane Road as I did, and who tended to keep any kind of emotion, good or bad, hidden from the outside world, was cheering too. No one said, 'Hey, calm down, it's a little insensitive to be going so wild about a mere goal so soon after so many died at a game.' No one, as far as I could see, was taking the time to gaze serenely into the distance and muse, 'This is all so trivial.'

To try and best explain why I was jumping up and down like a lunatic to celebrate a mere goal just seven weeks after 96 fans were crushed to death at Hillsborough, here's a piece I wrote for the *OneTouchFootball* website shortly after the terrorist attacks on New York and Washington DC on 11 September 2001, by which time I'd been living just outside DC for two years:

The People Who Played On (written October 2001)

> 'Every day, as soon as the evening meal was over, anybody who felt like it came to the field and kicked the ball around.' The football field referred to was in the Auschwitz concentration camp. The quote, describing a mundane kick-around at the end of a routine day, is from 'The People Who Walked On', a short story by the Polish writer, and Auschwitz survivor, Tadeusz Borowski, from his collection *This Way for the Gas, Ladies and Gentlemen.*
>
> Borowski's autobiographical narrator describes how he and fellow inmates, who have all been spared the gas chamber to become camp 'employees' (that is, slaves), build a football field, with one goal in front of the loading ramp where new arrivals exit the incoming trains. One Sunday afternoon, while keeping goal, he runs to retrieve the ball and notices that a train has just arrived, and that the passengers are disembarking the cattle trucks: 'The women, it seemed, were already wearing summer dresses; it was the first time that season. The men had taken off their coats, and their white shirts stood out sharply against the green of the trees.'
>
> The narrator returns to the pitch and kicks the ball out, but a few minutes later it goes out of play again, and once more he runs to fetch it, only to notice that the train has left and that all its passengers have walked off through the woods towards the gas chambers: 'Between two throw-ins in a soccer game, right behind my back, three thousand people had been put to death.'
>
> The story illustrates how desensitised we can become to death if our own survival is at stake. The football game is just one example of the everyday activities the inmates staged in order to construct an ostensibly normal existence for themselves. Yet, no matter how many times you re-read the story, it's striking nonetheless that in Auschwitz

they played football. It's shocking, yet simultaneously reassuring. There, on the site of the camp whose name above all others has come to symbolise the atrocities of genocide, prisoners still found time and energy for a game of football.

Over the past few weeks, Americans have tried to prove to themselves and the world that they're not scared of terrorism by continuing to watch and play all manner of sports. At first they said that in the light of what happened in New York and Washington, sport was not important. However, going to watch it or take part in it had become important instead, as had standing in a crowd and waving a flag and chanting 'USA! USA!' Never mind the score, feel the unity.

Yet as the American Football and ice hockey seasons have got into swing, as the baseball season concludes, and as the US waits to see if Michael Jordan can still successfully lob an orange ball into a small basket (one cartoonist depicted a sports journalist writing a column on how Jordan's hoop-shooting would heal the nation), it's clear that winning games has become important again.

In fact, the only game treated with the offhand dismissal that sport logically deserves in a time of war was the US football team's victory over Jamaica, which took them to the 2002 World Cup finals. ABC dropped its live coverage of the game and joined every other major channel by showing instead an occasionally flashing Kabul night sky on the day that the US bombing started.

Elsewhere, the sports sections are filled with the analysis, commentary and quotes of frustrated players, coaches and fans. My feeling is that people are discussing the Washington Redskins' start to the season more than they are discussing whether or not there is any point to bombing a starving, shattered country thousands of miles away. And it's hardly surprising, is it? I know which subject I feel more comfortable talking about.

On Sundays, the autumn season of the Second Division

of the Montgomery County Over-35s League also continues. For the first couple of weeks after September 11th it felt very strange, especially as people seemed to deliberately talk about the game, and nothing else. Six weeks on and everyone's cussing and cheering just like we were before. Ask me now, and I'll tell you that football's not important. Not the Montgomery County Over-35s league, not the English League, not the Champions League, not any bloody league. Yet watch me on a Sunday and you'd know I must have been lying, for there you'd witness me straining, sweating, swearing and celebrating along with the rest. Everything's back to normal, you see, and football helped us get there.

Well, except that now there's a war on.

Football, the Foundation of Normality

People were so shocked by 9/11 that they were craving a return to normality. One of the first things to cease in a time of war is organised professional sports activities. But this wasn't a normal war. Only on the first weekend after 9/11 did the National Football League suspend play. D.C. United didn't bother to complete their final two home fixtures of the season, but they were dead rubbers in any case so it didn't matter. If they'd still been in with a chance of making the play-offs, they would have played, you can be sure of that. Which begs the question, when does a game become too important to be cancelled just because 96 people died?

The game between Bradford City and Lincoln City stood at 0–0 the day of the Valley Parade fire on 11 May 1985, which killed 56 people. The fire started just before half-time. The Football League let the result stand. It was the last day of the season and Bradford were already Division Three champions, while Lincoln were safe from relegation. It didn't matter what the result was. Fifty-six people died while at a game of football whose result, it was known in advance, would have no effect on the outcome of the season.

Yet what if Bradford had needed three points to gain promotion? What if Lincoln had needed three points to avoid relegation? Would the game have mattered enough to replay it? Would the Football League have said, 'We know that 56 people died, but we have to know whether or not Bradford get promoted or Lincoln go down.' Would the clubs have said, 'Fifty-six people dying was a terrible tragedy, but still, the result is important. We have to play this game.' What would we as fans have said? Yes, I'm sure there would have been fitting tributes and minutes of silence and much poignant remembrance. But in the end, I know that I would still have wanted to see the game, know the score and celebrate the outcome.

Two and a half weeks after Bradford came the answer. Even after 39 mainly Italian fans had been crushed to death in the Heysel Stadium in Brussels before the European Cup Final between Liverpool and Juventus, the game went ahead. The official reason given was to avoid further crowd disorder. Yet I can still recall being astonished that Michel Platini and the Juventus players celebrated with such open gusto after they scored the penalty that won the match. Not that I was any better. Despite all the harrowing pictures of bodies being carried away on stretchers, I watched the game too.

Why did I not just get up and switch off in disgust, then go for a long walk? What was the point of being a football fan when the people that ran the game were so negligent that you risked death by fire or crushing when you walked into a stadium, supposedly to be entertained? If you couldn't be safe and relax while watching a game of football, where could you? *Perhaps it was time to take up another hobby*, I would have thought on this long walk, *like rambling or bird-watching. Something educational, healthy and uplifting.*

But no, I sat and watched the entire game. From start to finish. And just like those Liverpool players who said after the game that they never wanted to play again, but did, I was back at Sincil Bank just a few weeks later for the start of the 1985–6 season.

A number of fans, Liverpool or not, say the 1988–9 season should have been declared null and void, and that an asterisk should have remained next to a blank space in the record books besides 'FA Cup Winners' and 'League Champions' in tribute to the 96 Hillsborough dead. Fans of Arsenal, who took the First Division title from Liverpool in the most thrilling way possible via Michael Thomas's goal at Anfield in the very last minute of the season, might disagree. Morally, it's hard to disagree with those who say the Arsenal celebrations left them with a sick feeling of unease. As a fan, though, it's easy to sympathise with Arsenal, who had waited a long time for success. Liverpool had racked up a load of titles since Arsenal had last been champions in 1971. That year was important for Arsenal fans.

What, more important than the feelings of the families and friends of the 96 dead? No, of course not. But you know, life had to go on. Things had to return to normal. So my only defence for going mental at Orient is to see it as a moment of catharsis. There's only so much grief and depression and angst and sympathy that human beings are capable of giving out after a disaster that doesn't directly affect them. Much as we try, the lure of normality sets a certain limit. And then, sometimes without warning, we just explode. 'Gooooooooooal! Coops! Fucking magic! The Os are going up, wahaaaaaaaaaaaay!!!!!!'

Diary Entry for Monday, 5 June 1989

> Back to work and relative tedium, and watching the news of death in China (man-made), death in Russia (man-made but 'accidental') and lunacy in Iran (mass mourning of the Ayatollah, frenzied men beating their chests, hard-faced women shouting, 'Death to America', 10 killed in the crush), the importance of Leyton Orient gaining promotion to division three and two hours of uninhibited dancing at a party is put into even sharper perspective. On page 7 of the *Guardian* I barely read more than the headline of the report captioned '170 killed in landslide in Sri Lanka'. Is that all? The report on the sports page of the Orient v. Wrexham match merited more space than this cough drop of a disaster.
>
> Abstaining from a cigarette, helping out a telephone counselling service, putting 200 pounds in the building

society, writing articles on UK airport equipment companies, phoning Drew to arrange a weekend in Birmingham, phoning Helen to arrange going to Paris again next week – all things that would normally constitute a reasonably average day in my life, all things that did in fact constitute today, but things carried out with a vague feeling that in hours world history could overtake the lot, if it so chose, and wipe out the routines of such a mundane existence as my own. Which is relatively 'full' with a competent selection of variety. What I'm trying to say is, without sounding trite but failing miserably (and who cares), a random series of events and coincidences (i.e. history) – built on the basis of something like oppression (China, Iran) or carelessness (USSR, Hillsborough et al.) – could bring Queens Road [street I was living on at the time] or Thomas Telford House [workplace] to a pile of burned out bricks. And today it seems such a possibility that I can't take anything else seriously. It wasn't so at the weekend and probably won't be so maybe even tomorrow and more likely next week. But today that's what it feels like…

History is happening in China and Iran and it's exciting but also fucking terrifying. Two of the world's largest powers are shooting and shouting and the rest of the world stares, gob-struck, probably believing 'it' couldn't happen here (especially in the West), but today it seems inevitable to me that something will happen, or a series of things will happen, which will destroy the lifestyles that I and millions of others daily live without thinking life as such could ever end.

It goes on in this vein for another couple of pages. We're all doomed!

Football v. Turbulent International Events

According to the previous day's entry, I had wilfully enjoyed my weekend, dancing and watching football while Chinese pro-democracy students were massacred by government-controlled security forces and religious fervour was expressed through mass mourning in Tehran (I'm not especially proud of my description of events there as 'lunacy', but I was only 23, and that's what I wrote at the time, so that's what it seemed like to me), but by Monday, sober and faced with a return to the drudgery of work on a trade magazine mainly about equipment used at airports, world events had started to trouble me.

Yet even while noting my disapproval of the fact that the Orient v. Wrexham report in the *Guardian* took up more space in the paper than the one about 170 people being killed by a landslide in Sri Lanka, I'm fairly sure that I read the match report all the way through, while only reading the headline of the Sri Lanka story. Needless to say, picking up my diary now I have no recollection of the Sri Lanka mudslide, and I had to look up on the internet to see how many students were actually killed at Tiananmen Square. As for the disaster referred to in Russia, that was the Trans-Siberian Express explosion on 4 June, which killed 645 people when the sparks from two passing trains ignited gas from a leaking pipeline. I may have noted it in my diary, but I had to check on Wikipedia what the event was. I had completely forgotten that 645 people had died in a train crash in Russia that weekend.

I can remember that the weekend of the Orient v. Wrexham game was the weekend of Tiananmen Square. Or do I remember that the weekend of Tiananmen Square was also the weekend of the Orient v. Wrexham game? Perhaps the best way to work out the relative significance of these newsworthy events is to resort to the traditional male way of coping with difficult issues. No, not ending the chapter and never talking about it again. Let's try lists:

> Newsworthy events of the weekend 3–4 June 1989, in order of death toll:
>
> (1) Tiananmen Square massacre: 300–5,000 (estimated)
> (2) Ufa gas pipeline explosion in Russia: 645
> (3) Sri Lanka landslide: 170
> (4) Tehran mourning crush: 10

(5) Solidarity election win in Poland that triggered peaceful protests leading to fall of communism in Eastern Europe: 0

(6) Leyton Orient v. Wrexham: 0

Newsworthy events of the weekend 3–4 June 1989, in order of estimated geopolitical importance:

(1) Tiananmen Square massacre

(2) Solidarity election win in Poland that triggered peaceful protests leading to fall of communism in Eastern Europe (you could arguably exchange the first- and second-place rankings here)

(3) Tehran mourning crush

(4) Ufa gas pipeline explosion in Russia

(5) Sri Lanka landslide

(6) Leyton Orient v. Wrexham

Newsworthy events of the weekend 3–4 June 1989, in order of personal significance to Ian Plenderleith:

(1) Leyton Orient v. Wrexham

(2) Tiananmen Square massacre

(3) Tehran mourning crush

(4–6=) (can't recall them happening that weekend) Solidarity election win in Poland that triggered peaceful protests leading to fall of communism in Eastern Europe/ Ufa gas pipeline explosion in Russia/Sri Lanka landslide

I place the game at number one reluctantly, because I'd like to think I'm a better person than that, but I have to be honest. First, I was most involved in that event, actually witnessing it. It took up four hours of my Saturday in total. Second, it was the only event on the list that caused me to lose control. Third, I've replayed Orient's goals in my head far more often than I've replayed images from TV of Tiananmen Square, and probably talked about them more too. And although

I remember that Tiananmen Square depressed me like hell for a couple of days, as reflected in my diary entry, my shock and sadness soon subsided in the face of the fact that I knew there was nothing I could do about it. What were we going to do? Invade China, with me giving up my job on *Airports International* to sign up for military duty and certain death on the other side of the world?

On the other hand, I could at least have protested outside the Chinese embassy, or joined a lobby group or an organisation pushing for democratic reform, or looked to support the underground pro-democracy movement in exile, and written to my Member of Parliament, calling for UK government action. But I did none of those things. I didn't even keep the newspaper. But I still have my match programme for Orient v. Wrexham.

Programme Highlights

I haven't even mentioned the match programme yet, and with good reason. There's really nothing in it. Needless to say, it missed the deadline to incorporate any news about Tiananmen Square, the Ayatollah's death, the Russian pipeline disaster or the Polish elections, so as a preserved document it won't be much use to historians. There's an end-of-season feel to it, as if the editor couldn't really be arsed to hack out one more match magazine. 'Thanks to the supporters and the players and all the backroom staff for a great season,' and so on. The absence of the word 'Hillsborough' is interesting. Now it may be that the topic was tackled in depth in all the match programmes between Torquay (15 April) and Wrexham (3 June), but I don't have any of those. In the programme for the Wrexham game, Hillsborough was absent, but at the same time it was everywhere. Check out manager Frank Clark's column, ironically enough called 'Frankly Speaking':

> Your support on the night [at Scarborough in the play-off semi-final] was superb and a great help to the players in surviving the [on-field] barrage. Just as pleasing was the

> fact that the Police Chief on the night made a point of congratulating our supporters on their impeccable behaviour and good humour.

Further on he notes:

> Going back to last Sunday, I was delighted by the conduct of the supporters at the end of the game in respecting the request not to invade the pitch. I am asking for a repeat performance today! I am sure that, whatever the result, both teams will want to acknowledge their supporters and if everyone keeps off the pitch, then it can be an emotional and suitable end to the season.

Later in the programme, in what may or may not be an advert, is a picture of some fans in wheelchairs being pushed by other fans, and the headline 'The Caring Face of Football', with some text about how the Football Grounds Improvement Trust would be spending £1.25 million 'on improvements projects at Football League grounds, and areas for people with disabilities form a major part of this programme'.

The programme talks around the subject of death, but you can tell it's fully aware of football's very recent history. It probably reflected the feelings of the fans too. Seven weeks after Hillsborough we'd read and heard enough about the event, and discussed it enough too, to have had our fill of it for a while. There's only so much death a live human being can take. We were still very much *aware* of it, and so we'd do our bit by not rushing on to the field at the end, or by behaving in any way that remotely threatened to cause the death of another fan. Very good. Now let us watch the game, will you? It's Orient's biggest game for years.

How Male Football Fans Deal with Death in Western Society

0–5 years old: 'Grandma died? Why? When's she coming back? Can I have some ice cream?'

5–10 years old: 'Grandma died?' Begins crying. 'That's sad.' Stops crying. 'Oh look, Jimmy's here with his new ball. We'll be in the garden. Can we have ice cream after?'

10–20 years old: 'Me Gran snuffed it.'

'Really?'

'Yeah. Fucking funeral's on Saturday, I'm gonna miss the Burnley game.'

'Bollocks, I'll have to go on me own. Maybe you can flog your ticket to Bomber. Jesus, look at the arse on that.'

20–55 years old: 'Imagine, they just went to the game, same as you and I do every Saturday, and they never came back. *Never came back.* Think of all the times you've been trapped on the terrace in a crowd, but you never thought anything would happen. I remember one time at Grimsby v. Newcastle in the early '80s, we just kept getting moved along with the surge of fans whenever something exciting happened, and you really had to struggle to keep your feet. But we thought it was a laugh. You'd look around and laugh as you were being swept along, and then once the surge was over you'd try and find your mates again. It's frightening now, when I think about it. You couldn't have got out even if you'd wanted to.'

[Thinks: *But the most frightening thing is, that could have been me, that could have been me, that could have been me,* that could have been me, *and I'm still way too young to die.*]

'You going to the game on Saturday? Yeah, I don't much feel like it any more either. Still, see you in the Duke of Wellington about one, eh?'

55–Death: 'Yep, it'll come to us all one day, son, probably sooner than we think. Oh yes, I know, I'll probably be one of the next to go. Your grandfather had a stroke around my age. Well, I've had a decent enough life, though your mother might say different. Seen a few places, done plenty of things, produced a few kids, but there's not a whole lot left for me to hang around for now. I'll just be a burden. Everyone has their own time for signing off, and there's nothing more certain than death. Mind you, it'd be nice to see Newcastle win *something* before I go…' (Tails off, staring out the window as eyes become moist, hands fidgeting with the knob of his walking stick.)

11

Birth

FC Zürich v. Anorthosis Famagusta, UEFA Cup First Round, First Leg, Tuesday, 15 September 1998

Singled Out

Maybe it's a contradiction peculiar to the post-'60s generation – many of whose members shunned the idea of marrying and settling down in order to extend their youths into, through and even beyond their twenties – that we thought about death so much before we thought about birth. At an age when, biologically speaking, we should have been enthusiastically propagating, we were moping about in draughty rented London flats listening to music designed to induce introspective melancholia rather than a state of joy about living through melody, beat and sheer singalong harmony. The rave scene passed me by entirely – I didn't like the music, didn't trust the drugs (or have the cash to pay for them – my intoxication budget was bequeathed exclusively to Guinness) and I couldn't be up dancing all night if I had an important game to play the following afternoon in the Southern Olympian League Intermediate Division Two. Instead of proudly staring into the sweet, gleaming eyes of the next in line to the family surname, we were fretting about the prospect of nuclear war, global imperialism, the spread of fascism and the threat of environmental catastrophe. At least, that was the front we put on. Some of us were, it could be argued, given too many choices. In my early twenties I had qualified from university with a degree in German, and with no family ties to hold me back I could have done anything or gone anywhere. But I had no clear idea what I wanted to do or where I wanted to go, so I hung around in London for seven years doing a series of menial journalistic jobs that left me looking forward to a small number of things in life – beer, football, music and my next holiday.

So I was a harmless enough cog in the capital's huge grinding chain that wore you down, day after day, while affording you, as recompense, the opportunity to get drunk, cheer your football team, get laid every now and then, and go to just about any gig you wanted, if you could be bothered to work out how to get there and back without missing the last Tube and having to blow half a week's wages on a cab. Like everyone else around me, I veered between reasonable contentment and a sense of perpetual struggle on the road to nowhere in particular, depending on who was around at the time, how my job was going, who was sleeping with me and whether or not I was scoring goals for Nottsborough Reserves. It was easy to be principled about most things when you didn't have much money or own any property, and I always liked the idea of being able to up and leave at short notice to go and travel round the world. Which I never did, being prone to booking impulsive holidays or splashing my entire savings on a trip to the World Cup (Italia '90, to watch Scotland fail – and yes, it was worth it. I think).

The main advantage to life back then was its simplicity. I received a monthly pay cheque, and out of that I paid my rent, and then every three months my share of the electricity, gas and phone bills. Anything left over was for me.

In our house only Tim Bastard had a computer, a temperamental Amstrad word processor from Dixons. I couldn't understand what good it was when you could just as easily use an old 1950s typewriter like mine. We had a colour TV that got a lousy picture, and a small black-and-white one with good reception. I lent the latter once to a German friend who was staying in London for three months. The night I went to pick it up we went to the pub first, then I rode 6 miles home through London after closing time, half-cut, balancing the TV on my crossbar. Why would I waste 25 quid on a taxi when I could get it home by bike? One night, I almost crawled from Leytonstone to Walthamstow after taking two hits from a chillum. I didn't know what a chillum was. I thought it was just a different method of toking on a joint. The stoner friends who'd watched me go through several phases that night – hysteria, delirium, catatonia – laughed for several months about how I'd apparently swum home through the sewage system, as I'd disappeared to the bog and was not seen for several weeks. Still, I was conscious enough to take three hours staggering back to the flat rather than spend any cash on a taxi.

I didn't appreciate all that at the time because I was just as burdened and depressed by the shackles of the five-day, 37-hour working week as everyone else. And I can remember feeling so directionless in my pointless job on the airports magazine that I applied to do a teacher training course, but changed my mind when I got a new, equally pointless job at a small news agency, where you proofread tedious business-news press releases and added a headline. And I can remember being lonely enough to reply to a singles ad in *Time Out*, as a consequence of which I spent an evening in the company of a pretty, intelligent woman, but all the while I felt wretched for not behaving like my real self, and then felt guilty for years afterwards because I never called her as I'd promised I would, though it's doubtful she was waiting by the phone. And I can remember being stuck on the Tube, or stuck on the bus in traffic, or riding my bike or stumbling home through London at three in the morning, dying of cold and too stoned to think, except for wondering how long I was going to keep living like this and how long could the human body stay fit enough to tolerate such abuse.

Fortunately, as I approached the end of my twenties, it became time to sell out. The end of youth had long been holding up a sign that said, in bold black type, 'OVERDUE!' It's just coincidence that it happened at around the same time as the FA Premier League replaced the old Football League Division One, and the 'Champions' League replaced the European Cup.

'Historic Day'

A friend of mine in the Nottsborough football team, Darren Venn, worked for the Football League. When we went to training way down in Surrey on Monday nights, I'd go over to his office to get a lift. It was always a bit of a thrill for me to go into the Football League and see the odd famous face, or pick up some free shin pads or boots. One evening we got into his car, and he said, 'Well, today was a historic day for English football. Next year the first division will be the Premier League, run by the FA. It was inevitable.' You could tell he was already thinking about his next job.

I thought he was exaggerating. To most football fans at the time, the difference looked cosmetic. It was still 20 teams, with straight up and down promotion from, and relegation to, the second division. It seemed daft that the second division would now be renamed Division One, but no one was chaining themselves to the railings at Lancaster Gate about it. It was only when, some time later, you read the figures for the TV money the Premier League clubs were going to get from Sky that you realised the smaller league clubs had been shafted and left behind, and that the top level of the game didn't give a shit about the teams who, for decades, had provided them with many of their best players. Well, you might have realised all this at the time if you had been reading the requisite newspapers and fanzines, or even paying attention to the bloke from the Football League who was driving you down to Monday-night training at Worcester Park, but I wasn't.

At the time, I was too wrapped up in all the things discussed above to read much of anything besides novels whose anti-heroes half lived in my head by proxy for a few days until I started the next one. Much as I was into football, I wasn't politically into it. I'd never realised you had to be, because, naïvely, I thought it was a game, and I thought (even more naïvely) that everyone else involved in the game viewed it as an untouchable, sacred institution. It wasn't there for people to make money out of. It was a game. It was *the* game.

Selling Out: A Personal Odyssey

Sell-Out 1, Aged Six. Becoming a Manchester United Fan

A crime, of course, but it didn't stop me 'properly' supporting Lincoln City, unlike many of my school mates, who scorned local teams in favour of Liverpool and, later, Nottingham Forest, who *almost* counted as local. After looking at my very first league table on *Football Focus* (or *Football Preview*, as it was back then, with Sam Leitch) one Saturday morning and seeing that Manchester United were eight points clear, and quickly deciding they were definitely the team for me, I suffered 20 years of (relative) privation before they would ever be so far ahead again, punctuated with the odd FA Cup win, when the FA Cup still seemed important. In self-defence, the more successful they became, the less interesting they seemed to me as a club, and now I can barely be bothered to look out for their results or their latest super-signing, let alone watch them on TV.

I certainly fit the demographic of the archetypal distant MUFC fan. I've never been to Old Trafford. I have no desire any more to do so. I've seen them live a total of eight times: five times in London in proper competitions and three times on their money-making US tours (see 'Success' chapter). I've never put a penny into the club's coffers, unless you count whatever it was I might have paid for the chipped 1977 FA Cup Winners mug I still possess. I'd probably get a fortune for that on eBay from Johnny-come-latelies trying to shore up their long-term fan credentials.

Yet despite all these mealy-mouthed self-justifications, I can't alter the fact that I cared about them for a long, long time. True, six is maybe a little young to be adjudged as having sold out, but how I wish I'd had the gumption and the independence of mind to shun the seeming necessity of following a big team. Every small-town kid did it, with Leeds, Chelsea and Arsenal enjoying big numbers in Lincolnshire thanks to the live televising of the early-'70s FA Cup Finals. Young kids still do it today, judging by the replica shirts in the playground. Yet it might have been the one time when a sharp crack to the side of my head from my dad would have been a decent idea, accompanied by the order 'Ye'll support yer local team, laddie!' Then again, years later I tried convincing my nephew in Dresden, who was seven at the time, that supporting Bayern Munich made absolutely no sense for him, and all it achieved was to make him more determined to cheer their every kick.[1]

Besides, who says you can't have two teams? Shouldn't I have supported Market Rasen Town, whose ground was a five-minute walk from my house, ahead of Lincoln because they were more local? As a matter of fact, I did support them, in a way. I used to go down to The Ropewalk to play in a kick-about adjacent to the main pitch, and though we rarely cheered home goals, because we weren't actually watching (most weeks I had no idea if it was even the first team or the reserves who were playing), I bought enough packets of savoury vinegar crisps to keep the club's snack-shop accounts nicely ticking over.

Sell-Out 2, Aged 26. The Transition from Vinyl to CDs

Now something like this may not seem such a big deal, and you're right, it's not. Only, as you will see in the forthcoming sell-out stages, I am the worst, most dishonest kind of sell-out. What's that old saying about the one who holds out longest from selling out is just the guy with the highest price? That's what comes to mind whenever I finally cave in to something I've been ranting and raving about for the longest time.

I would never abandon vinyl for CDs, I often said. Like the disappearance of the old First Division, I refused to believe it was going to happen. Vinyl had been around all my life, and it wasn't just going to go away overnight. There were millions like me who wouldn't stand for it. CDs were for yuppies, because they cost twice as much as

1. As a teenager he became a Dynamo Dresden fan, but hardly an avid one. He usually needed me to tell him where they were in the league, and if I went to a game with his father, my brother-in-law, he'd find an excuse not to come along. A thoroughly wasted youth.

LPs. CD players were for yuppies because they were expensive, and because in all the adverts the yuppie twats who were smugly hawking the ease of operating a CD player looked exactly like the kind of yuppie twats you'd expect to have a CD player. These were the contemptible people who'd said goodbye to youth aged 22, the day after leaving university. And then I'd go on and on about how great it was to take the vinyl out of its sleeve, and then out of its inner sleeve (why?), and how CDs didn't get the same depth of sound (as far as I've ever noticed, this is completely untrue), and how I wasn't going to get ripped off buying the same LPs on compact disc that I already owned on vinyl. No, brother, those ultra-capitalist, multinational media magnates are not going to get their hands on *my* cash. Every record I own has its own scratches; they've become part of the song. In this way, each LP has its own personality. And tell me, how can you appreciate the sleeve artwork of an LP on one of those poxy little CD cases?

The conversion was as swift as the Premier League's creation. I became involved with an American girl who was in London for only a short time. I went over to visit her in Philadelphia, and she, knowing my passion for music, took me to some CD shops. They were so cheap. They'd be so easy to carry home. What the hell, I was on holiday. And the girl could not understand why I was so resistant. They'd had CD players in America for years. The way she put it, my bolshie stance all of a sudden seemed atavistic and quite ridiculous. I flew home, more chronically besotted than before, and with 12 CDs in my case. The first thing I did when I got home was to dump my luggage and head straight back out to Richer Sounds at London Bridge, to spend the last of my savings on a new CD player.

Oh, I'd still keep all my vinyl, and I'd never buy something I already owned. And I do still have all my LPs and a turntable. Only now, vinyl is fashionable again, and because of the internet no one, absolutely no one, still buys CDs. Why would you? My daughters can't understand why I haven't binned the lot. They serve no purpose and take up space. And if I hadn't caved in and sold out for the intervening quarter of a century, I could now be the world's most righteous living vinyl collector.

Sell-Out 3, Aged 26. Getting a Driver's Licence

You see, there was this American girl, and as well as not understanding what I had against CDs, she also could not understand why I was 26 years old and didn't have a driver's licence. Well, you don't need one in London, I said. One thing that became clear to me during my two weeks in America, though, was that if I ever dropped everything to go over and live there, for whatever reason (because, say, I was besotted with an American girl), I was going to need to be able to drive. There wasn't a local bus that would take me to the local train or underground station, and if you wanted to walk there wasn't a footpath either. You went by car. Everyone did. The planet has gone and sacrificed itself for the convenience of suburb-dwelling wealthy Americans. You can make a speech about this in the US and everyone will listen politely, and then someone will say, 'Okay, so do you want a ride or not?'

When I came back to London I immediately booked driving lessons. Under pressure from my mum, I had taken lessons as soon as I turned 17, because she said that's what 17-year-olds did. I hated driving and I hated driving lessons. I was crap and nervous, and once scraped my mum's Ford Fiesta on our front gate seconds after I'd assured her I could get into our driveway, no problem. She didn't take it well. Still talks about it, in fact. Another time, I almost killed us both at a roundabout in Lincoln and she gave birth to a quintuplet of Tasmanian devils, which, even collectively, made less noise than she was making in the passenger's seat. When I was 18 I took a test, one Monday morning. My mum was away in Scotland for the weekend, and I drank so much to quell my nerves that I vomited all night. Hungover, I failed so miserably (at one point, at a T-junction, the examiner had to press the emergency brake to prevent a serious accident) that the examiner, after curtly informing me of my failure to reach the standards required by Her Majesty's Department of Transport, stormed out of the car and slammed the door, leaving me with a sheet of paper disfigured by more scores and crosses than the first draft of Donald Trump's inauguration speech.[2] My instructor, a usually genial Scotsman called Harry, was also unhappy – I'd broken his run of something like 471 consecutive passes. I told him I'd been feeling unwell (true), but not that this was down to a crushing hangover. 'Why did ye no tell me, Ian? I'd have called it off,' he admonished, then drove me to the train station in the kind of Scottish silence I hadn't experienced since having afternoon tea with my great-aunts as a tongue-tied wean.

After that mishap, I refused to drive any more. I maintained that it was better for the environment if less people drove. The train, the bus and my bike were fine by me (although this didn't stop me taking a lift if one was ever offered). Not driving was another component of my carefree, car-free twenties, and I wore my failed test as a badge of anecdotal honour, all the while imbuing my lack of a licence with an ecologically principled hue that was blown out of the water the minute this American girl said, 'You're 26 and you don't have a driver's licence? Why not?'

'Why not? You know, it's like that CD thing. It's for... yuppies, or something. I can't afford a car. I like walking and biking. You're right, though. Maybe I should take some lessons.'

I returned from the US in October, and by January I'd passed my test, thanks to a balding but brilliant instructor in Walthamstow called Mark who yelled at me whenever I made the slightest mistake. When I told him how astonished I was at having passed, and having passed so well, he grinned and said, 'That's because I bollocked you to a standard way higher than you needed to pass.' I bought him a box of chocolates.

Considering what a huge sell-out this was on so many levels, I was in an unbelievably happy mood at having gained my driver's licence, even allowing for the fact that the signals from my American girl had turned from positive to intermittent over the course of the grey winter. I jumped around my bedroom at 9.30 in the morning playing loud music (on my new CD player). I made jokey, flirty conversation with two Jehovah's Witnesses who came to my door (usually they went away with their ears burning). And that evening I went for

2. 'No, Mr Trump, you cannot say that you'd rather fuck a dog than a liberal. Not any more.'

the ultimate in decadent celebration – I took my flatmates for pizza at Oz's in Leyton.

Now I live in Frankfurt and don't have a car, because we don't need one. I go everywhere by bike, or I walk, or I take public transport. It's like with vinyl – if only I'd waited long enough, I'd be the righteous prophet who'd warned people never to change, never to sell out (although my 16 years living in the US might have been a challenge). Can I claim to be selling back in?

Sell-Out 4, Aged 27. Buying a Car

You didn't need a car if you lived in London, but then I got a job in Reading, in the newsroom at BBC Monitoring, a branch of the World Service located in what looks like a huge old public school in Caversham. It was an institution that seemed to provide employment for people who have either failed to make a decent career elsewhere (either in the BBC or out of it), or who were borderline certifiable. I felt immediately at home.

I could have moved to Reading, but then I could have taken a sharp knife to my own jugular too. I could have travelled by train, but an annual season ticket was so expensive that, taking into account the reliability of UK public transport and the fact that I would finish some shifts at midnight and be too late to take a train back, I opted to buy a car and spend several hours of my life in traffic jams in West London or on the M25 instead. Even moving from Walthamstow to Kensal Rise in North-West London didn't help all that much, although it brought me closer to my new girlfriend in West Hampstead, a vocal environmentalist who, like myself in a previous incarnation, never once turned down the chance of a lift in the despised polluter, despite the rail line that easily linked our two respective flats.

Almost all the money I'd saved from working in London for five years went into paying the deposit on a small red car whose make I've already forgotten. It had no cassette player, so I blew another 130 quid on that. Over the next year and a half, until I left to live in Germany, I spent most of the rest of my savings on maintenance and petrol.

When I sold it for less than half of what I'd paid, the remaining cash covered the rest of the loan payments and left me with 700 quid.

Seven years as a working professional, and all I had to show for it was seven hundred pounds and a passable knowledge of the best way to negotiate the Hammersmith flyover. Selling out has never been so expensive, although it did make it easier to make the trip to watch Lincoln at Wycombe Wanderers one rare Saturday afternoon when I was neither playing nor working. They won 3–2, so at least I have that precious memory whenever I wonder how I made it to 30 years of age, asset-free.

Sell-Out 5, Aged 29. Moving from the BBC to Knight-Ridder Financial News

I left the newsroom at a noble, world-renowned public service broadcasting corporation to edit financial news in Frankfurt at an agency that served banks and all those other evil capitalist establishments I was 'against'. I went from the good guys to the bad guys, simple as that. From the neutral and reputable crisp tones of the impeccable Beeb to the hectic, manic world of newswire journalism, where a second's delay in reporting the latest central bank interest rates caused your superiors to crap their pants and throw themselves into the tempting dark waters of the River Main.

True, they were offering me a permanent contract and better pay, whereas BBC Monitoring was managed by such a bunch of prevaricating clowns that every month myself and several colleagues were given a new contract to tide us over until the next one, all the while uncertain if there would even be a next one because no one above us could make a long-term decision. The new Birtist doctrine flogging the virtues of an internal market had thoroughly confused the old-timer Trots and Stalinists who still believed in the virtues of public service broadcasting and thought that it owed them a living too. However, the rest of us were dispatched to all-day workshops filled with jargon about core activities, streamlined modules and producer choice. I didn't understand a word of it.

And I wanted to go back to Germany, always had. I also wanted to leave my girlfriend, only I behaved dishonestly, trying to convince us both that me moving abroad was of absolutely no significance to our relationship. When I arrived in Frankfurt and found that my temporary flat had no telephone, I just laid back for a month with a crate of beer, went to Eintracht Frankfurt games (Bundesliga! UEFA Cup!), watched trans-European football on cable TV and enjoyed the sound of silence, punctuated only by the odd moment of crowd noise and the reassuringly recurrent clichés of the excitable commentator.

After a couple of months, I broke up with her, because I was already preparing myself for new ways to sell out. I was nearly 30, after all. Where the hell was my house in the suburbs, my wife and two kids?

Sell-Out 6, Aged 30. Moving to Switzerland

Before we get there, we have to travel via Switzerland. 'It's a funny old place,' my mum once wrote to me while I was living there, because they wouldn't grant me a work permit (she was much more bothered about this than I was). It annoyed me that she said this, given that she didn't live there and knew nothing about it, but she was right enough, it *is* a funny old place. One of those countries you just never think about, except in passing conversation. 'Yeah, he's off skiing to Switzerland, yuppie cunt.' Or, 'What was the name of that Swiss team who knocked Celtic out the UEFA Cup a few years back? Chateau Xanadu or something?' Looking back, I find it hard to grasp that I lived there for three and a half years. I still find it hard to get a handle on the very idea of Swissness. The only interesting theme in Swiss literature is the country's identity crisis. 'Who are we? What is our point, besides having a few nice lakes and spectacular mountains?' I talked to some Swiss students in Basel in 2016, when I was at the university for a conference about the aesthetics of football (it's very important to fly people in from around the world to discuss these things), and asked them about the Swiss identity crisis and how it had affected them when growing up. They hadn't the slightest clue what I was talking about.

Switzerland is like those infuriating agnostics in religious discussions who refuse to commit to either belief or disbelief. The supposed neutrality is just a ruse to avoid making a decision or taking a stance. Switzerland is one big fence-sitting cop-out and, worse still, it's proud of the fact. They are proud to be boring and conservative. Secreting the money of the deeply immoral despots, dictators and criminals of the world is no big deal. 'If we didn't do it, some disreputable little Caribbean island would do it instead.'

Yet being boring really bothers them too. The mass circulation daily gutter rag, *Blick*, would big up anyone who might be seen as an ambassador for the country to the great outside world beyond. In the late 1990s Martina Hingis was the world's number-one female tennis player and made the front page most days, not just because there was nothing else to report – at least not from Switzerland, and *Blick* didn't give a bugger beyond that – but because she was the balm to the mass inferiority complex of a country with nothing else to offer the world besides the Red Cross, expensive chocolate and a lakeside bolthole for the unnecessarily rich.

So, Mr Principles, what was a politically perfect radical like yourself doing there?

Actually, I loved it, especially Zürich, and not just because it had two professional football teams. I loved the lake and the mountains. I loved the lack of a threat. My true petit bourgeois colours began to show. I had a wife and a baby now, and I didn't want anything to harm them. In the space of a few months, I went from being a boozy bachelor living it up in high-finance Frankfurt while working a reasonably high-pressure job to being a stay-at-home dad with a little blond baby while my girlfriend and wife-to-be went to work, in a city where I barely knew a soul and couldn't understand the local dialect. I read books, read the paper, dandled the child, went shopping for groceries and then cooked dinner. Sell-out bliss.

Sell-Out 7, Aged 30. Becoming a Parent

When some of my friends had started to become parents a couple of years earlier, I had felt a genuine sense of betrayal. I raged against babies and kids because they were a threat to my lifestyle. I couldn't be doing with the idea that I would phone up a mate to meet for a drink, and he wouldn't be able to make it because he had to stay at home to *look after a fucking baby*. That was not a young person's thing to be doing. Drinking in a smoky pub was much more healthy for people of our age. 'You going to the match on Saturday? What do you mean you can't make it because you're taking a walk with a pushchair down to the park? What the fuck is that about? Do it in the morning, or on Sunday. And no, I certainly do not want to come along.'

I was actively hostile to the idea of parenthood. I made it clear to my girlfriend (the one I abandoned in order to move to Frankfurt) that I never *ever* wanted to be a father. Got that? When close friends brought their two-month-old baby to a party one night, I was horrified. 'Can't you keep that thing at home?' I refused to even look at it. Damn, I was a tough guy. As well as being obnoxious and repetitive and protesting way too much.

No one seemed even slightly surprised when I told them just over a year later that my new German girlfriend was pregnant already. They congratulated me, and all the while I was waiting for them to go, 'Ha ha ha, and you said you never ever wanted to be a father. What about that, eh?' Such gloating is, I know, generally reserved for five-year-olds, but there wasn't even a mention of my deeply held opposition to paternity. This was either because they knew already I'd been protesting way too much, or because they remembered all the other ways I had sold out previously (see above), and one more sell-out was no big deal. 'The car-driving, corporately employed careerist is now becoming a father, just as we knew he would.'

It's possible I clawed back a grain of credibility in the eyes of a few people, mainly female friends, by giving up my job to stay at home and look after the newborn. And by living illegally in Switzerland, because we weren't married, but that was hardly heroic given that immigration officers were unlikely to be knocking on our door in the middle of the night. In the main, though, since selling out was expected, at this age anyway, judgements ranged from the jocular to the non-existent.

Football and Parenthood

I thought that once my child was born, I would not have the time to watch another football game for the next 20 or so years of my life. I would be too busy. I'm not sure what I was going to be busy with, but when your wife is pregnant for the first time you get all kinds of knowing comments from Experienced Dads about being up all night, wiping the shit off tender butts, taking walks in the park on Saturday afternoons with the pushchair while everyone else is at the game, and watching endless nursery-rhyme videos instead of the match on TV.

In fact, all our newborn daughter seemed to do was sleep. A few days after her birth, I tried an experiment by watching Spain v. Scotland in the semi-final of the U21 European Championships with her placed on my lap. When Scotland scored, I half jumped up and went 'Wahaaay!' and she woke up and cried. Then she went back to sleep (Scotland inevitably went on to lose 2–1, so it was appropriate that this disappointment marked her first game). During interruptions in play, I could look at her and go, 'Aaaaaaah.' This was a dry run for the entire Euro '96 tournament, which kicked off a couple of weeks later, and I ended up watching a higher percentage of games than I had at USA '94, when I'd still been in a job. Fatherhood was working for me.

Come the new Swiss season a month later, I started going to watch the home games of both Grasshoppers and FC Zürich. Mostly, they were on Saturday evenings or Sunday afternoons, and my wife, having been at work all week, loved to hang out with the baby for a few hours. For me, it was the best way to escape our small flat and enjoy some fresh air and relief from the feeling that I wasn't constantly protecting my infant from some unspecified danger. I went to tons of games, many of which I can barely recollect, against the likes of Aarau and Servette and St Gallen. I loved being able to walk into the stadium five minutes before kick-off, buy a sausage, choose a seat, and then sit back and watch a game of football. Often the sun would just be going down behind the main stand at the Grasshoppers' Hardturm stadium as the players lined up to kick off. Who were they playing today? Bern or Basel? I didn't care. It was just a beautiful sight, and I felt like the luckiest bastard in the whole world.

Celling Out at FC Zürich v. Anorthosis Famagusta

I went to watch Grasshoppers, but I became a fan of FC Zürich, even before I realised this was politically more expedient and that the vast majority of lads on my Sunday football team were lifelong FCZ fans too. The club just had a better feel to it, in much the same way I immediately preferred homely Orient to vitriolic West Ham when I lived in East London. FCZ were rubbish compared with Grasshoppers, but they scraped fortuitously into the UEFA Cup thanks to a fourth-place finish and the Swiss Cup winners Servette ending above them. And then, all of a sudden, they assembled quite an attractive team consisting of both ageing and young Swiss players, up-and-coming Brazilians, Burundian asylum-seekers and the classy South African striker Shaun Bartlett.

This game took place just a few days before the birth of my second daughter. A few months earlier I had sworn in disgust when someone sitting next to me at a Grasshoppers game had answered his mobile phone and started a long conversation while the game was actually taking place before him. Like all things you see for the first time, it's shocking. Now every second fan spends half their time recording the 'experience' and taking selfies and sending texts, though at least the highly asocial habit of long phone conversations has been culled back to, 'Yeah, Row Z, I can see you, I'm waving at you now…'

Still, way back in 1998, I took a cell phone to the game as well. It was my wife's work cell phone, and I had it switched on in the event that she suddenly started to give birth. I didn't want to be one of those dads summoned to the hospital via the PA while everyone thought, 'What a wanker, his wife was nine months pregnant but he went to the game anyway.' At the same time, I didn't want to miss the game. This was FCZ's first UEFA Cup season for around 15 years, and they had comprehensively overcome Shakhtar Donetsk of Ukraine in the preliminary round. They were building a decent team that might even challenge for the Swiss title. Across the city, Grasshoppers had whacked up admission prices by as much as seven times for their Champions League qualifier against Galatasaray,[3] while neighbourly FCZ, the proletarian club in contrast to the self-appointed aristocrats of Grasshoppers, advertised their game with the slogan: 'Come and watch European football at Swiss league prices'.

'There's something special about UEFA Cup games,' said FCZ captain Urs Fischer in the match programme. That something special was mainly the fact that they weren't playing Lausanne, Aarau or St fucking Gallen yet again. When they beat Donetsk 4–0 in the preliminary round, the crowd had responded in a manner that was far more animated than if the opponent had been Sion or Neuchâtel. It wasn't just the midweek floodlights, which for many fans somehow make a game more special, but the imminent risk and excitement – next round we could be playing a club from England, Spain or Italy. Against Famagusta they won 4–0 again, and I was going nuts, mainly because I knew that, a second-leg suicide excepted, there was going to be another floodlit midweek UEFA Cup tie a bus ride away from my flat, and this time the opponent could be bigger still.

I went drinking afterwards to celebrate, and it was only on my second beer that I remembered the phone in my pocket. I took it out and checked that it was still working. It seemed to be. A drunk fan gave me a giant polystyrene 'Z' he'd been holding up as part of the terrace choreography. I took it home as a souvenir and placed it in our attic storage space (we left it there when we moved to the US the following year). I expect it was just the euphoria of the evening. What could be more invigorating than a 4–0 UEFA Cup home win?

3. I had a letter printed in the Zürich daily *Tages-Anzeiger* complaining about this. I proudly showed this to Marcus, an American journalist at Reuters in Zürich who had got me into country and the blues thanks to the musical powers of the bong. He read it carefully, then said, 'Well, Ian, that really needed to be said, so it's good that you stepped up to the plate.' I didn't show the letter to anyone else after that.

Birth

Happily, my second daughter, Natascha, didn't arrive during the match, and so I didn't miss any of FCZ's four glorious goals. She came six days later, while my wife was absorbed watching Bill Clinton's testimony to the House–Senate committee on the Monica Lewinsky case, which was being broadcast in full by CNN for the first time on the evening of 21 September. When I pointed out three times that her breathing indicated birth was imminent, she snapped at me to shut up (hormones raging), so I sat eating dinner until she decided it was time to go. She almost gave birth in the car, especially after I took a wrong turn, but we made it just in time, popped the kid out, and I was home by midnight.

My first daughter, Nina, had been born the day of the 1996 Champions League final. It's an established joke in the family by now that I rushed home that evening in time to see the game, but it's not actually true. My wife, Conny, went into labour at eight in the morning, and Nina arrived at 3.20 in the afternoon. It's a fact that I didn't *completely* forget that Juventus were playing Ajax that night, but there was a lot of standing around that day, despite all the excitement, so that was probably one of a hundred things going through my mind. It just so happened that by the time I came home, with mother and baby settled down and sleeping at the hospital, the second half was about to start. Yet I spent the entire half, extra-time and the penalty kicks with the sound turned down, calling everyone on both sides of the family to tell them the news, and afterwards had little recollection of anything that I'd only half watched to start with.

FC Zürich continued their UEFA Cup run in the autumn of 1998 by knocking out Celtic and then giving AS Roma a torrid time before they succumbed 2–3 on aggregate, mainly thanks to the diving gifts of Francesco Totti. The four games against Shakhtar, Famagusta, Celtic and Roma at the time represented the most memorable cup run of any team I'd followed (usurped only by Lincoln's FA Cup miracle of 2016–17), and those games reflect the easy bliss of my life at the time, and the privilege of being a happy young family in a safe, beautiful city. Conny had three months of maternity leave, while I was working on a casual basis for cash in hand as a reporter at a news agency. It's true, there was an insane neighbour who lived directly below us who tried to make life hell at every opportunity by complaining about the slightest noise, but we refused to let her dominate our lives and either went on the counter-attack or completely ignored her, depending on our mood. Her life was so bitter and lonely that it was difficult not to have a strange kind of sympathy for her, even while I wrote an epic, unprintable but cathartic poem that envisaged my own part in her painful and grisly demise.

Overall, though, despite a three-night stay in hospital for Natascha at the age of two weeks for a mystery virus, we had no reason to complain. Especially not me – reborn as a father, it turned out that having children had not altered my life as radically as I'd led myself to believe. Football was still there, ticking and kicking away in the background, and life went on around it.

Programme Highlights

Swiss match programmes, at least the ones produced by Grasshoppers and FCZ, were dull, colour-shy affairs in an unwieldy A4 magazine size that made them most useful as improvised seat cushions on cold winter days. This being Switzerland, they had lots of adverts for banks. The Famagusta programme contained one for Credit Suisse, a half-pager that said, 'We like playing passes to FC Zürich. What's your next goal?' I've no idea what it's supposed to mean, but it may have shed some subtle nuance in translation. The full-page one for UBS didn't try the lame football analogy, striving instead for the all-embracing, transparently bogus corporate cliché I can best loosely translate as: 'Now we're concerned about something important. About you.' Yes, UBS was telling its customers they were important. Our account was with UBS, so I'm sure this left me feeling all warm and wanted.

There was also a full-page ad for the dubious beer Feldschlösschen (try ordering one of those at midnight), showing a jubilant, half-dressed team standing and cheering over an ice-cooled giant bucket of the stuff, and the slogan 'Ole Ole Ole... until Feldschlösschen. Life makes you thirsty.' Though it doesn't state that Feldschlösschen makes you headachy after three bottles, and that it also makes you want to go home, drink several pints of water, lie down and never touch alcohol again. To this day I'm convinced that the tastelessness of Swiss beer at that time was a subterfuge government plot to wean the workers off drink. When the team I played for, Wacker Selnau, won the 1998 Zürich Alternative Championship (a league founded on anarchist principles similar to the Wilde Liga in Bielefeld), we drank something entirely different, probably procured on the black market, as the highly protectionist Swiss economy at the time excluded the import of decent beer. In the end, the resulting headaches were much the same, but at least it took us several hours of concerted drinking to get there.

Apart from the ads, the only article of interest was a look back to FCZ knocking Galatasaray out of the 1963 European Cup thanks to the toss of a coin, after a two-legged tie and then a replay in Rome that went to extra-time. There was also a roller-coaster account of how eight away fans had made the away trip to Donetsk that can best be described as a primary-school creative writing project still in its first draft. 'At 7.50am, a little later than scheduled, we landed safely back at Zürich,' concluded the understandably unsigned report, followed by a list naming the eight fans who made the trip and discovered that in Donetsk, 'most of the streets are lined with trees'.

The Final Sell-Out

It's possible, of course, to renounce everything in your life and take the righteous course back to responsible living. It would be nice to report that after living in Switzerland, we returned to the UK to set up a co-operative community run on anarchist principles of mutual aid, whereby we lived on a self-sufficient organic farm outside of the system, consuming only renewable energy, working the land by hand and travelling by horse or bicycle.

In reality, we moved to the US, the home of naked, all-consuming ambition, where making money and trampling on the weak is not just an unfortunate by-product of capitalism, but a way of life to be proud of. With our two kids and our two vehicles, we settled down in our first owned home in a faceless suburb on the doorstep of the world's most reviled government. It was as if, having gone through the first stages of selling out, I was unhappy with the half-arsed way I'd gone about it, so now I was going to go the whole hog.

And, unlike most US cities, Washington DC did at least have its own professional soccer team.

12

Reconciliation

Boston United v. Stevenage Borough, Nationwide Conference, Monday, 8 April 2002

How Books Are Supposed to Conclude

Take any writing course, or talk to a literary agent trying to flog your sorry prose, and they'll tell you that all good books and films must end with redemption and reconciliation. The main character must have *learned* something for the whole writing, printing and page-turning process to be legitimate. Never mind that this rarely happens in real life. Somehow, in the realm of literature and celluloid, we writers must condescend to show you readers that we are here on earth to move forwards and progress. So the central figure starts out as a woman-hater, or a Jew-hater, or something reprehensible, and by the end they have realised the error of their ways and learned to love women, Jews, blacks, Muslims, themselves, and in the process have become well-meaning, well-rounded and valuable members of society. Hurrah! And you, the reader, apparently like that too, because any time I've deviated from these rules in my various speculative scripts, novels and short stories, I've been told by the publishing industry's many experts that they simply 'won't sell'.

Even the memoir of someone who considers himself to be reasonably well rounded, if not necessarily an indispensable member of society, must conclude in this way. Even when writing about something as inconsequential and as parallel to the relevance of meaningful human endeavours as sport, I'm afraid we must finish up with a satisfactory closure, whereby you end the book with the sense of having gone on a bit of a journey, albeit one that mainly encompassed various football stadiums in Lincolnshire, Scotland, London and German-speaking mainland Europe. All that swearing, crying, kissing, hoping, despairing, loving, dying and breeding had to take us somewhere other than to another turnstile in another ground, hadn't it? Well, of course. And you have to agree that the next appropriate stop on our minor odyssey through life and football would be on a Monday night in south Lincolnshire, watching non-league football.

We Are Family (Sort of)

For the first time in over 25 years, my dad, my mum, my sister (Carol) and I went to watch a football match together. I couldn't date exactly when the last time the four of us had been in a stadium, side by side, but it was sometime around the mid-1970s, when my sister was still not quite too teenage to disdain a Saturday afternoon where she might conceivably be seen in the company of her parents and younger brother, doing something as uncool as watching football. It only happened once or twice a season, and I can only remember one specific game, a 2–0 Lincoln City home victory over Workington, when we went with family friends. The eldest boy of the family was in her class, and they spent the entire 90 minutes discussing what they liked and hated about their various teachers, and it annoyed the hell out of me that they weren't interested in the game. I remember thinking, *When are they going to shut up?*, but they didn't, at all.

In the '70s Carol professed to support Celtic and Liverpool, mainly to annoy me even more and – coincidentally, of course – because they were winning almost everything in their respective leagues. When they won, she gloated, but when they lost, and I gloated back, she completely ignored me or said she didn't care about football anyway. She fancied Kenny Dalglish and put posters of him all over her bedroom wall, and that annoyed me too. It wasn't like she ever actually watched him play, or watched anybody play for that matter, apart from her occasional enforced two-hour sojourns at Sincil Bank. She just fancied him. Huh, typical girl.

By the turn of the century, though, she was genuinely interested in football, living in Leeds and, properly enough, being a Leeds United fan, with no trace of her previous incarnation as an undedicated follower of British football's two most successful sides of the 1970s. Kenny Dalglish now meant the same to her as he did to millions of other football fans – he was just a miserable old Scot. Liverpool had become another way of saying 'expensive but mediocre', like a number of their Premier League counterparts (Leeds, at least, were about to become something more original – expensive but crap). Celtic, if you could be bothered to look, were still regularly Scottish champions, albeit with the help of, on average, maybe one and a half Scotsmen per season. My sister, meanwhile, actually went to watch Leeds play when her schedule allowed – she was managing a pub, so evenings and weekends were mainly occupied – and was the proud owner of not one, but two LUFC replica shirts (home and away) bearing the name of that shining young model of professional behaviour, Alan Smith.

My mum had gamely gone to watch Lincoln on her own once or twice after I left home, but was put off for decades after an unfortunate choice of seat at home to York City one Saturday afternoon. She thought it would be wise to sit at the end of a row close to the exit so that she could beat the crowds on the way out, or if she needed the loo. It was also the seat closest to the refreshments stand, so the whole afternoon people were pushing backwards and forwards past her to buy a cup of tea and a Wagon Wheel. Eventually, she let out her anger on some innocent punter, telling him that no, she didn't want to move her legs again, thank you, and he responded that it wasn't his bloody fault that she'd decided to sit there, luv. The only time she goes now is when I drag her along, and even then, she usually makes the case for a stroll around the cathedral grounds instead.

My dad, like me, will still go and watch almost anything if he has company, and so didn't need much persuading to go and see Boston v. Stevenage. He wouldn't have gone so far as to *suggest* it, but he certainly wasn't opposed.

Finally, there was me, having to live with the nagging fact that I was from Lincolnshire and had been to Lincoln, Grimsby and both Scunthorpe grounds, all of them several times over, but I had *never been to see Boston United*. There had been one opportunity, years back, when we'd ended up in Boston on a Saturday afternoon and had looked to see if there was a game on. Boston's reserves were at home, and though I was still keen, I couldn't persuade my dad (this was just outside of the jurisdiction of the 'almost anything' cited above).

Now I was living in the US, a long way from the original Boston, but here was an opportunity that might not come again for a long, long time. I knew as soon as I saw the fixture in that morning's paper – one of only a handful of games taking place across the whole country that night – that I had to be there. I had returned to my roots, and I needed closure on my senior Lincolnshire football stadiums.

Never Come Back

Football managers and players know it well: you should never go back to an old club for a second spell if you were successful there the first time around. It may not necessarily work out badly, but it hardly ever turns out better than before. It's never quite the same – the players are all different, as are the club's personnel, and the chemistry that led to that first spell of success will be impossible to replicate. When Colin Murphy came back to Lincoln and led them out of the Conference and back to the Football League, it was a worthy feat, but hardly the same as missing out on promotion to Division Two by one point back in 1982. Yet somehow the lure is irresistible, as though the old stomping ground represents a safety net, where you know that no matter how much you fail, all will be forgiven because everyone still remembers the glory you brought the first time around. You're in the Hall of Legends, and even if you turn incontinent and piss on the floor, someone will clean it up with a kindly smile, and no more will be said as they lead you back to your plinth for exhibition.

All through my teenage years, I moaned about Lincolnshire. I wanted to be seen as Scottish, and taken seriously as Scottish, because

Scottish bands were hip and Lincolnshire bands were... non-existent. I went to Scotland, to my dad's, four or five times a year and came back complaining that whereas Scotland was beautiful, Lincolnshire was flat. Where were Lincolnshire's great works of literature? Scottish football fans were feral and true, while Lincolnshire fans were fickle moaners who could barely raise a song. In Scotland, despite the weather, people were friendly and funny and, when appropriate, displayed a brilliant, savage wit. In Lincolnshire people couldn't be bothered to do anything but atrophy. That, at least, was my perception. I couldn't wait to leave.

God, how I must have gone on about it, and how I wish I could go back and edit some of the things I went on about back then. In short, I thought that I was better than Lincolnshire, and Lincolnshire people. I was going to go off to that smart university place and be dead clever.

In later years, when I was working in London, my mum would often ask me if I fancied coming back to live in Lincolnshire one day to 'settle down'. This idea was so ridiculous to me that I'd scorn her for asking, and couldn't understand why she wasted her breath. 'Never,' I said. 'Never ever ever ever ever, so don't even think about it.' Which she didn't, until she asked the next time I was home, or when she was down visiting me in London and wondering aloud how anyone could possibly live with 'all that filth and traffic and noise'.

Gradually, I started to care less and less about 'being Scottish', recognising that whatever picture I held in my head of the Scottish character was probably both idealised and thoroughly inaccurate, and that it had absolutely nothing to do with me as a person. My dad will still maintain that my 'Celt genes' influence certain aspects of my behaviour,[1] but as it's not something that's easy or worthwhile to prove, then we should let it go. In the meantime, instead of telling people I'd just met that I was Scottish, I told them that my parents were Scottish. I grew up in England. It was like admitting to a part of my past I'd once considered shameful, but now I had come to terms with it. I became almost defiant about it. 'I grew up in Lincolnshire, okay? Anyone got a problem with that?'

1. Not sure which ones. Stoicism? Losing? Loving the rain?

The next step went beyond accepting my past and the fact that Lincolnshire had a far greater influence on my life than those unquantifiable Celt genes. I started to become interested in the county's history, and began collecting books on Lincolnshire folklore, oral histories, Lincolnshire folk songs, what the Romans left behind, and which villages sprang up when and where and why. I had my mum post six Ordnance Survey maps to me of the entire county, and I laid them out on the floor, studying the roads and places I knew, or where I'd once played football or village cricket. More astonishing still were the places that I didn't know. Although as a family we'd taken walks in the countryside perhaps every second weekend, I'd only a vague idea of where we'd been. Now I saw on the map Roman roads, Viking burial mounds and monastic ruins, as well as intriguing place names. I couldn't believe that when we'd done an O-level course module on local history, I didn't care about anything besides handing the project in as quickly as possible and getting it out of the way. Education is criminally wasted on the young.

Two days after the Boston United v. Stevenage Borough game, Tim Bastard and I took a road trip around Lincolnshire. 'What the fuck are you doing that for?' asked everyone we knew. It was hard to explain. Like me, Tim usually only went back to Lincolnshire to see his family. Like me, he'd moaned about the county during his youth, and how he couldn't wait to leave and explore the big, exciting, sophisticated world beyond.[2] And now, like me, he was fascinated by the idea of Lincolnshire and what it meant to us, both now and then.

This is not to say that we viewed the place any less critically than before. We just wanted to view it from a different angle, hopefully to see more than apathy, potato fields, alienating RAF compounds and greasy bikers who liked beating up 'pretty boys'. And I suppose it wasn't a bad excuse to try out some countryside pubs and sample their ales, while banging on about the past with the wisdom of all our considered retrospective insights.

As we drove from town to town, through village after village, from pub to pub, musing aloud in fields about barely visible barrows and

2. See *Small Town England* by Tim Bradford (Ebury Press, 2010).

ditches and pointing up the county's hitherto hidden qualities, it's possible that we were subconsciously preparing ourselves for turning into old farts who wanted to settle down somewhere a little quieter than, say, London or Washington DC. Not necessarily Lincolnshire per se, but somewhere like it. A place where our kids could complain that nothing ever happened, and that the people were all backwards, and that they couldn't wait to leave for the proper world. And then we could spend the next 20 years asking them if they didn't fancy coming back one day to live there for good and settle down.

And increasingly there had been a part of me that every Saturday morning, at around 10am US Eastern Time, had started to wish that I could, right at that moment, be taking my seat at Sincil Bank, in the stand that had replaced the old open terrace, with the view of the South Common ahead of me and, high to my left, the cathedral, magnificent as ever on the hill by the castle, overlooking the city and the stadium. In my head, we were living a few miles outside of Lincoln, in a village a bit like the one my mum lives in now, with a church and a friendly local pub. I'd maybe dropped off the girls at my mum's for the afternoon. The wife had gone shopping. I finished my Mars Bar and read the match programme, or the *Deranged Ferret* fanzine I'd contributed to years ago, and then looked up to see the two teams ready to start another game, the visitors probably Torquay or Wrexham. I felt the profoundest inner contentment. And then… *Oh fuck, 1–0 down already. Bloody rubbish. I don't know why we bloody bother, really I don't.*

I think it was the last bit I *really* wanted.

Boston v. Stevenage: How It Happened (Bear with Me Here)

It may not seem a huge deal that a family of four would go to watch a football match together, and in a way it wasn't. We were sitting around in my mum's living room, wondering aloud what to do on a Monday evening in Lincolnshire. That weekend, we had all met at my cousin Luke's wedding in Leeds. I came from the US, my dad from the South of France (where he'd retired to an isolated farmhouse with his second wife for a life of perpetual curmudgeonry), my mum from Lincolnshire, and my sister was already there. After the wedding my dad was staying at his sister-in-law's in Lincolnshire for a few days to look up old friends. My sister came back to my mum's to spend a few days with me before I flew home.

That Monday afternoon my dad had come round like a moping teenager to just sort of hang out at his ex-wife's, and said he had no plans for the evening. And so we thought we should do something together, which wasn't something that had ever gone well. In the 1970s this meant trips to stately homes (I would always throw up, usually in the car because I was too afraid to admit I was feeling ill), Sunday walks in the Wolds (my sister in a perma-huff, walking either 100 yards ahead or behind), a day in Skegness but with none of the fun (I wasn't allowed to waste money in the arcades), or weekends with relatives or family friends my parents would complain about all the way home. Whatever the trip, my sister and I always, always wanted to stay at home.

I proposed Boston United v. Stevenage Borough. Boston was a club that had been striving for Football League membership since the 1970s, when they won the Northern Premier League a number of times, but their league applications had always been rejected by the stitch-up that was re-election. Now they were on the verge of automatic promotion to the fourth division. 'It should be quite exciting,' I reckoned out loud to a reluctant gang of three. There were only six games left until the end of the season, and they were just ahead of their nearest competitors, Dagenham and Redbridge.

My dad gave a doubtful smile, my sister didn't say anything, and my mum said, 'You must be kidding.' Someone suggested the cinema, but there was nothing on that all four of us wanted to watch. Going out for a meal on Monday night didn't seem right either. After all, we'd just spent the entire weekend sitting around and stuffing ourselves at a wedding. There was a short silence. I could *feel* Boston United v. Stevenage Borough hanging ripe from a low branch, just waiting to be plucked. What else was there to do? My mum looked at me, laughed and caved in. 'Alright, let's go to the football,' she said, and immediately I set about laying out the timetable we'd need to get down there, park, find a fish and chip shop, and settle down with the match programme in a decent seat.

Boston v. Stevenage: Why It Was Significant

It wasn't just that we were going to a game, the four of us. There could hardly have been any occasions at all since 1979 when we were sitting in the same room together, alone, as that original family unit of four. And yet, despite a bitter 10-year battle over maintenance and other money matters, including court appearances, court summons, never-ending mutual recriminations, hurt and slander, sneaking lawyers, threats and sleepless nights, here were my mum and dad chatting away, drinking afternoon tea and eating cake, and I was probably reading the paper, and my sister was probably waiting for something bad to happen, but the worst that ever happened now between my mum and dad was the occasionally bitchy, back-stabbing comment under the guise of a humorous remark. And for years, at least until my mum lost a ton of weight, my dad would confide in me, after seeing my mum, that she was looking older and had put on weight. And then my mum would confide in me that my dad was looking older and had put on weight. Perhaps 'confide' is the wrong word, given that I would delightedly tell one parent that the other had said exactly the same thing (neither thought this at all amusing).

My mum and my sister had had so many fights down the years that this book would need a separate appendix to list them all. One way or another, we'd all had our moments, like in any family, although in some families it's possible that the rifts we had experienced would have been well beyond repair. Family members, though, however much they are thrown together and forced into each other's company and compelled to make an effort to get along despite a million differences of opinion, have an amazing capacity to heal. Arguments that in friendship would have simply meant a permanent severing of all contact are, within a family, somehow either forgotten or forgiven, or both. Apart from the extremely dysfunctional cases (rather than the averagely dysfunctional cases that most families are, like ours), families can *correct themselves*. Once you get used to the idea that, short of changing your identity and moving to El Salvador, you cannot swap or drop your family, you learn to love it, albeit in a qualified way. Families are a need more than a want. Your family will exasperate you, baffle you and drive you to tears, but it's painful as hell to imagine what it would be like if they suddenly weren't there. Oh, go on – say it. Just like your football team.

Here we were, sitting around in my mum's small living room, laughing and joking, taking the piss out of each other and getting ready to go to a football match. It had taken well over two decades of divorce, tears and recriminations to get us back to this point, where we were all finally accepting the other three family members for what they were, and so were now relaxed enough to sit in each other's company without the sense of an imminent storm. It didn't feel unnatural, and I didn't even think about it much until afterwards – I was probably too focused on the game and getting there on time. It's also possible that my mum, dad and sister all felt and saw it in completely different ways. And unless you're actually in our family, it's not an event of much significance. Still, in 1981 or 1984, or even as late as 1995, it would not have seemed possible. With compromise, calm and the knowledge that we would all be together for a limited time, the reunion, if you like, had been possible. And not just that, but satisfying too.

Especially as we went to a football match. Wahay, York Street finally crossed off my list!

Okay, to the Game at Last

It was 0–0.

Oh Dear

Even 0–0 games have their stories, although this one's mostly told. My anal planning served us well, despite protests from everyone else that we were leaving way too early. We drove 40 miles down to Boston, my dad telling stories of the countryside he'd travelled for years on his rounds, and at last I was an attentive listener, thanks to my new-found interest in all things Lincolnshire. He even knew when strange kinks or unpredictable bends were coming up, and over-helpfully pointed them out to the driver (myself), making me feel like I was 17 again. It's peculiar how parents never stop being parents.

Boston were close to gaining promotion to the Football League for the first time in their history, and when we got there we found that, according to the match programme, 'on Police and Safety advice' (not sure why 'Safety' is capitalised; perhaps it was the fabled and caped Captain Safety who oversees all toddlers' playgrounds in the US, who flew to Boston, his or her arm raised and fist clenched, and delivered the warning), the club had decided to make the main Finn Forest Stand all ticket, 'as we have not got computerised turnstiles'.

Could someone perhaps have *counted* the number of tickets sold to see when the stand was full? Apparently not. Instead of having two lines of paying customers that led straight into the stand, there was now a single line of fans queuing for entrance into a tiny room, where an elderly woman with a biscuit tin sat using a pocket calculator to work out the cost of four times £9.50. Welcome to the nearly big time. Consequently, kick-off was delayed by 10 minutes to let everyone in.

In a column at the time, I wrote:

> Although the 0–0 draw that followed was absorbing enough due to its speed, its hardness and the need for a positive result, the unremitting tendency to welt the ball downfield through the air betrayed nervous legs that would rather play safe for a draw than risk a mistake and the loss of a point. The Stevenage defence sucked the ball in and spat it back out without ever looking in much trouble, while news came through of a Dagenham victory elsewhere, leaving the clubs level on points but Boston ahead on goal difference. The 3,800 home fans sang sporadically and without conviction.

Programme Highlights: 'We Know Where You Live'

In the programme that day, general manager and club secretary John Blackwell wrote in his column about the 'hurt and distress' caused to Boston United by 'the anonymous woman' who had written to the local paper, the *Boston Target*, criticising the facilities at the club's Study Support Centre, a noble club endeavour to provide extra education for local kids who had fallen behind at school. 'I am asking the person who wrote the letter to come forward, name yourself to the club (although we know who it is) and let us show you the facilities, meet the people concerned and get the true facts and figures regarding our Study Support Centre.'

Although she might want to bring security, or at least let her family know where she's gone.

The woman's 'misleading letter' is mentioned elsewhere in the programme, and together with the biscuit tin incident illustrates the vicissitudes of running a small-town, small-time club with an important place in its local community. 'Many thanks for all your e-mails and kind comments praising our coverage of the Yeovil and Southport games,' wrote BBC Radio Lincolnshire's Scott Dalton. At this level, people still listen and care. In a way, it was a refreshing change to get my ticket and change from a woman staffing a biscuit tin, like I was entering the Sunday school tombola. It wasn't professional, but it was rustic. It was very Lincolnshire.

On the other hand, I can understand why the letter writer to the *Boston Target* wished to remain anonymous. It was cowardly, perhaps, but you can see from the reaction how people in small organisations respond to criticism. Would anyone have even noticed if the club had ignored the letter completely? Would Manchester United have gone out of their way to harangue the author of a critical letter to the *Manchester Evening News*? It reminded me of the time a friend and I, as teenagers, wrote a letter to the *Market Rasen Mail*, complaining about being unnecessarily hassled on the mean streets of Rasen by an aggressive copper merely for standing still (it counted as 'loitering', although loitering was about the only thing to do in Market Rasen).

They didn't print the letter, but the editor – whose main achievement was to keep news of any interest or consequence well away from the pages of his crappy rag – was kind enough to show it to his mate, a police officer I'd played football with a few times. The cop in turn came up to us in the pub one night to tell us in forceful language that we had a bloody cheek writing such a complaint, and that if he'd found us standing still on the pavement, then he'd have reacted in exactly the same way.

If I were to seriously entertain the idea of returning to my roots, with an idealised vision of cosy Saturday afternoons at Sincil Bank, I'd do well to remember people like that. There are very few secrets in a small town. There's no chance of you changing your name to Mr White.

Love and Unity in the Finn Forest Stand

With the gutsy slog of Boston versus Stevenage being played out before us, there was little need for the four of us to talk to each other, besides muttered observations on the game or the people around us. It felt comfortable. Although I always missed my wife and daughters like crazy when we were separated by 3,000 miles of Atlantic Ocean, this evening with my 'old' family felt gratifyingly familiar, when it could so easily have felt strange and awkward. The fact that it had not been planned in advance was definitely a help, because no one had had the time to build up a sense of apprehension. And if we had gone out for a meal, the obligation to make conversation might have led us to places we were not yet ready to visit. The past, for example.

In the Finn Forest Stand, though, there was no question of going there. Football is all about the present, and the immediate intensity of the game taking place before you mostly keeps you rooted in the here and now. All previous defeats and indignities are forgotten or forgiven, even if only temporarily, when a fine move or a 30-yard strike allows for the unleashing of that immediate *sensation*, like watching a spectacular firework. Sometimes I think the whole point of football, if it has one at all, is to allow that moment of joyous celebration to kick you into remembering that you're alive. Or is the goal a transitory trick that fools you into a momentary joy from which you then have to execute a depressing climbdown?

That there were no goals for Boston on that evening strikes me as appropriate, at least for the four members of our family. My guess is that while we were watching the game, we were also all involved in our own contemplations. They might have been no more profound than 'It's nice that the four of us have come to watch the game together after all these years.' Or they might have been along the lines of 'If we hadn't had the intervening 25 years apart, we'd probably all have killed each other by now.' The point is that we were there, for better or worse, sitting together. In the background was a game of football. Its individual kicks and grunts were forgettable, but its actual staging in that time and place were now a part of our history.

13

Success

Major League Soccer All-Stars v. Manchester United, Friendly, Wednesday, 27 July 2011, New Jersey

'To burn always with this hard, gem-like flame, to maintain this ecstasy, is success in life.' Walter Pater, *The Renaissance*

'How can they say my life isn't a success? Have I not for more than sixty years got enough to eat and escaped being eaten?' Logan Pearsall Smith, *Afterthoughts*

These two opposing views of achievement attest to the fact that success is, of course, relative. By the time I watched this game in 2011, I had been a successful stay-at-home dad for 15 years. I had successfully published a book of short stories that no one read.[1] I was still scoring goals, albeit for a men's over-35 team. I had enough to eat, and I had escaped being eaten. If that sounds like a complaint, you've misunderstood Logan Pearsall Smith. But to always burn like a hard, gem-like flame? Bloody hell, that sounds like a lot of hard work, even if you're somehow maintaining a state of ecstasy. Aren't you supposed to *enjoy* success?

In 1984 Billy Bragg put it another way. With my mate Drew I interviewed him for the Birmingham University student rag *Redbrick*. We were the newspaper's music editors (unelected positions that afforded us the right to be obnoxious in ink), and Billy was riding a wave of popularity that saw him touring the country on an eclec-

1. Taking 'no one' not quite literally, but I'm rounding the figure down by formulating the ratio of world population to world sales of *For Whom the Ball Rolls*.

tic bill with Japanese musical performance artistes The Frank Chickens and gynaecologist-turned-country-singer Hank Wangford. We asked Bragg if he thought people were getting bored with his one-man/one-guitar format. 'No, they're getting more fucking interested if anything,' was his testy response. 'I'm satisfied with what I'm doing, I'm making a living. In my terms, this is success. I don't want to be seen as a chartie like Wham! and Spandau.'[2]

I was 19 years old and didn't really agree with the singer. I know this because my mum proudly kept a scrapbook of all my early student articles, which were mostly about music. This scrapbook is now safely in my possession, but my greatest fear is that I will die and it will fall into the wrong hands. It's like Bill Hicks's routine about him getting killed in a car accident, and then his parents coming to clean out his flat and finding his massive stash of porn. This scrapbook, however, is much more shameful than a video collection that Hicks described as including *Clam-Lappers*, volumes 1 to 27. I should really destroy it, but it serves to remind me that as a teenager, I knew nothing, and really wanted to tell the world all about the vastness of the nothing I knew. Also, I'm too vain to burn anything that has my name at the bottom of it in bold black print. So I'm running the risk that the public discovery of this scrapbook could destroy my colossal legacy as a writer of obscure football books and a blog about how amateur referees get yelled at every weekend.

Back to the pop charts of the 1980s, and my awkward, indie-devotional writings on that particular subject. This was my profound and important manifesto: if only singers like Billy Bragg had a platform on *Top of the Pops* and non-stop daytime Radio 1 airplay, then they would replace 'charties' like Spandau and Wham! as the singers of choice among the country's youth. Not only would people now realise that they had been blessed with the same good taste as myself (and how extremely grateful they would be for that), they would also

2. When I say 'we' interviewed Billy Bragg, what I mean is that Drew asked the questions and I took notes, because I was too shy to speak. In between songs at a concert broadcast on BBC radio a few weeks later, Bragg referred to the interview because we'd talked about Subbuteo, and he was getting all nostalgic. 'One of my favourite interviews recently was with a little geezer from a fanzine...' he started. No mention that 'the little geezer' (Drew) was with 'an awkward, taciturn, frightened-looking geezer' too.

follow the political goals of their new idols. Together we'd kick Maggie Thatcher out of power with consciousness-raising protest songs, dancing and singing along to great music all the way.

So I thought success for folk singers like Bragg who could write funny, political songs (even though their voices weren't up to much) meant being high in the Hit Parade, as my mum still called it. My sister's former flatmate Melanie once said, in response to my sister's complaint that she had just played Toni Basil's 'Mickey' for the 34th consecutive time, 'You can't criticise my taste in music – all the records I buy get to number one, so they must be the best.'

It's not just Melanie's taste that is beyond criticism, but her logic too. She *knew* success. Success meant being at the top. Success meant being at number one. The best-selling single song that week in the UK. The best-selling, the best-sold. In capitalism, there is no other criterion for success. On your terms, Billy, you can call yourself a success. Sure, go ahead. But will Melanie buy herself a copy of 'A New England' and play it 34 times back to back, marvelling at the cleverness of the line 'It's wrong to wish on space hardware'? No, she won't, because she's never fucking heard of you. And she's never fucking heard of you because you're not at number one, you loser.

Which diverts us from the topic of my embarrassing and deluded righteousness as a truly odious music critic, and nicely on to Manchester United.

So this game took place in New Jersey, just across the river from New York City – ultra-capitalism's first stop – in a purpose-built soccer stadium owned by the Red Bull corporation. To all intents and purposes, though, it took place in New York itself. It wasn't a game at all, really, it was the focal point of a week of 'events' vaguely related to football. Manchester United, for the second year running, were the guests of Major League Soccer (MLS) for the MLS All-Star game.

All-Star games are a big deal in US sports. The leagues who run them say that they are a way of acknowledging the prowess, skills and endeavour of their best-performing players. There may be the tiniest bit of truth in that, but in reality the All-Star game is about selling the sport, selling the league and selling the players. In terms of competitiveness on the field, there is no game with less meaning. A pre-season friendly between Alfreton Town and Clipstone Welfare has 10 times more meaning than the MLS All-Star game. On this particular night, MLS is trying to sell its league and players to an enduringly sceptical US public. Manchester United are here to extend its market reach. Essentially, one is trying to use the other to win over the purchasing power of the same group of fans. Or 'customer market segment', if you prefer, and both US sports executives and Manchester United generally do prefer the language of being up their own commercial arses.

As it does every year, MLS strained to endow this game with significance. In the match programme, writer Simon Borg was tasked with telling the spectator why this game mattered. I felt for him. He had rent to pay and a fridge to fill, I'm sure. And there he was, commissioned with selling a burst balloon and a slice of stale cake in a knackered portaloo to someone used to attending celebrity weddings on a Pacific island. If I ever meet him, I will congratulate him for his sincere effort to fulfil a nigh impossible task, armed with only the 26 letters of the alphabet. He scrapped away like a technically limited bunch of thrown-together no-names playing one of the biggest clubs in the world.

The headline was honoured with block capitals: 'REMATCH SHOWS WHAT ALL-STAR GAME IS REALLY ABOUT: COMPETITION'. 'Manchester United again?' began Borg. 'That was the reaction of some when the Red Devils were announced as the opponent in the 2011 All-Star game. But those are the people that don't understand why the MLS All-Star Game has become the best all-star game in all of US professional sports: because it's a real competition.'

That's true. Get someone to manufacture a trophy, and the game becomes a 'real' competition, in that it's not a more abstract, computer-based competition like FIFA 18 or Fantasy Premier League. Alfreton Town and Clipstone Welfare could just as easily get the home team's left-back, an apprentice metal-worker, to smelt down some old five-pence pieces and forge a cup. Now the two teams are no longer playing a pre-season friendly, they are battling it out in early July for the Bob's Chippy East Midlands Challenge Trophy.

Without a piece of silverware as an incentive, Wayne Rooney and Javier Hernández, for example, would not have looked at the MLS All-Star trophy and said to each other, 'We've *got* to have that. Yes, we really, really have to have that cup in the Old Trafford trophy room. We'll put it right next to the three European Cups. Tonight, we have to *compete*. Enough of climbing up the Empire State Building, sampling the Manhattan nightlife, boat trips up and down the Hudson, the musicals on Broadway and the multi-faceted culture, cuisine and architecture of the amazing Big Apple. It's time to get serious about soccer.'

It wasn't just the trophy that would get the players going, though, argued Borg. 'After Chicharito & Co. handed the MLS Select team a sound 5–2 defeat last summer,' he said, 'there were few true MLS fans who didn't want another crack at Sir Alex Ferguson's side right after the final whistle.' He then post-supposed a series of 'what if?' questions, such as 'What if ex-Manchester United idol David Beckham [had been] fully fit to play against his old club?' These were presumably the questions that 'true' MLS fans were asking 'right after the final whistle'. The naysayers, on the other hand (and I was probably among them), were dooming the whole idea with their typically negative analyses. Borg didn't post-suppose what *they* were saying, but it would have been along the lines of 'Our best players humiliated again in a meaningless exhibition game. What was the point?'

Borg bravely ploughed on in his quest to imbue the game with competitive pedigree. 'Along with all the [imaginary] questions,' he wrote, 'there was also the pinch of regret that a great opportunity had passed for MLS to show that its collection of All-Stars, gathered together at the last minute, could defeat – and perhaps even outplay – mighty Manchester United.' A win could have 'sent another loud message to the world establishment coming on the heels of the USA's performance at the 2010 World Cup. This year the statement can be made. In a bigger way.'

As some people[3] say in the United States of America, 'HELL YEAH!'

If the column had finished there, I don't think anyone on the pro-

3. Drunk fraternity boys.

gramme's editorial board would have complained. Borg was on a roll, though, and there was no stopping him. 'The 2011 match will be held in the biggest media market in the country,' he went on (not really sure what that means, but 'biggest' must be best, so let's skip on). 'If the MLS All-Stars can pull off the upset of [*sic*] the English Premier League champs, it could make larger waves than if it had happened in Houston [in 2010].' If they can, if they can, if they can, scrunch your eyes closed and wish, wish, wish, and it might come true. We are, after all, on the same continent as Disneyland. Press the point home – one last rallying call for a meaning to this game! We're nearly at the finishing line with our arms aloft. We're cheering you on, Simon, you and your unlimited stamina.

'This is a must-win. Yes, a must-win.' Yes! 'The last crack at the Red Devils. In a sports landscape that is becoming known for overlooking what fans want, MLS has handed the league's real fans the grudge match they wanted. And you are here.'

It's a grudge match now – do you hear? Are you angry, *true* MLS fan, about that 5–2 defeat last year? Does it still rankle? Show how *passionate* you are about MLS then, get behind this randomly assembled coterie of mainly mediocre talent and let them know that they must win. They *must*. Because if they don't... they will have lost. The absence of success cannot be tolerated. It's neither American nor United Mancunian.

A Revolutionary Idea – 'Accept Defeat as Part of the Sport!'

The Spanish coach Vicente del Bosque knows plenty about success. He led Spain to the 2010 World Cup and the 2012 European Championship titles. Yet in a remarkably sane interview after his retirement, he questioned the media hyperbole when covering football, and made a plea for a fresh perspective on the importance of winning. Talking just after the 2016 European Championships, del Bosque said that after Spain beat the Czechs and Turkey in their first two group games, even a critical radio station was saying, 'We have the best national team, there's no team better than us. Then when we lost to Croatia in the last minute [in Spain's third group game], everything switched back to the negative. This extremism! Either you have to put up with the most over-the-top praise, or the complete opposite. How I wish that people would take things in a more sporting fashion.'

'So you're saying that we simply have to accept victories and defeats?' the reporter asked him. 'Yes!' del Bosque responded. 'The unsporting attitudes put across by some media are very bad for young people. The media believe that only victory counts. Before the European Championships, someone on the radio said that we had a duty to win. A duty! We have a duty to do everything to win. But there's no duty to win. Or again recently, I heard this praise on the radio for the Italians: *Look how patriotically they reacted to defeat! How many tears they shed!*

'Of course it was painful for us to lose. But do we have to cry to show that we love our national team and our country? Seriously? That doesn't make any sense. You don't have to cry because of a defeat. That's sport! Defeats are simply a part of the game. When I was at the draw for the European Championships in Paris and all the coaches posed for a photo, I was thinking: *Only one of us is going to win, and the other 23 are going to have to put up with being labelled losers*.'[4]

This reminded me of my own message put out on Twitter, just as the Championships were about to start and every hack in the universe was posting links to their lengthy tournament previews. I've no idea why anyone bothers writing these and who bothers reading them – they're forgotten the moment that the first ball is kicked, and unless someone predicted that Portugal would beat France 1–0 in the final after extra-time, I doubt that anyone went back to check whose previews were even vaguely pertinent.

Anyway, my own forecast went like this: 'My Euro 2016 preview: 24 teams will start, only one will win. That team will bounce up and down holding trophy aloft, looking pleased.' (It garnered the massive total of two 'likes' and four re-tweets, but relatively speaking it was a success – that's far more attention than most of my tweets get.) This all seems massively, overwhelmingly obvious. So that begs the next question: why does the media react so incredulously, so harshly, with

4. *Süddeutsche Zeitung*, 16/17 July 2016.

such 'extremism', as del Bosque puts it, when England, for example, lose to Iceland? Or Germany lose to France? 'Oh my God, what went wrong? What are the answers? How can we do better next time?'

A game of football was lost. It was always going to happen, except for the one team in 24 that wins it. Why are you so surprised? Why does it matter?

In truth, most fans do not see such a defeat as the tragedy that the journalists want to portray. No one's expecting them to see the game as some kind of success, along the lines of 'Well, England scored a goal against Iceland, so I'm happy with that.' Here's what really happened, though: millions of England supporters got up the next morning and continued with their lives. Was there a mild sensation of melancholy for a day or so? I can't say. There seemed to be a great deal of dark-humoured resignation among the English people I called (concerned as I was, I wanted to know how they were coping), mainly along the lines of it being a punishment for the Brexit vote four days earlier. No mass suicides, though.

It was the same in Brazil after the 1–7 home defeat in the 2014 World Cup semi-final against Germany. Media coverage centred on the imminent collapse of civilisation, because apparently Brazilians care more about football than anything else in the world – that had been as far as much foreign media coverage had gone up until that point. How important this tournament was to Brazil. True, there were massive social and economic problems for the vast majority of its citizens, and there were quite a few questions asked about the costs of staging the tournament and the building of new stadiums at a time when the money would have been better spent on health, education and housing. Questions about the razing of favelas, with the response that the clearances were to make way for new infrastructure. But that was precisely why the World Cup was so, so important to Brazilians, you see, because if everything else in their lives was so poor and desperate, at least they might be cheered up by winning the World Cup (no word on why they weren't still happy about the previous five triumphs). The sticking plaster of success on a mountain of heaving misery.

Yet when they lost 1–7, the journalists who scouted around town looking for the mass of inconsolable Brazilians found only shrugs of resignation. 'Life's shit, what can you do?' It turned out that people were still concerned about the social and economic issues, and that these were in fact much more important than a game of football. It could also have been that they knew their football, and had been watching Brazil's defence carefully throughout the tournament. It was clear that a hiding by a good team like Germany was long overdue.

A Spanish friend texted me the day after the 2010 World Cup Final: 'I am the happiest man alive!' One year later, he was in the middle of a bitter divorce and his world had collapsed around him. His fall reminded me of a piece I'd once written for *When Saturday Comes* about a study that proved a nation of people whose country had won a major tournament would, one year on, be no happier overall than any other country. Why should they? Sport does not have that power. It's about the thrill of the moment, not about strengthening the spirit of humanity.

The Meaning of Fireworks – A Theory

I happened to be in New York on a short family break when the All-Star game was being played. For several years, I'd been covering the US game for a variety of publications and websites, but a combination of waning ambition and the increasing unwillingness of media bodies to pay journalists for their work meant that my career, in this respect, had stalled. It had not been a success. I was now occupied more by working as a youth team coach and a referee, and was still running an old-men's team that coughed and stumbled its way around the rutted fields of Maryland on a Sunday morning. I would, though, occasionally ask for accreditation to write the odd piece for the *When Saturday Comes* site, which I'd churn out after the match, and which would be edited and published by the time I woke up the next morning.

Among us low-paid and generally denigrated enthusiasts who used to make up the bulk of the press box at games in the US (and probably still do), there are a handful of quite famous sports writers who occasionally pontificate about soccer. The days when they would be wheeled out by their editors to flame the sport and mock it as communist, feminine and un-American over a column of 700 entertaining but largely fallacious words are thankfully over. That week, George Vecsey of the *New York Times* had done MLS the favour of trying to talk the game up. You can see how this might have happened. The league badgers the paper about its negligent coverage of the game. A soccer-sympathetic writer like Vecsey feels bad for them and agrees to write a piece. And then he pens some thoughts that leave him open to attack from cynical US-based British hacks like myself, sitting around in the media room eating free chocolate brownies and scoffing at the idea that there is any point at all to the fucking All-Star game.

I did enjoy the occasion of the All-Star game. I played in the media tournament somewhere in Manhattan and got a free shirt and a lovely see-through medal for being on the winning team. We beat a team with Greg Lalas in it, Alexi's brother. Greg once played a handful of games in MLS, and he didn't seem any better than the rest of us, allowing me the delusional thought, *Yeah, sure I coulda made it here.* I loved being in New York, but then I always love being in New York. Who doesn't? I also loved sitting around with the éminence grise of US soccer journalism, Paul Gardner, swearing at MLS and laughing at George Vecsey. I think that the Red Bull Arena, despite its name and owner, is one of the best soccer stadiums in the US. Ultimately, though, I had to write about the football, and the football that night wasn't good. These are the opening two paragraphs I came up with right after the final whistle:

> Respected *New York Times* sports journalist George Vecsey previewed last night's Major League All-Star game against Manchester United in New Jersey as an 'increasingly meaningful liaison'. He was far from alone in the US media this week in trying to talk up as a significant challenge a game that's just one more stop on United's brand-enhancing, cash-generating US tour. But any question of the game being an encounter from which we could glean anything other than shallow conclusions about MLS or Manchester United (apart from confirming that signing Ashley

> Young will not bring them any closer to Barcelona this season) was moot by half-time, with United almost walking their way to a 2–0 lead on nicely worked goals by Anderson and Park Ji-Sung.
>
> Dimitar Berbatov added a third shortly after the interval in that casual fashion suggesting he'd rather be ordering a portion of fish and chips, and the usual flood of second-half substitutions rendered the contest as a competitive clash of 11 versus 11 absolutely void of all tension and interest. Danny Welbeck rounded off the scoring with a long-range shot. Any meaning spotted by Vecsey in this liaison must have evaporated in the smoke of the pre-match fireworks, whose sparks and explosions inspired most of the night's biggest cheers, alongside two parachutists landing on the field, and a linesman getting knocked over by the ball. It was one of those crowds where you felt they'd cheer either side scoring. Which is all very nice, but somewhat parallel to the whole point of having two sides at all.

You can argue that the game was an easy target for a quick and sarky column, but in truth I'd tried for several years to work against the image of US soccer as a joke or an inferior product (if you like). And there was nothing I hated more than a European journalist flying over for a voyeuristic glance at the US game and coming out with this kind of writing. I'd also been arguing for a long time, however, that for a league to grow up (and MLS desperately wanted, and still wants, to be seen as a serious, grown-up league), it had to take criticism on board and not be afraid to talk about its problems in a serious, grown-up manner. That was a problem, though. It implies that not everything is a success.

There's little patience in America for people who might think that success takes time. There's also little scope for any definition of success that doesn't involve making money. MLS always refuses to release its accounts, and everybody knows that's because the league is not yet making a profit (though some individual teams are). On the one hand, this lack of disclosure smacks of paranoia and an operative secrecy that cocks a snook at the public's and the media's right to know. Transparency is surely a *good thing*, after all – like democracy and equality. On the other hand, if MLS released its accounts before it has become a profitable concern, you just know what the cry would be from a society that always has an eye out for the short-term gain – 'Failure! You're losing money!' And that cry of glee would be all the more shrill for being applied to the apparently un-American pastime of soccer. 'Look, we told you so, soccer doesn't work here, how many times do we have to prove it?'

This is why an event like the All-Star game might be seen to be important. We send up fireworks, lots of them. The swirls, the explosions, the spirals and the smoke all make this look like an almighty Event. It's like judging the success of the Olympics on its opening ceremony. A country or a league like MLS has to seem capable of Staging the Event. Never mind how much that costs. Never mind how little relation that has to the actual sport. This is visual public relations. And as I observed in the final paragraph of my column, they finished off the night as well:

> There were fireworks after the game too for the couple of thousand who stayed around to watch United pick up the massively prestigious All-Star trophy. It was the least they deserved for having paid well to see a pedestrian exhibition game, and belated compensation for an all-round lack of heat, fire and fizz on the football field. But I still don't get the meaning of fireworks.

Now, though, I think that I *do* get the meaning of fireworks. The fireworks are there to distract from the fact that sport has no inherent meaning at all, and that when you stage a game where success culminates in such an anti-climactic end – 'Manchester United have won the MLS All-Star Trophy!' – then you need something else on top. Before you can ponder the significance of Rio Ferdinand lifting that trophy, your head is turned. Whoa, hear that fizz and look at that bright green sparkle in the sky!

It's like telling someone who points out the unconscionable disparity between rich and poor in America, 'Yeah, but look at all the fun everyone has on the Fourth of July!'

Trophy Clubs

In the chapter entitled 'Hope' I wrote about my delusional belief during the 1980s that Scotland would win the World Cup. As I write, Lincoln City are close to the promotion places in League 2 (Division Four), after winning the fifth-tier title last season. The club is carefully planning for more stringent, less successful times, having been on the verge of bankruptcy on four occasions during the past few decades. They are canny realists. At the same time, a lot of Lincoln fans see no reason why we shouldn't keep getting promoted – up to the Championship, at least. Maybe they're right. It happens now and again to other small clubs, like Blackpool and Bournemouth. If we don't believe it's possible, why are we watching at all?

At the same time as I nurture hope, the idea of success scares me. I'm not used to it. We may succeed in climbing higher up the Football League, but then we have further to fall. Success incurs envy, resentment and, thanks to the financial rewards for success, the inevitable accusations of greed – all negative things. You wonder if you'll be one of those fans who preferred it when you had the whole stand to yourself to moan about how shit everything was. And while there's not a second when I wouldn't be cheering Lincoln on, every game, all the way to the Champions League group stages, I worry that it would leave me incapable of coping with defeat, as Vicente del Bosque said of the Spanish. Would I really want my club to be just like Chelsea?

Put another way, is success over-rated? If you get the chance, ask the president of German fourth division side Rot-Weiß Oberhausen, Hajo Sommers. If you don't get the chance, here's an interview he gave with *11 Freunde* in late 2016. The magazine describes how there's one thing above all that gets on his nerves: tradition. Every time a fan comes up to him and starts a sentence with the words 'I've been watching this team since 19XX…' then he knows that a complaint's coming up. 'Oberhausen,' wrote the magazine, 'cannot be a contented fourth division team where people are happy that there will soon be a new, club-run pub at the stadium. Or that the youth academy only just missed out on achieving One-Star status, sensational for a fourth division team. But still, fourth division, not first division, which Rot-Weiß Oberhausen once was – from 1969 for four short years. "It's an absolute burden to have to reach the level you once achieved in the past," says Sommers.'

On the other hand, fans love to talk about the past, when their team was good, or merely better. Maybe Sommers is taking them too literally. Even if Lincoln suddenly plummet back down the divisions and end up in the Northern Counties East Football League playing Eccleshill United, we'll always, always have the memories of the 2016–17 season – winning the National League title, sold-out home games and making it to the quarter-finals of the FA Cup. It was surely better for Oberhausen to have played four years in the Bundesliga than never to have played there at all.

That was the 1970s, though. Leicester City winning the Premier League in 2016 was an aberration, condescendingly tolerated by the mighty precisely because it was so clearly a one-off.[5] The owners of big teams are not into winning trophies for the pride of the city and its supporters, they're in it for the reflected glory. For the Qatari government, say, to polish its totalitarian image. To make Russian or US billionaires look like big shots in the corporate world. Trophy-winning clubs have become trophy clubs. Losing out on honours is not simply a case of being second best on the field. It's bad for business.

This doesn't make the emotions of their true supporters any less legitimate when they celebrate winning the Premier League or the Champions League. It just makes me glad I'm not one of them. And there's a major plus-point about both of those competitions that is worth never losing sight of: look at all the clubs that *don't* get to win. Ha!

Success v. Happiness

Speaking of the Champions League and endlessly winning titles, I

5. And lest we get too romantic, plenty of money was spent on that team too. It wasn't exactly a collection of bony, raw talent scalped from the rutted back alleys around what was once Filbert Street.

have a friend called John who is the worst kind of Bayern Munich fan. He doesn't live in Bavaria, and he wasn't born there either – he's from Chicago, and lives just south of Frankfurt. His youngest child, Louis, is now also a Bayern fan. Like his father, he has no obvious connections at all with the club or the city. I met him when he was 12 years old. Look, I know, he was just a boy, but I wasn't going to let him get away with being a Bayern Munich fan. Louis had to be told that he was going to spend his life being vilified by all decent, right-thinking people. Supporting a strong, dominant club led by the perennially hateable Karl-Heinz Rummenigge and convicted tax fraudster Uli Hoeneß was in no way going to prepare him for the disappointments that life and destiny were already rigging up along his path.

Louis didn't care about what I had to say about his team, and showed no signs whatsoever of renouncing his support. He showed me a picture of himself with Toni Kroos. Once or twice a season his dad takes him down to Munich, and for some fantastic amount of cash they stay in the team hotel for two nights and get to not only watch a game, but to stalk the players in the lobby and bombard me with gloating selfies. Bayern stroll their way to a two-, three- or four-goal win against some back-pedalling paupers from the north, and John spends a few more hundred euros in the club shop buying Louis a bedspread and a mug that says, '*Mia san mia*'.[6]

'Why don't you support Eintracht, your local team?' I asked Louis. 'Because I support Bayern,' he replied. 'What connection do you have to Munich?' I retorted. 'I'm a Bayern fan,' he said, logically. We went for a walk through the vineyards near their flat in Bensheim on a chilly but tranquil autumn afternoon. We climbed up a hill, and then had lunch at the top. We talked about football for much of the time. At the end of the afternoon, Louis still supported Bayern Munich.

I'm annoyed by fans of Bayern Munich in the same way that my sister was annoyed by her flatmate playing Toni Basil's 45rpm 7-inch single 'Mickey' over and over. It's the sound of success. When John crows about another Bayern victory, 6–0 at home to Werder Bremen, he might as well be repeatedly chanting that you, Mickey, are so fine and that you blow my mind, hey Mickey! Just typing that out

6. Bavarian for 'We are wankers but we don't give a shit what you think.'

has already annoyed me, and made me wonder whatever happened to Toni Basil. Who the hell was she, anyway?

Thank you, high-speed internet – it turns out she's not just a singer, but an actress, a dancer, a film-maker and a choreographer too. She's done tons of stuff in her life, including the video to 'Once in a Lifetime' by Talking Heads, a song I still revere almost 40 years after it came out. She's active even now in the entertainment field, and I can well imagine that she has been a ground-breaker and an innovator in many of her professed fields. But why do we know and remember Toni Basil? We know and remember that she annoyed the tits off us for her cover version of a song by 1970s British combo Racey, a group best described as the groomed and grinning poster-pop beige-boys, whose asinine output may in itself have been solely responsible for the spewing, spitting outburst that briefly battered our lives as punk rock. No one is thanking Toni Basil for having a massive worldwide hit with 'Mickey'. On the contrary, when it comes on the radio and we can't get it out of our brains for the next four days, we are hating Toni Basil for the net-loss contribution she's made to our lives.

For that, she (and Racey, Gawd bless 'em) no doubt banked enough cash to finance all her future choreographic projects. 'Mickey' helped her achieve success doing what she wanted to do – and there's nothing wrong with that. A friend who's part of the Mancunian music world once told me that Manchester film-maker and artist Ed Barton wrote 'It's a Fine Day' after maintaining during a discussion with friends that any twat could write a pop hit. He proved his point when it got to number four in the UK charts, sung by Opus III, and was used by Coca-Cola to sell its dark fizzy drink product. Success! Ed used the proceeds to finance what he really wanted to do for years to come. And 'It's a Fine Day' is a terribly annoying song, though not quite as much of a mood-killer as 'Mickey'.[7]

So here's why meritocracy is a myth: it's possible to make it to the top not on merit, but by deliberately being crap (Opus III/Toni Basil) or by pricing out the competition and buying success (Bayern Munich and too many others to mention). Once you've achieved success, you just point to success as proof of your merit. It's easy. 'Look,

7. Ed's solo album *And a Panda*, on the other hand, is magnificent.

we have fans who weren't born in Munich and have no connection with the city at all. The world is our market!'

Maybe it's natural to resent success – success is the unnatural state, after all, the outstanding outcome. Is it necessarily the desirable goal in human terms? Bar the admirable dropouts, why do most of us play along with the sham of meritocracy? What are people going to do in the Kingdom of Heaven for eternity? Why is there rarely a discussion about an alternative? The majority of us should concede that we are just happy to be taking part, happy to be here, muddling along, pottering about, taking small pleasures where we can, trying our best to be halfway decent people, struggling with all our own and the world's contradictions. Who cares about the trophy? When you're being held to that standard, you have to keep it up and do it all over again – there's already a new season looming. You have to polish the fucking thing. You have to put up with the negative losers who say, 'So what? It's just a fucking trophy. It doesn't *mean* anything.' You're wrong, it means we won (Louis would probably say). But what does it mean that you won? What next, you high-achieving, hit-writing, goal-tallying, fortune-accumulating, eternally gloating Number One?

You poor successful bastards, I feel so sorry for you. You win 19 times in a row, then you don't know how to handle it when you lose at home to Mainz. It's a fucking crisis, right enough. Or you win 19 games in a row and everyone sneers that you only did it because you bought all the best players in the league, and a few more from abroad; that you lobbied hard to create the Champions League so that you and your rich pals from Manchester, Paris, Madrid, Turin and Barcelona could bully your way to the league's top positions every year and all reach the last eight of the self-appointed world's best club competition. You win 19 times in a row and no one loves you, no one thanks you, except for all the fans and the hangers-on, but they would love you anyway. There's no *respect* for those who succeed like this, thanks to moaning buggers like me.

Lincoln's success in 2017, when they won the National League and reached the FA Cup quarter-finals, will last me for as long as it takes us to achieve the next honour or promotion. To return to the quotes that kicked off this chapter, we're more into the idea of eating, and not being eaten (Logan Pearsall Smith). Because I don't believe that Bayern Munich fans really *feel* Walter Pater's constant ecstasy when they're well on their way (which they are as I write this sentence) to their sixth successive Bundesliga title. John and Louis down in Bensheim are no happier on a day-to-day basis than I am up here in Frankfurt. But they do love their football, and their fandom is just as legitimate as mine, just as valid as the obsessive's and much more so than the hooligan's. We're all part of the sport. Meanwhile, thanks to them, I've realised why I value Bayern Munich's size and success: it's to make me feel morally superior. And who doesn't like that?

Success, Nonetheless

Another friend of mine, Lane, once ran his own business, but after a few years it went bankrupt. He picked himself back up and tried a different approach, operating independently without the burden of overheads such as staff and offices – that is, he worked out of Starbucks on a laptop. One night after a few drinks I dropped in a reference to him being a failed businessman. 'Well, Ian,' Lane replied, 'we can't all be like you, making millions out of freelance journalism.'

That was a canny comeback. My career effectively disappeared when websites and publications suddenly stopped paying freelancers round about 2009. For a couple of years I'd almost been making enough to have survived without my wife's income if I'd lived alone in a one-room bedsit on the wrong side of town and Washington DC had had a network of bicycle lanes. Phone calls and emails asking for submissions were a reasonably common occurrence. Then, almost overnight, newspapers and websites either stopped using freelancers completely or meekly offered you a platform for your work, 'even though we can't pay you right now'. Or their fees were lousy in relation to the amount of work that needed doing.

When I returned to Frankfurt in 2015, I thought that I could maybe do what I'd done here before – work as a desk editor in a news agency. 'Those kinds of jobs don't really exist any more,' someone told me. There were, however, lots of 'journalist' and 'writer' jobs at companies that were looking for staff to promote their products on social media. 'Are you passionate about social media?' the job ads would ask. Maybe I would have been 30 years ago, if social media had been around back then. 'They'll take one look at your date of birth and shred your CV without reading the rest,' Neil (see 'Kissing' chapter) told me with a certain grim satisfaction. He wasn't just saying it because I snogged his ex-girlfriend in 1980, though; he was almost certainly right. Most of the applications I sent out didn't even warrant the courtesy of a standardised rejection email. My complete lack of passion for social media was coming across loud and clear.

With one daughter having left home, and the other about to follow, and with my wife's career showing no signs of easing up, I tried to take stock of where I was at, aged 50. I was refereeing every weekend, and mainly enjoying it, apart from the days when I came home and wordlessly stalked to the fridge and took out a beer and then sat down and said, 'I don't want to talk about it. All the world's an arsehole.' I was writing regular pieces for *When Saturday Comes*, the only outlet still willing to pay me for my troubles. I'd enjoyed writing two football books, one fiction and one non-fiction, both of which had brought in just about enough money to commission an artist to rapidly draw a picture of a roof over our heads. And then my literary agent dropped me overnight, without any warning at all, and I felt like a teenager being dumped by the girl everyone else had known from the start was way above my station.

So I took the train from Frankfurt to London and for four days sat in Tim Bastard's kitchen, where we drank coffee and beer and indulged in a casual mid-life crisis. We laughed and we... no, we didn't actually cry. We just laughed, and afterwards we said that we both felt much better. I started coaching again, a boys U14 team, and relished being back on the training pitch, telling lads to be on their toes before they got the ball, shouting with glee when they strung five passes together. Then I had a medical scare that saw me hospitalised for two nights and attached to a heart monitor. The following weekend I spent in a hospital in Scunthorpe with my dad as he lay in bed attached to various tubes, and he told me several times that his time was up, he'd had enough.[8] I left with heavy eyes, not wanting to believe what was happening to someone so close to me who'd been there from the moment I'd swum free of his bollocks.

And the weekend after that, I was back in Frankfurt, out on the football pitch on a parky but peaceful autumn Sunday afternoon, refereeing the usual fractious adult men, watched by barely enough spectators to change a light bulb. Running up and down that pitch I felt serene and happy. I believe that it is an immense privilege to enjoy, even for odd moments, that equanimity and sense of pure pleasure. I was back out on the damp grass, back to normality, back to where I felt most at home, completely at ease. Creating my own micro-version of success, quietly flowing as a tiny microbe within the magical, maddening game of football to help me keep a grip. Heeding the advice I give to all the players – whether refereeing or coaching – just before every match:

'And please, for Christ's sake, don't forget to try and enjoy the bloody game.'

8. He hadn't. Happily, thanks to medicine and willpower, he kept going.

Acknowledgements

A huge, unlimited 'Thank You' to all the readers who had faith enough in this book to fund its publication, and to magnificent Lincoln City FC for its invaluable support. Thank you as well to Mark Brend at Unbound for his unstinting enthusiasm for The Quiet Fan. My agent Kevin Pocklington at The North Literary Agency deserves massive credit for taking me on in the first place, and having the belief to persevere with such a commercial liability. Rich Guy, Andy Lyons and Tom Hocking at *When Saturday Comes* have backed this book from the start, and my writing for several years. I will also always be grateful to Ian Preece, Drew Whitelegg, Tim Bradford and Carol Plenderleith for reading and commenting on earlier drafts of this book. Gratitude and endless love go to Conny and my daughters Nina and Natascha, who never stop supporting and encouraging me. And finally, a gargantuan shout of appreciation to the three meticulous editors at Unbound, whose names for some reason we are not allowed to know, but who superbly guided this book through its structural, copy and proof-reading edits. If I ever find out who you are, the first few rounds are on me.

Patrons

Moray Allan
Alex Anderson
Jason Ballinger
William Blanchard
Aifric Campbell
Jane Chamberlain
Paul Colley
Nathan Duin
Lynn Genevieve
Otto Gonzalez
Derek Hammond
Simon Harper
Pete Harris
Hallvard Johnsen
Sam Kelly
Carlo Navato
Kevin Pocklington
Derek Priestley
Bartley Ramsay
Philippa Rose
Stephen Ruddick
Mark Sanderson
Raymond Smith
Matthew Smith
Rosslyn Spokes
Mark Stanton
Mark Taylor
Ellen Thalman
Adam Tripi
Alex Usher
Doyle Waldrop
Gretchen Woelfle